THE
RIVEN
COUNTRY
OF
SENGA
MUNRO

Renée Carrier

For my Jeff

PART ONE

My daughter would have been twenty-nine years old this year. I rediscovered her face in the dancing spray of a wave, as I reached for one more home, on another longing shore.

. . . . My name is Senga. It was not always. I grew into it, you might say. I was born old, am older still, and, like a dormant tide before it turns, embracing its own mighty waters far out at sea, somewhere deep and mysterious, I've lived that holding back, a stagnant and rotting stillness.

Think of waiting to leap in at school-yard jump rope, weight braced on forward leg, hands and arms gauging the coming crest of the rope. Invariably, I would miss my chance and down would descend the rope to rise up on the other side, leaving me to return again to my lack of skill—or courage. At long last, life intervenes and what science calls "critical mass" is reached; some molecule drops over the edge, to be followed by another, then another, and the great turning—or Thing—is accomplished. The almanac tidal tables aren't always precise, I've learned, at least in the so-called affairs of men; or, of women.

CHAPTER 1~FALLING WATER

The Black Hills

1994

Senga Munro arched her back then leaned on the hoe a moment to listen to a raucous conversation between two crows. June had stirred much weather talk among the residents of Sara's Spring, Wyoming. It had rained nearly every afternoon and gardeners' green beans had to be replanted, having drowned. After tossing her long, honey-colored braid over her shoulder, she bent once again to the hoe as her daughter Emily dropped in seeds. When Senga finished tamping the soil over them, she asked the young girl to go turn the water on at the faucet.

Y'all, leave 'em alone, please. This to the birds, about the seeds.

It had become habit, her dialogue with nature. And there was always Hermione, the witchy scarecrow. Upon completing the chore on the rare, sunny Sunday morning, Senga thanked Emily for her help.

"Now what?" sighed the girl.

She regarded the child who seldom pushed circumstances, and her heart enlarged for this most willing companion and daughter—a wild and untrammeled beauty. Head cocked, Senga listened inwardly. *This day of no rain demands further time outdoors.*

"Let's go for a hike."

Face scrunched-up, Emily said, "But we always hike on Sundays, Mom."

"No-no, I don't mean here—I mean, um, a destination hike," Senga suggested. Eyes wide for emphasis—"You know, *to* somewhere—and back, of course."

"O—kay. . . Where?" the girl asked as she reached for the hoe, the can of seeds and the pair of sawed-off broom handles, wrapped with twine, and used to measure tidy rows. Senga took the hoe and together they turned toward the tiny rented house in Sara's Spring.

Due to their home's unconventional floor-plan and size, they jokingly referred to themselves as *The Borrowers*, after one of Emily's favorite childhood series. "Well, how about Spearfish Canyon? To one of the falls?" Spearfish, South Dakota lay across the state line, an hour's drive away. After considering, Emily agreed.

The odometer on the older Honda Civic read 180,543 miles. The vehicle needed several issues addressed, but managed to continue running, owing to Senga's diligence in having the oil changed regularly, a habit ingrained in her by Emily's father before he left for the last time. A singer-guitarist working solo gigs, he'd found the trade unprofitable in rural America. Nevertheless, he contributed, if erratically, from "The Road," and made the rare unannounced visit if passing anywhere near the small town.

The air blew fresh into the open car window, and the sun shone through high stratus clouds, with no rain forecast until Tuesday. Senga and Emily rode in silence, neither commenting on the absence of a working radio. Then, as though by spirit summoned, Emily began humming one of her father's tunes, "Whiskey in the Jar." Senga inhaled, drawing the sounds into her, recalling its levity (the song *was* funny). Stronger poignancy of loss followed. "You miss him," she stated quietly when the humming stopped.

"Mm, I guess, Mom. . . I'm not sure what I miss. You?" She turned in her seat to face her mother, unflinching in her directness.

"I miss, ah, your father's—stupid jokes." She chuckled wryly, retrieving the sentiment from a heaviness that might have dampened their excursion.

In Spearfish, Senga turned south onto Highway 14 and entered the gorge. The creek flowed whitewater-fast, paralleling the twisting road. Dappled sunlight played off high limestone walls, streaked with the black and red stains that marked their geology.

Arriving at the trail head, Emily gathered up her day pack, containing water bottles for both, and two extra-large peanut butter cookies. Senga had thought to include her *Peterson's Guide*, in case, remembering Morels grew in the area; but she wouldn't need a guide for them, as false Morels were obviously so . . . well, false. On second thought, she left the guide in the pack, zipped it and helped Emily slip it on.

"Okay?" Senga asked.

"I'm ready. Are you, Mom?" Emily asked as she brushed wispy strands of hair away from her face. She was growing out bangs, and that morning Senga had brushed her daughter's hair into a pony-tail, fastened it with a covered elastic band, then tied on both a blue and a green ribbon: "One for the sky, and one for the Earth," she'd declared to her daughter.

"Just a sec. My stick. Okay, you lead—oh, wait, I need to lock the car." Senga made sure the locks were all down, placed the key in her pocket, arranged Papa's loden-green fedora on her head and finally grabbed her walking stick while nodding to Emily to proceed.

The trail was well used and maintained. Senga occasionally liked to hike where human effort enriched an experience of the outdoors, though she recalled heated discussions on the subject—wildness versus convenience—with Emily's father. She and her daughter soon found their stride on the smooth trail through the undergrowth, though the footing was slick with moisture. In the middle of June, the air felt cool at 4,500 feet. Beside them, steep canyon walls rose hundreds of feet. Mountain goats and Big Horn sheep inhabited the area, often spotted on impossibly narrow ledges, high above the trail.

Senga hoped they might see one today—a wild thing in the wild.

They met several hikers returning from the falls, at least three groups, Senga later recalled: a family of four, a young couple and the two gentlemen who reversed direction to fall in several paces behind them. The men spoke in quiet tones, the language not English. After a quick, furtive glance behind her shoulder, Senga guessed they were father and son by their resemblance.

The gently elevating trail led hikers through an audibly diminishing chorus of bird call, barely perceptible over the stream's torrent. The deafening noise of the cataract prevented quiet conversation. Alternating between a smile and intense concentration, Emily turned intermittently to her mother, who clearly reveled in the hike and being in the company of her daughter.

At last it appeared; the waterfall, proverbial force of Nature, over a hundred feet high and, justly, "Elemental Queen" of this part of the forest. Or so Senga thought. "My Water is Life," it proclaimed. She and Emily stood transfixed, her hand reaching for the girl's shoulder, to pull her close. They remained so until the hikers behind them caught up and, stepping off the trail, they let the men pass. The younger one smiled warmly in greeting.

"Let's climb up along the waterfall!" Emily leaned in to be heard. "I see where a trail winds up that way." She pointed toward an outcrop, halfway to the top of the waterfall. Senga thought a moment.

"Okay, Em, but we'll have to take it slow—I'm better on level ground."

After recovering what they had lost (the supposition), Senga noticed the two men, sitting on a long, flat stone, following their progress up the steep terrain. Emily frequently offered her mother a hand for support and vice versa. When their goal was achieved, Senga wondered if their observers could hear the girl's exuberant *Woo-hoo!* over the din of the falls. The view from the crest deserved a long moment, Senga thought, and she moved to a better vantage point.

Calf muscles burned and upper arms ached from the use of the walking stick, but exhilaration won. Emily had claimed a dry, sunny spot to sit on and removed the cumbersome day pack. Opening it, she called to her mother, "Snack time?"

"Yes! After I catch my breath . . ." After several moments, Senga accepted the proffered cookie and water bottle. "Isn't it gorgeous? What a view . . . thank you for coming, Emily," she added, self-consciously.

"Oh, Mom, you're so funny. . . No, this is great. I *love* it," and standing up, she turned slowly around, halting at the sight of a regal juniper tree whose trunk measured sixty inches or so. Wrinkled purple berries (actually cones, she knew) adorned sweeping branches. Emily stepped over to it. "Look, someone's tied something here—" She drew aside the branch, exposing a red cloth, its edges frayed.

"Don't touch it, Em. Please. Remember? It's a prayer cloth," Senga cautioned, rising with some effort to join her daughter. "You see, some people—Indians mostly—will say a prayer and leave these in the trees. It holds their prayer. The candles we sometimes light in churches? Same thing, at least, *I* think it is." She smiled at Emily's bewilderment.

"We've seen them at the Tower, too." Senga pinched off a small sprig of juniper and rubbed it between her palms. She brought it to her nose for its sharp scent, then held it out for Emily to smell.

"*Mmmm.*"

The nation's first national monument, Devils Tower (patently mistranslated), had been named "Bear Lodge" by at least two peoples—the Cheyenne and the Lakota—for the species that once inhabited the area. Local residents crept around the devil by simply calling it the Tower. Senga wondered if it pissed him off, being ignored like that.

"Did you know that in Tibet—that's a country China invaded in the fifties—prayer flags are used much the same way?"

"O—kay." The corners of Emily's mouth slowly curved into a grin. "Then, let's leave one too. Here!" she said, yanking elastic and ribbons from her hair. She passed her mother the green one (the one she'd prefer), keeping the sky-blue for herself. Holding the ribbon between her lips, she pulled back her hair using both hands, and replaced the elastic.

"So what do we do first?"

"Well, we each make a wish, then choose a branch to hang it from . . . that's it, I suppose. Oh, and remember to greet Grandma Juniper." Their ancestor.

Senga drew a breath, noting her words, then, closing her eyes for a moment, sighed. Choosing a branch at eye level, she tied the green ribbon with care.

Emily followed suit, taking longer, and fixed her ribbon to the branch below. Senga gazed at her daughter, memorizing her features at this tender age of nine.

"What is it, Mom?" Still as the blue air on this rare day. *And what is so rare as a day in June? Then, if ever, come perfect days; Then Heaven tries earth if it be in tune . . .*

"Oh, nothing," she said, James Russell Lowell's lines having said all. Then, not as afterthought, but with certainty, "I love you, Em . . . Well, I guess we'd better start down. What do you think?"

Emily nodded assent, adding, "I love you, too, Mom," and both turned to where the pack lay. Beyond it, the lip of the falls shimmered, a moving horizon, the fast water disappearing over its glinting edge, like hundreds of white, translucent serpents slipping over, into infinity.

"Look!" Emily pointed to the men below and waved. They waved from where they sat, necks craned, staring up from beside the far bank of the pool into which the heavy, white curtain of water fell, producing a misty cloud of spray. "They look like miniature railroad people," Emily commented.

"Or Borrowers." Senga reached to help with the pack, adjusting the straps evenly, then turned and stooped for her walking stick. Upright again, she glanced back. To see Emily stumble then slip on a wet stone and fall backward, mouth and eyes open in disbelief and terror, arms flailing before her.

"*Mamaaa!*"

"*Em-ily*—*!*" The scream caught in her throat then sprang free in anguish. Clamoring frantically on her belly to the edge, she helplessly watched her daughter fall off the earth, down, down, and against a blue sky, the color of her eyes and her ribbon, into the green backdrop of surrounding pines. Until she could see her no more.

The younger of the two men told her with great sorrow and care, that her daughter could not have lived long and would not have suffered. She had fallen, not into the water, which might have saved her, but onto the rock-strewn bank. Deeply shaken, the older man had hiked out immediately to seek help, instructing the other to stay.

The younger man had searched for a pulse on the child's neck and wrists and, after removing the pack, had gently lifted the child from the stones and carried the precious burden to the stone bench-slab, where he had waited.

Senga had hurried down the steep cliff trail, emerging from the shrubbery at the base of the cliff, the front of her shirt soaked, her walking stick, jeans and hands smeared with mud. The image of her Grannie Cowry's sorrowful face in her mind's eye offered no word.

Halting a moment at a loss, she looked around, and up, from where she'd hiked, as though waiting for her daughter to catch up. But no—

There's my Emily—lying in that man's lap.

Twisting her head and neck to the top of the falls, she then trained her vision down its thunderous length until it rested where the backpack lay. The man slowly shook his head when their eyes met. Senga stepped warily to him, over several yards of shoals, then, she crumpled to the ground, in a slow, but graceful descent, like the ballerina in Swan Lake. The man leaned over and tenderly passed the girl into waiting arms.

Rocking back and forth, she murmured Emily's name, over and over, through choked-back tears. The man lifted a small flask from an inside pocket, unscrewed the top and raised his brows in question. Their eyes locked and, without looking away, she pulled her trembling hand from under Emily's broken body, took the flask and, putting it to her lips, she swallowed a long, burning gulp of whiskey that relaxed; then, still considering the man—as though holding his gaze might ward off grim reality—she slowly held out the container to him, nodding once in thanks. Then was she able to peer into her daughter's now dull eyes and search her too-still face, to love it, to learn it, and finally, with her fingers, to gently pull down the eyelids and kiss each of them.

"I . . . I did not close her eyes. I thought perhaps you. . . Her eyes were *so* vivid, so blue, like the sea." The man said he'd let them be, so her mother could see them once more.

With detached observation, she noted the man's eyes. Like sapphires under water.

There was blood, issued from a wound on the side of Emily's head. A small, jagged point of a rock appeared to have pierced the temple, the man explained. He rose to step over to the area, reached down to pick something up and returned— showing Senga a similarly shaped stone, which he then let fall to the ground.

"I used my kerchief," he told her haltingly, ". . . to clean her face," then he'd tied it around her head.

Blood lay matted in the hair, the hot metal smell filling Senga's senses, its taste searing the back of her throat. Blood created its own synesthetic impression; an original memory.

She turned vacantly to the falls, compelled by calling waters and the ever-echoing sound of Emily's cry. Mama. A sense of the surreal gathered around her, like wisps of corner-of-the-eye motions, as though she'd been removed from All Things, except this child in her lap, whose mighty spirit yet clung between worlds, betwixt the dock and the boat. Senga knew this, and knew that this man knew it.

"What—what had you lost?" she asked after a few moments.

"Pardon?"

The waterfall roared on, her unwitting adversary.

"You and your . . . friend . . . were looking for something. I—I saw you from up there," she spoke louder, her voice trembling, and gestured to the top of the cliff with her chin, where she and Emily had been. She labored to wrap her mind around it. *Only a little while ago. . .*

"Oh . . . It was careless of me, really," he admitted. "This flask, you see, it had fallen from my pocket when I reached for something and, as it was a gift from my, ah, late wife, I was obliged to return for it." He turned from her to the waterfall.

She detected an accent. Sing-song. His expression bespoke both perplexed wonder and deep underlying sadness.

"Ah," Senga acknowledged, pulling Emily's head closer to her breast. "I'm grateful you and your friend were here, Mr. . . um . . . Mr.—?"

"My name is Sebastian, dear; Sebastian Hansen. I am here with my father, Henrik; we are on a little holiday. We live in Denmark, you see, but have relatives in Spearfish."

She heard calm reserve, and empathy.

"Mm, well," Senga replied, "It seems I needed you very much today, Sebastian." Then her efforts to shield this stranger failed and a slow, tentative mewling rose from her depths, to become a wail, with tears streaming down her face, as if her heart had sought and matched some resonating frequency of the falls themselves. Two instruments responding to that which must be answered.

The man moved quickly down beside her, to lay his right arm gently, but firmly, around her shoulders; his left arm and hand resting on Emily's leg, he gathered the wrenching *pieta* of mother and child unto himself, to wait, to attend, as Senga keened her slow rocking arpeggio to the thundering drone of falling water.

CHAPTER 2~IN THESE HILLS

Western North Carolina

1960

The boy led the healer along a hidden path only a rabbit could follow, *or make*, she decided, as she meandered back and forth behind her young guide. With kit bag slung across her body, her keen eyes ranged between rough ground and swift feet ahead. She needn't have demanded why on earth they'd had to struggle through the knotted rhododendrons, when far easier routes existed. She knew the reason.

After a quick turn north and several more minutes west, below the ridgeline and past the old mine, a light, gurgling noise alerted her to the creek, flowing their way. She heard the whiskey still before seeing it, by the aptly named thump barrel. When the thumping stopped, she knew the 'shine would come.

A man addressed her young guide when they entered a grove of evergreens, brilliant in the slanting rays of the late hour sun. He gestured for her to follow, after a terse nod in greeting—"Grannie Cowry."

The honorific title signified Aggie's role as healer and midwife—not that of grandmother—though her age might have supported it.

"What's he done," she asked the man, accepting a quick cup of fresh water from her guide with a nod of thanks. She then lifted a corner of her work apron to wipe perspiration from her forehead and the back of her neck, her dark hair conveniently pinned up in a two-braided crown against prickly heat. As she smoothed the apron over her shirtwaist dress, she regarded the man impatiently, for his slow answer.

"Broke a leg."

She'd learn soon enough how seriously.

"It's my little brother," he continued. "He's worked only a couple months as look-out."

Like it don't give the boy call to make a mistake, Grannie silently retorted. They crossed the grove.

The flies were thick and grasshoppers thicker, drawn to the smell of blood, but mostly, to sweet mash. Early September, even in the higher hills, brought sticky air; it seemed the insects stuck to it.

"Where's my husband?" she asked.

"Oh, tending the fire. Didn't see 'im?"

"No." She'd brought an extra pasty for his evening meal. He wouldn't be home tonight.

Grannie halted to study the scene before entering the shady space. Laid out before her on a hasty bed of boughs and grimacing, a young boy, maybe fourteen, murmured in pain. Beside him on a tree stump, sat an older man lost in a daydream, it appeared to her. She frowned, her thick black brows nearly meeting above her eyes, then—

"Go find me a long, straight stick, about yay thick." She held up two fingers. "Go on, now." This to the daydreamer.

Rising, the man returned her expression and made off, shooting a sidelong glance to another bystander.

The break was bloody. "What's your name?" she asked her patient as she approached.

With a groan, he told her.

His brother described the boy's tumble, down the dew-slick side of the ridge early that morning, and pointed in the direction.

"I-I tripped. It h-hurts real bad, ma'am," said the boy.

"Has he drunk any water? Get me some now," she ordered the brother, who quickly brought over the tin cup, filled creekside.

Setting to work, she cut away the blood-damp pant leg. She'd seen worse, but wasn't going to say so, and summoned an idle spectator to help yank calf bones back into place. The boy screamed through teeth clenched on the leather strap she carried for the purpose. He could be heard above the thumping. After ordering the men to keep a better hold on the boy, she doused the site with antiseptic, cleaned it, sewed the tear, applied a salve and wrapped it. Then, aligning the stout stick, she wrapped it to the leg.

"Can y'all make a crutch?" she asked no one in particular and several responded they could. "He needs to be carried home now and put into bed to give that leg time to stitch. I know where you live, son. . . I'll take your ma some comfrey leaves—unless she has some growing?"

His pain smelled like rotting lettuce.

The boy's face glistened with sweat as he shook his head and, leaning over, she wiped his forehead with her apron tail, doused in cold water, then told someone to give him a small glass of 'shine to dull his senses. She had aspirin tablets with her, quicker than brewing willow bark tea, and gave him two. Though she knew most folks kept them on hand, she wrapped several more in a square of cloth for him to take home, stuffing the wad into his shirt pocket.

"No? Or, you don't know?" The comfrey.

"I-I don't know, ma'am," he said, wincing.

"I'll take her some tomorrow and have a look at you. You'll be all right. Just be careful getting home. Wish y'all had a wagon here. . ." She stood, glanced around, then told the onlookers. "See if y'all can't fashion a cot and carry him out. I swear. . ." she sighed again, surveying the operation, if that's what it could be called.

In the near distance, the "hog still" squatted on the ground, an area dug out beneath for fire, the flue pipe sticking up behind. She spied her husband twisting a hardwood log into the hot fire. After lifting out the cloth-wrapped pasty, she gathered up her equipment and returned it to her kit bag. Then, ignoring his cohorts, she made her way across the grove and handed the pasty to her husband. He smiled and, saying nothing, set it aside, intent on his task.

The still was fenced off against the real hogs that roamed the woods. Three fifty-five-gallon barrels stood beside and beneath the boughs of a giant spruce. The smoke rose straight up, to be counted in the far view as only that which gave the mountains their name.

Ramshackle came to mind, but she recognized a certain symmetry in the doings, what she and her husband had deemed more necessity than choice, given the extra income and medicinal value. She sighed, turned and was gratified to see two men lashing together a litter of sorts. These were resourceful folks, if stubbornly bent on a way of life. Precisely what necessitated her choices, when she made them.

She accompanied the boy and his carriers through the tangle of rhododendrons, stopping once to readjust his brace, then to continue alone to where she'd parked. Once there, she expressed appreciation for her strong constitution and good balance and sent a good thought to the boy for his healing. *Well, you surely won't be back for a while,* she predicted, and then she spotted it. How had she missed it before? A handsome, mature specimen of ginseng, or 'sang, as it was known—its red berries and palmate leaves waved at her from behind an old hickory tree trunk. "I thank you," she muttered, noting the exact location. She would return for the roots in winter. Her work as healer was always compensated.

Two days later, a 'shine buyer arrived well before dawn and waited for Grant Cowry to exit the house first, then the old garage. The buyer knew to stay in his vehicle until Grant, or Papa, as he was known, brought the box of whiskey, topped with firm tomatoes, four ears of corn and two bunches of turnips. The customer hurried out and around to open the truck door so Papa could set the box on the floor boards with care. After fiddling in his wallet, the man handed over several bills and they nodded their goodbyes.

Papa stood by until the truck reached the bottom of the long sloping drive and turned west onto the road, beams of light illuminating the early morning mist coming off the creek.

He turned and strode farther up the hill purposefully, with an easy stride. Hands in pockets, one fondled the folded bills. When he reached the flat stone, he sat and waited for dawn.

His forefinger nudged up the brim of the loden-green fedora he wore. His wife, Aggie, once told him he took after a woodland spirit. "A tall one." A fondness for plaid shirts and a particular wool vest further made her case. His complexion in all seasons ran between translucent and ruddy, and his once auburn hair was flaxen, to eventually turn white. He wore it to his shoulders and tucked behind prominent ears. "What they're for," he'd quip.

The high, east side of the tobacco barn grew rosy with a shaft of sunlight, even as the land below remained dusky. Hillside tree crowns shone yellow-gold. Returning his gaze to the barn, he watched as light crept down long vertical planks, as though great hands held to it a thousand candles. The warming glow on the weathered wood lit long-held memories as the sun entered their valley.

Yesterday evening, he transferred the wilting and sticky tobacco leaves from the scaffold in the field into the barn to air-cure, a chore requiring the help of his wife and daughter. They took care with the leaves, mindful not to bruise or damage them.

His father and grandfather had worked Burley tobacco on this hilly, forty-acre farm, as had their wives and children. It proved a stable and resilient crop—though the livelihood was considered subsistence farming—and so, the 'shine.

After inspecting the leaves once more, he returned to the house, the sweet green filling his nostrils. As he opened the door to the screened-in back porch, he saw his daughter Lucy tuck in the summer quilt on the bed where she slept on too-warm nights. *Clack!* the door sprang shut behind him.

"Mornin', Lucy dear. Ready for some oatmeal? We'll be leaving soon . . . your mama's champing at the bit, I expect."

"Yes, Papa, I am and she is."

It was autumn, and Aggie Cowry was due to enter a midwife nursing program, to improve her skills. In 1925, Mrs. Mary Breckinridge founded The Frontier Nursing Service in eastern Kentucky. It was located 170 miles away, through the mountains. The school had eventually inspired wealthy philanthropists—how Grannie's tuition was provided.

The program would require attendance for several months and Papa could see the wisdom of the plan. He supported her decision to attend and could take care of their daughter Lucy "just fine," he'd declared, with a dash of bombast for her sake.

A practitioner at the clinic in town had submitted Grannie's name and address to the school, writing, they were, "most fortunate to have Mrs. Cowry's skills and dedication in the county, and might there be a program designed for the older student?" Grannie was in her late forties.

She received the scholarship after being visited by a traveling nurse who, herself, had matriculated at the school. Professionally garbed in uniform, cap and cape, she was a short woman, middle-aged, who stood up straight and sat down neatly with perfect posture. She did not cross her legs. *Do they teach you that in the school?* Grannie wondered. The woman drove a sensible Jeep Woody and spoke in clipped syllables as though she'd spent time in the Army.

She asked to see Grannie's records, then quoted Mary Breckinridge; "You must be able to show progress or demise."

Grannie detailed several case histories, drawing examples from her extensive log. After all, she'd been healing in these parts for nearly thirty years. She took care to omit certain practices—catching babies for one—that could land her in trouble with the authorities. Considered a, "special case" (given Grannie's age), the nurse recognized the potential for the community.

"You must be the youngest-looking Grannie I know," observed the nurse, after reading *Grannie Cowry* under a remedy. She would learn to respond to "Mrs. Cowry" in class.

"I suppose folks thought I looked older than my years when they started calling me that. My daughter calls me 'Mama,'" Grannie quipped, her eyes smiling. "But you must know there are lots of grannies my age—and some much younger—in these hills," she added with a pointed look at the woman, thinking, *She must be pullin' my leg.*

The nurse smiled slyly, then offered to help her fill out the application. Several weeks later, the invitation arrived in the mail to join the next class.

Grannie felt butterflies in her stomach. The mountain folk who relied on her care and medicinals promised they'd do their best to stay healthy and not die, nor have babies in her absence (tongue-in-cheek). Everyone knew she wouldn't abandon them for a puny reason.

She sat on the porch in her mother's creaky rocking chair, slowly sipping her second cup of coffee, its heat warming and soothing her aching hands. Whenever she suffered from insomnia (as she had the night before), she imagined herself beside a desert well in old Palestine, waiting for Jesus to come by. He'd always request a drink of water; she'd always draw the water for him; he'd always thank her and they'd always scrunch down together on the shady side of the well, against the cool stones. There she'd ask him questions, and, invariably, in the course of listening for his answers, she'd fall asleep.

Someone other than Jesus once told her there were no answers, only choices.

She and Papa practiced neighborly charity, buried the dead and visited the sick—a given, in her case. Both tried to give their daughter direction, with Papa's emphasis on example, with Scripture pointed to when that example failed. And when it did, lessons in forgiveness and forbearance found their opportunity. Grannie forgave his occasional mean drunk (when his behavior upset Lucy) and, ignoring the imbalance, he forgave his wife's irritation and occasional harsh word.

He's taking pains, Grannie later thought as she studied her husband. After eating a bowl of oatmeal with Lucy, he shaved carefully, trimmed his sideburns, bathed and proposed to dress in "Sunday best" for the trip. He owned a suit for funerals, but Grannie insisted it wasn't necessary, suggesting instead, flannel trousers, a long-sleeved shirt and his vest. He folded his jacket into the trunk in case he needed it.

Going out the door, he plucked his fedora off the hook, having brushed it earlier.

Lucy too dressed carefully and fixed her hair in the style she knew her mother preferred—a side part with a barrette keeping it out of her eyes. The girl was thirteen years old and not passing through her first change well, though Grannie reminded her the time proved difficult for anyone her age. Hair the shade called "dish-water" hung lank to her shoulders, despite her efforts; Grannie preferred the straightforward barrette solution and one hundred daily turns with a brush, but Lucy usually pulled it back in a pony tail—expediency over patience.

Plainly nervous, the girl fidgeted constantly. Her fingernails, chewed to the quick, worse than usual. Lucy fretted her coming absence—the fingernails but one sign. Papa mentioned possible weekend trips to the school (travel being a rare pleasure), and this seemed to please her.

They were almost ready: Papa in the driver's seat, Grannie beside him, Lucy rushing to gather her "trip things": a movie magazine; her geography textbook; the novel for English class, *The Lion, the Witch, and the Wardrobe;* and two boxes of Cracker Jacks. Papa asked her to grab the Brownie camera. By car, the school lay almost four hours away.

"Well now. . ." Grannie addressed her husband, then her daughter in the back seat, ". . . will y'all be all right here?"

"I reckon, Aggie. . ." Papa answered, studying her features, ". . . though the girl might get tired of oatmeal after a while," and he grinned at both, started the car and backed away from the house and their mountaintop.

Grannie gazed out the window to her home and surroundings. *Please watch over them . . .*

Grant Cowry first saw Agnes Mac Kay at a funeral. "Truth be told," she would correct him; "it was the burial, not the funeral." He had stared at the woman the entire length of the prayer, he'd recounted later, long enough to form an attachment of such feeling that his sentiments were impossible to contravene. They would be married some three months later.

Burial concluded, they slowly walked back down the hill.

Aggie was a tall woman of sturdy build—"handsome," he'd emphasized; he admired her self-possession, never calling it such. She'd practiced her healing arts for several years by then and hadn't made time for courting—saying so when he didn't disguise surprise at her age.

When she asked what he did, he told her he farmed tobacco and also helped out at one of the stills.

"Is that how you got that?" She pointed to an ugly scar on his forearm—Papa had reached up to adjust his hat.

He let drop the arm. A burn, two-inches-by-six-inches, had left a white scalded patch of glassy-smooth skin.

"You and some hot mash came together, I reckon. . . Oh, don't look so surprised—I see it too often. Hurt pretty bad, didn't it?" she said, her eyes twinkling into his. Aggie had been only momentarily appalled, he thought; not at the injury, but the reason for it. She'd rallied, adding that they—the healers—depended on the whiskey, "For *medicinal* purposes," she'd suggested, giving him a hard look.

"Peeled the skin right off—right then," he said, looking down. "I ran to the crick and let the water run over it for a time. When I got home I put some salve on and wrapped it—kept it clean though, like my momma told me. This was years ago. I ain't bothered by it now—except it might bother someone seein' it.

"There's going to be a runnin' tomorrow—want to come see?" he asked her—foolishly. He couldn't show her the still's location.

"Seen one runnin', seen 'em all. No, sir," she said, "Don't want nothing to do with that part of the business."

"But it *is* a thing of beauty. . ." Papa told her. To no avail.

He continued to supplement their income through sales after they were married. A false bed in his pick-up truck hid a layer of pint jars, some painted white. . .

After driving for two hours, Papa stopped at a roadside gas station to fill up. Aggie and Lucy welcomed the opportunity to visit the outhouse. Lucy reported it reeked when they returned to the car. He told the attendant he'd pay inside and emerged with three ice-cold Coca Colas, passing these through Aggie's open window. She set them down beside her. The clinking of the glass bottles promised refreshment as Papa opened his door and slid under the steering wheel.

"The fella in there says there's a *scenic* overlook," he emphasized the word, "About twenty miles up the road—a good place for a picnic, he told me. How 'bout it?" He twisted in his seat to address his passengers. His stomach had been steadily growling and just then loudly complained, due to contorted posture. Lucy burst out laughing.

"We better get something into you, Papa, before we start looking good," Aggie joked. He raised an eyebrow in her direction, smiled, but quizzically; his wife seldom made jokes. She stood on the serious side of things; any rare attempt at humor tended to the dry variety.

The picnic basket held cold fried chicken, potato salad, a half-pint jar of bread and butter pickles, biscuits spread with butter, summer apples and chunks of pound cake. Aggie had baked three of them last week and frozen two for later. Lucy knew her way around the kitchen and Papa liked to grill.

After their meal, he brought out the Brownie to snap a picture of his wife and daughter. "Say cheese?—now, don't fret, woman," he said as Grannie then turned to repack the basket.

The highway twisted through the mountains and Lucy complained, as the old Buick swayed around the curves like a reeling drunk. Papa rolled down his window to allow more air to reach the back seat.

"That better?" he asked after a moment, glancing in the rear view mirror. She nodded. No one spoke, except to call out an odd tourist trap, or rather an oddity erected to lure the unsuspecting.

Papa found a place to park. An impressive old lodge dominated the grounds. They learned it was the home of the school's founder. A guide showed them to Grannie's room and introduced her roommate: a petite, young girl whose face was covered with freckles and hair the shade of red that often earned its owner the nickname, "carrot top."

The rest of the afternoon passed in touring the grounds, and she and Papa posed in front of the school's entrance for another picture. At the welcome reception, their eyes grew wide at refreshments presented from bowls of sterling silver, crystal decanters and silver trays.

Papa had decided earlier that he and Lucy would leave after the reception. The journey was not so long and early September enjoyed a long twilight. As they hadn't discussed staying overnight, Lucy wasn't disappointed, but Grannie sensed her road-weariness, and sadness at leaving her. They embraced long. This was their first separation and the knowledge arrived as an unkind surprise, the kind that plucks unawares like an errant branch on a dark path.

"Write to me, Lucy. Please?"

"Yes, Mama. And we'll be all right," she said. "You'll be home for Thanksgiving. I saw the calendar in the dorm; you have five days of vacation." Lucy announced this but missed the shadow cross her mother's face. Those days free of classes were designed to give students time to study and catch up on coursework; Grannie didn't plan to visit until Christmas. She said nothing, but embraced Lucy again, then reached for her husband.

Grannie noted Lucy watching them—*Is it then so unusual?* she wondered. *Why, yes, it is.*

Papa stepped back and, placing his hands on her shoulders, he looked her in the eye and smiled, "You know I'll be thinking of you."

She nodded. Then he turned to their daughter.

"We'd better go on, Lucy dear . . . come on, now." Papa motioned to his daughter and Grannie watched as they crossed the road to the parking lot.

As they pulled out, she raised a hand to Lucy's tentative gesture at the window. Then Grannie turned and, with heaviness of soul, strode to the large tent where the reception was winding down. A malaise disallowed full anticipation of the coming months. "*What have I done?*" she whispered.

CHAPTER 3~HARD PLACE

"Did you hear that?" Papa asked as he busied himself at the stove.

"The crows?" asked Lucy.

"No, after them—that."

"Someone's at the door," and Lucy rose from her chair at the kitchen table, where she had been waiting for a bowl of oatmeal. The light knocking sounded again and she called out, "Coming!" The screened-in sleeping porch lay off the kitchen facing north, where the temperature at night permitted better sleep than the stifling bedrooms upstairs. A pair of twin beds with handcrafted frames, painted white, and a small table set between for a lamp furnished the space at the far end of the porch. An oval braided rug she'd done in blues lay on the wide plank flooring.

Lucy crossed the few steps to the porch's screen door and opened to a young man stepping down backwards, whose appearance, and odor, caused her to rear back. Papa came forward from his position directly behind her and inquired, "Yes? What can we do for you, young man?" in a formal tone, as he wedged himself in front of her.

"Good morning, sir, I was wondering if you might have some work today."

Papa studied him for a long moment, then turned to Lucy and, with a smile, asked her to dish up her breakfast and clean up, but to leave the pan on the stove—he'd return directly. She nodded but followed her father and the man—boy? She couldn't tell.

The boy—and this was what Papa judged him to be—had stepped off the bottom tread onto the gravel drive, one hand still resting on the railing as he looked up into Papa's eyes. *Never wavering*, Papa noticed, *or is it defiance?* He made a rapid assessment, deciding the kid looked as if he'd been sleeping in his clothing for several nights. *Fine-looking boy, though*, he added, and wondered if he lived in the county. He didn't recognize him.

Of medium height, well-proportioned but too thin—judging by the slightly sunken cheekbones—the boy's complexion gave him a bright, ruddy look. He looked hungry, though. Papa thought his eyes queer; light brown with specks of yellow in them. The eyes had a way about them, but he couldn't say what.

Aggie had been away at school for six weeks or so now and he wished he could just go into the next room for her opinion.

"What's your name, son? And where're you from, if I may ask?"

"Oh, I ain't from around here," he said, looking in the direction of Papa's tractor, parked in front of the big shed. "My name's Kenny Mason. My folks used to live in these parts long time ago, but moved over to Tennessee a while back. Pa's gone; Ma's making do, I guess. Haven't seen her in a month of Sundays. . . My sisters still live with her though, so I guess that's something."

Papa didn't know any Masons; people came and went, so he dismissed the background questions. "What can you do, Kenny?" They needed someone at the still, too.

"Oh—"

Before the kid could reply, Papa decided to hire him, right then and there, without considering several factors—he later realized—and he invited Kenny to bring in his pack, which lay at his feet on the gravel. Doubtless everything in it would need to be washed; but first he invited the boy to take a hot shower, and to, "use lots of soap!" He led the new hire to the bathroom—the boy repeating "much obliged for this, sir," too many times.

Papa saw Lucy staring wide-eyed at this strange behavior, knowing her mother would have given the kid the third degree and then sent him on his smelly way with a biscuit or two in his grubby hand.

When Kenny walked into the kitchen wearing a pair of Papa's too-long jeans rolled up at the hem and one of his clean white t-shirts, Papa invited him to sit down and eat a bowl of cereal, and would he like some coffee? A place had been set at the table, including a glass of milk and two slices of buttered toast on a saucer.

"Yes sir, please, and thank you," he replied, to Papa's amusement. Lucy stood at the stove, paralyzed—the large spoon hovering over the bowl.

"Well, Lucy," Papa began, ". . . Are you going to give our guest that bowl, or what?" At which Lucy blinked and sputtered, "Oh!" She plunged the wooden spoon into the pan of cereal to stir it, then filled the bowl and set it down in front of the boy.

"There's milk and sugar," she said, unnecessarily, pointing to them on the table, while Papa poured up a mug of coffee. She returned to the sink and resumed her task of washing morning dishes, giving the occasional sidelong glance in the boy's direction.

Papa thought Kenny was doing a good job of restraining himself as he ate. He wanted to ask him how long it had been, but didn't. Kenny added more milk and another heaped tablespoon of brown sugar. When the bowl was empty, Papa told Lucy she'd better refill it, that it looked like Kenny still had a hole in his stomach, at which the boy smiled.

"Papa makes the best oatmeal. . . He adds pecans, raisins, butter and lots of cinnamon."

"It's right good," said Kenny. "Best I ever tasted," he added, still smiling, and Papa wondered if the boy was merely a flatterer or genuinely impressed. He knew he made good oatmeal. He cooked it every weekday morning; Aggie (usually) fixed weekend breakfasts. Now this scene looked strange to him and he suspected Lucy felt the same way—her Mama not being there in the kitchen with them while someone else was. Almost a betrayal of sorts.

Lucy's Saturday chores included laundry—today the added burden of this bag of stinking clothes. She set about it all with grace and Papa felt a pride.

He and the boy worked out the details of his employment: help with fall plowing, wood cutting and whatever fixin' needed to be done before winter. He would sleep on one of the cots on the sleeping porch (necessitating Lucy's return to the stifling second floor). When it turned cold, they'd think of something else. The boy seemed agreeable and grateful and they soon found an easy rhythm and routine.

In truth, Papa enjoyed the presence of another male. Outside his "business buddies" at the still and having the occasional neighbor to supper, he seldom met with other men, and having this congenial young man to work with, ordinary day-to-day life took on more interest.

A letter from Grannie contained several thorny questions about the new hire. *Lucy,* she wrote her husband, *told me about the boy and says you seem to like him a lot, but she feels a mite confused about him.* Their daughter had confessed the boy "sometimes seems creepy," but "he's nice to look at."

On a Friday night in mid-November, Papa and Kenny returned from a long day in the back-country tending to the still where the boy had been passing more time, employed as a look-out. Kenny asked to drive, but Papa, who'd been drinking, would have none of it and he became surly. He seldom drank, but when he did he grew mean and became another person altogether—a deranged demon—*saying and doing crazy things,* his wife had once dared tell him.

He began the harangue by calling Kenny poor white trash, that he didn't have a pot to piss in and that he was a stupid ass who'd never go anywhere. If he was merely goading to get a rise out of his passenger, he didn't succeed. Kenny said nothing in response—his face turned to the window.

Papa drove the pick-up to the small garage, switched it off and they stepped out. After several missteps and much heaving, Papa gained the kitchen porch door. Kenny didn't offer to help, but let himself in, crossed the hall to enter the bathroom, emerged shortly and escaped to his room— Grannie's small pantry off the kitchen, where they'd moved one of the cots. Kenny closed the door.

Papa sat in the front room, a quart jar of new whiskey in his hand—this resting on the table next to the chair. The radio was dialed to a local music station. He hadn't eaten well during the day and the effect of alcohol poisoning soon became evident. He hollered for Lucy to get downstairs right *now*, the command drowned by a flood of derision and cursing.

"You sleazy, stupid whore. . . You—*slut*. . ." His words slurred as he spit them out. "Bith! Geth the hell dow' here, you hear me?"

He hissed and tore at this quarry, a known—yet unknown—adversary, a prey to devour who hid cowering behind the drink, unrecognized, inhuman; soulless—not his daughter, then. His own voice echoed in his ears, like someone pouring gravel into a cement mixer, and it roared into his head.

Utterly powerless to end it, he heard what he was saying through the strangled speech, but understood it strangely; a consciousness apart, as if he were witnessing the madman hurling the vitriol. With eyes shut tight, he struggled to stop the mechanism of his rage. Succeeding, he slowly opened one eye to find Lucy before him, unworldly, shrunken somehow. *Is she cold? She's shivering,* he noted through the miasma of drunkenness; and more, that her shoulders slumped, and her lips quivered.

"I'm here, Papa," she muttered as she reached out slowly to place a hand, tentatively, on his forearm. He gasped and jerked back, the half-filled jar of whiskey knocked over and spilled onto the rug. Turning from her innocence (and her eyes), he buried his face into the crook of the wing chair and he shuddered and he wept.

After several moments, all was quiet.

In the morning, other than presenting a quiet and bleary-eyed countenance, Papa set about preparing the usual oatmeal, greeting Kenny and his daughter in turn as each shuffled into the kitchen. Papa glanced sidelong in Kenny's direction, to catch him watching Lucy.

The trouble began when Papa had errands in town and wouldn't return until after dark. The school bus stopped at the bottom of the long hill. Lucy stepped off, walked the few steps to the mailbox and removed a few pieces, delighted to see her mother's handwriting. She trudged up the drive, lugging her books in her arms.

When she reached the house, she felt, rather than heard, an eerie silence, as if it was alive. As she set the mail on the dining table, she wondered what was amiss and recalled her father's errands. She climbed the stairs to her bedroom, saw the open door (she always shut it upon leaving in the morning) and Kenny standing in front of her dresser, examining photos she'd stuck around the edge of the mirror.

"Kenny. What are you doing?" she asked, having paused at the doorway.

"You're home. Good. . . Oh, I was just looking at your stuff—didn't think you'd mind and all," he ventured, adding, "Here, let me take those books—they look heavy. A lot of homework, Lucy?"

She felt nonplussed. She couldn't think what to do or say as Kenny reached (with filthy hands in need of washing) for the books, which he placed in a heap on top of her dresser. Then he moved toward her, wearing a closed-mouth smile. It did not reach his eyes. He turned toward her bed, sat down and patted the space beside him.

"Come here, pretty Lucy," he said, and she did. He spoke with smooth flattery as he guided her onto her back, lifted her skirt and violated her. She said nothing. By simply turning her head to the wall, she "left," just as she had learned to do when her father began his increasingly frequent tirades. A kind of paralysis heeled her to submission, mimicking the night terrors she experienced: when she thought she was awake, she couldn't move or utter a sound.

This felt—similarly heavy. But now there was blood and there was pain, which she ignored, minimized and ultimately, over the following weeks, endured.

On occasion, Kenny would hold a grimy hand over her mouth to prevent her cries from escaping. She learned some pain would not be stifled.

But on this day, her father was away and there was no one to hear her.

Before Kenny left, he told her she'd better keep quiet about what had happened. She lay on her bed until she heard the front door close, slowly sat up and felt a slick sensation between her thighs. Crimson blood. She rose, jerked the bedding off and rushed to the bathroom to wash, first herself then the sheet. She found a pail under the bathroom sink in which to soak it and left it in her room, going about these tasks in a slow-motion dance with denial and disbelief. She would never speak to her father about it because, *It's not real,* her mind told her.

Kenny demanded she come down to his bed at night or he'd tell her father "things," and so she did, careful to avoid the one stair that squeaked. She knew where to place her foot.

Lucy's appearance faltered, but Papa couldn't quite decipher it. He noticed she didn't spend as much time in the bathroom in the mornings before school. He could've simply looked at her, but his capacity for caring had been interfered with, interrupted or stolen.

After Lucy's teacher telephoned him one evening, he approached his daughter, asking if anything was wrong. It seemed her school-work was suffering. Papa watched Lucy's expression change to one of alarm as her eyes darted this way and that, as if she were looking for someone. *Kenny?* Kenny wasn't in the house; he was staying up at the still and not due to return for two more days. Then Papa scrutinized the girl carefully, *for the first time in weeks,* he lamented, having just realized his wife would return the following week for Christmas break.

Lucy regarded him anxiously, which frightened him. *A right haunted look,* or *hunted,* he amended.

"Lucy, tell me what's happened."

"Nothing, Papa," she answered. "Why?" Spurning a reply, she turned and trudged up the stairs to her room and shut the door.

He walked out to his pick-up, where he kept a jar of 'shine behind the seat, and proceeded to obliterate the past thirty

28

minutes of his life. But niggling awareness, like a bee sting, would not be ignored. He added up small observations and inklings, calculating how his own behavior had contributed to consequences (even through the present fog of intoxication), whereupon he opened the door to the truck and threw up onto the gravel.

Admitting his culpability, he felt sore afraid—for Lucy, for his wife and, last—for himself.

After pouring out the remainder of the whiskey, he uncovered a second stashed jar and repeated the action. He sat in his pick-up all evening after returning briefly to the kitchen for a strong cup of coffee, a glass of water and a hasty cheese sandwich.

At ten o'clock, he slowly climbed the stairs to Lucy's door and knocked.

She said nothing.

He opened the door to find his daughter curled up on her bed, facing the wall, still dressed. He crossed to her bed and sat down on the edge.

"Lucy, dear—" and he reached out his hand to her back. She flinched.

"No, Papa . . . please . . . I'm okay."

"I don't think you are, Lucy. . . Please tell me what's wrong."

She shifted onto her back and stared at him long, now with accusation. "You *know* what's wrong. I'm not going to talk about it with you. . . I want Mama," she said, turning to face the wall again. Sighing, he rose. Near the door, he sank down into her desk chair, folding himself into it, melting into its hardened capacity to receive a great weight. And with elbows resting on the desk's surface, he covered his face with his large hands in shame for what he had done and for what he had failed to do; for what he was going to do and, finally, for his daughter's lost trust.

Lucy did not offer to comfort her father and after several moments he stood, took his handkerchief out of his pocket to blow his nose and stepped out of her room, shutting the door quietly behind him.

Downstairs, he crossed to the gun rack above the mantel, chose the twenty-gauge and the box of shells below it. In the

29

truck, he stowed the shotgun beside him, started the engine, backed out of the drive and drove the distance on back roads to the hidden turn-off to the still.

His mind felt grainy, like a television screen after programming ceased for the night—an image of white and black snow and the sound of static.

After parking the truck where it wouldn't be seen, he lifted out the shotgun and pulled two shells from the box. Then, he set off in the direction of the old mine shaft. An indifferent moon aided his efforts.

After reaching the mine and making a quick survey, he traveled quietly through the cold night, brushing past the tight shrubbery, the laurels and rhododendrons whose exposed roots could fell a man, until he reached the narrow earthen path. He discerned the pumping of his heartbeat, not unlike the sound of the thump barrel. Arriving at the shack where Kenny slept, he pushed open the make-shift door.

"Boy?" Papa called, shotgun raised to his shoulder.

Kenny woke with a start and, when his eyes adjusted, scrambled back against the wall, yelling, "What the fuck! What did she tell you?!" Moonlight shone on wide-open eyes, filled with surprise, fear and now dread.

"That's all I needed to hear," and Papa lowered the shotgun to the boy's chest and pulled the trigger.

The shot reverberated through the woods, the echo winding round on itself in the thin, dark December air, allowing for the punky sound that accompanies a met target. Papa expected company directly, so he pulled the body outside and used the sleeping bag as a shroud. He cleaned up as best he could, then removed the body to the nearby abandoned mine shaft—including the boy's gear—and covered his tracks. It required the rest of the night.

Blood is black in the dark, he noticed with odd detachment.

Lucy had left for school by the time he returned home the next morning. After wiping down the shotgun he replaced it on the rack, then ran the hottest bath his skin could stand.

CHAPTER 4~BLACK

Five Years Later

She's blooming," Grannie declared during the second trimester. In the late third, after a dose of castor oil in orange juice and a bumpy back-woods ride (it was all back-woods), Lucy delivered a healthy, rosy-colored girl, caught (as they say) by Grannie.

Agnes Maria Munro was born on a sweltering August day in 1966 on a mountain in western North Carolina in her mother Lucy's pink-and-white childhood bedroom. Father and Grandfather waited on the vine-laden front porch, drinking Pabst Blue Ribbon beer and listening to a turned-up radio broadcast of a late-summer Atlanta Braves baseball game. Lucy's pregnancy had gone well.

Lucy and Andy Munro chose their mothers' names for their baby, Grannie's first true grandchild. And the Braves won the game—further cause for celebration.

Three years passed. Andy joined the Army for the benefits; moreover, because so many friends were leaving to fight in Viet Nam, some returning, many not. The Army ordered him to Ft. Benning, Georgia, to boot camp, while the child and Lucy returned to the mountain for an extended visit. When Andy learned he'd been posted to Fort Bragg, two hundred-forty miles from the mountain, his wife and daughter joined him, only to learn he had pending orders to Viet Nam. Papa and Grannie once again helped them return to the mountain.

Andy served one tour of duty then returned to the United States, where he worked as a civilian mechanic. He reenlisted for a second tour, settled his wife and daughter in post housing, and arrived in Viet Name three months prior to Saigon's fall. A "freakish mishap" took him on April 30, 1975 in an example of bitter irony, his daughter would later learn; the date signaling the final hours of the conflict.

She'd never been to a funeral and this was her Daddy's. The cat got a hold of her tongue, but good. After the morning funeral and internment at the Main Post Cemetery at Fort Bragg, there followed a small reception at the funeral home. Her mother told her grandparents she wanted to be alone for a spell, so Papa and Grannie took Agnes to the post's stables to spend the afternoon. "Something familiar might help the child," said Grannie.

The smell of horses, fresh hay and regularly oiled tack brought comfort. Agnes headed for a particular stall, stepped in and clung to its occupant's neck. The horse nickered and stood by patiently. Before her father had left for the last time, he'd shown her how to call the stables early on Saturday mornings to reserve a horse for an hour's ride. The stable became refuge; horses, her friends.

Later, when Papa pulled up to her house, she saw several vehicles parked on the street. One, an ambulance with flashing lights. A woman introduced herself to Papa as, "your daughter's neighbor" and said she'd been asked to watch for them and take them to her home next door, and that a woman from Family Services would be by.

Agnes wondered why the neighbor lady was ignoring her and, as if the woman heard her thoughts, she said, "Why don't you go on to the back yard with the girls and watch them," she suggested, adding in an audible aside to Grannie, ". . . to give her something to do." Her grandmother would have none of it and wanted answers. Now.

"What's happened?" Grannie demanded, but in a controlled manner, looking from the woman over to Lucy's home and back to the neighbor. She started for Lucy's door.

"Aggie," Papa reached for Grannie's arm, "wait now."

"I will *not*," she replied, eyes and voice determined, and she marched toward the house where two young men struggled to pull a gurney through the front door. Her Grannie made an inarticulate sound, and Agnes noticed that the windows to the left and right of the door, including the large picture window facing the street, were blackened with something.

What's this . . . Paint? Grannie puzzled. On the gurney lay Lucy, covered with a blanket, wide straps securing her in place. Her face appeared to be streaked with soot or something. No . . . it was painted black and poor efforts made to wipe it off so as to leave her eyes owl-like. Lucy's normally ash-brown hair was daubed in careless fashion with black where the hairline met her delicate forehead. *It'll have to be cut off.* Lucy looked drowsy, her eyes half-closed as she moaned. After calmly examining her daughter's appearance in a clinical manner, her mother alarm now clamored.

"What's happened to her? Where are you taking her?" she cried, as the ambulance pulled away. Looking for someone who could supply an answer, she shook her head at her husband who stood back with Agnes and the neighbor, shielding the girl from the sight. Grannie saw the neighbor place a hand on Papa's forearm and speak to him, and she watched them turn and walk toward the adjacent house. Papa glanced over and down every few steps through an obstacle course of two tricycles, a small red wagon, several dolls and a scattered tea set.

Grannie steeled herself and entered Lucy's house.

After some time she knocked lightly on the neighbor's door and was shown in. "I'm Arlene," said the neighbor, gesturing to a seat next to Papa in the small living room. The woman offered a glass of iced tea and Grannie accepted the drink mechanically, while two glasses sat untouched on the table beside the couch.

"You go on now, girlie," Papa gently pressed his granddaughter, who slowly reached for the hand of Arlene's three-year-old daughter. Agnes gave him a beseeching, side-long glance. Arlene's five-year-old followed them through the kitchen and out the back door, but only after the woman assured Agnes that her momma was all right and that everything would be just fine.

Grannie leaned toward Papa to say the woman from Family Services would arrive directly.

A serious, middle-aged woman wearing a uniform with two metal name badges—one that read "Family Services" and the other "Mrs. Rupert Black"—came to the door, was shown a seat and offered a similarly ignored glass of tea. She asked Arlene to repeat to Mr. and Mrs. Cowry what she had conveyed earlier and this Arlene did, in what sounded to Grannie like a school assignment recitation, the details a struggle to recall.

"I was in the front yard with my girls and we heard this noise, and when I looked over I saw the windows all covered in black something, and screaming like someone was being killed. So I hurried the girls into our house and called the MPs." She paused to take a breath and continued. "We saw them arrive, and could hear their knocking like they were using those heavy sticks they carry, you know? And calling out—loud. They must've got in, 'cause an ambulance came shortly . . ." she said, one hand holding the other and rubbing it nervously.

Everyone sat still for a moment then Grannie began. She'd spoken with an MP.

"It looked to him, he told me, like something just snapped in our Lucy. When the ambulance came, the police told the driver that Lucy was naked when they got there, so one of them found her robe and she fought with him to put it on, crying that she didn't want anything touching her. He said she was babbling something like, 'No light, no light,' then she started screeching and sobbing. . .

"The driver told him that one of the MPs—those are the police, Papa—found and removed a—what did he call it? Oh Lord . . . 'a small caliber hand gun'; that was it—from the kitchen table."

Papa sucked in his breath. "Oh no-o-o," he moaned and hung his head.

Grannie continued. For all her usual aplomb, she'd simply stared at the MP in disbelief, she now told them, adding that she'd gawked similarly at the room's walls, which had been painted in slap-dash fashion with coal-black paint, including the windows and the mirror hanging behind the couch; greasy, black splotches of paint had dripped, or been spilled, on the furniture. She remembered thinking—in the way the absurd mocks pragmatism—*Why couldn't she have used a water-based paint?* The room looked as if it'd been tarred. Someone had turned the lights on, Grannie added, in order to see anything.

She related all this mostly to Papa; the two other women just happened to be there. Fixtures, like the drapes.

The house reeked of cannabis; it smelled stronger than what she remembered. In the past, she'd occasionally used the herb to treat a child's asthma, or nausea; some pains—like headache—and hysteria; but that was long ago. Combined with the odors of wet paint, stale cigarette smoke and spilled whiskey—these filled her nostrils and she began to gag. With hand to nose and mouth, she rushed to the bathroom, where she vomited into Lucy's filthy toilet.

Having regained her shaken composure after several deep breaths, she rinsed her mouth, cupped her hands to the water and brought it to her face, then used toilet paper to dab herself dry. The face of an old woman stared back from the mirror. She lifted her hands to adjust an errant bobby pin.

Grannie was accustomed to a body's various odors and the necessity to uncover possible causes for an ailment, but her daughter's choosing to ally herself with these poisons, to deliberately despoil herself with them, this she did not comprehend. *And yet—you do—don't you?* came the question raised by her soul.

Agnes heard every word of her Grannie's discourse. Having ordered the two young girls in her fiercest tone to stay in the back yard, she crept to the side of the cinderblock house to an open window and leaned against the wall to listen, her hearing fine-tuned to auscultation. A trance state descended upon her, meeting the concentration required to hear, to bear witness, to know; and after, strangely detached, she simply tucked the knowledge away into one of her many inward boxes.

In the following weeks, at her new school down the mountain from her grandparents' farm, she explained her mother's absence simply: "She's sick." When asked "Why?" she answered, "I don't know." In time, the inquiries ceased. Papa and Grannie never discussed it. At least in her hearing.

Her mother had suffered an acute "nervous breakdown," as it was then known. *Nowadays*, Senga would later ponder, *the phrase is mental breakdown, or psychotic break, so, still—a break,* manipulating the words cat-and-mouse-like: heartbreak, break-up, break-neck speed, breaking, brakes, braking—*ahh, when it all comes to a grinding halt*—a foregone conclusion.

Lucy entered a hospital to undergo long-term psychiatric treatment. Which may or may not have contributed to further difficulties.

Senga (then called Agnes) would always wonder.

CHAPTER 5~THE TEACHER

The girl's been with us for two years . . . On an early morning in May, late spring in Appalachia, Grannie stirred from sleep, sensing knowledge like a nudge, and then, much as one wakes and simply chooses which shirt to wear that day (when only one is hanging in the closet), her mind was decided: her granddaughter would be her student. Apprentices—young plumbers, carpenters, masons, electricians and so on—paired with experienced old-timers to learn a trade. The daughter (or granddaughter) learning homemaking craft wasn't accorded the distinction, Grannie concluded wryly.

She'd simply use the word "student."

Later, from her rocker on the front porch, her thoughts drifted on the mist that rose off the creek bed far below in the valley; a weaving, ghost-like thread, white then gray, playing with bright sunlit patches shining above and beneath. The county road followed the course of the creek but, early on a Sunday morning, few vehicles passed. *Ah, there go the Wilsons.* She rose and turned to the screen door just as Agnes bounded through.

"Whoa, dearie, my coffee!" she cried, raising high her mug.

"Sorry, Grannie," the girl called back, as she darted down the steps.

"Hey, come back here! I want to talk to you."

"Right now?" asked Agnes, and perhaps thinking better of it, she climbed slowly back up the steps and sat down on the porch swing—impatiently, Grannie noticed.

"Where are you all fired up to get to?"

"Mary Ann's mare foaled during the night; she just called and asked me to come. Right away."

"Yes, and you may, but I have something important—too—to talk with you about. There's time, and this won't take long," she added, knowing the girl was raring to go.

After gaining her full attention, Grannie asked Agnes if becoming her student was something she might be interested in—which was important, as she wasn't going to waste her time, nor anyone else's. Her daughter Lucy had never shown an aptitude for the work. Never taken to it. Maybe she was too close to it, Grannie had decided, what with her sickness and all. Grannie doubted her own ability to heal her daughter's ailing spirit, and there lay the trap, she knew. Ruefully recalling the shoemaker's son having no shoes and risking the sin of pride, she remembered Jesus' pronouncement, "A prophet is not without honor except in his own country."

Even the medical doctors cautioned against treating their own if they could help it. And yet? And yet she wondered if she was somehow ignoring, or overlooking, another means by which to help her daughter. *Mayhap* flitted by the periphery of her mind, though not long enough to arouse curiosity. It settled in a hidden corner, just behind her eyesight, poised to appear when summoned.

Grannie allowed the girl a moment longer.

"Well . . . that's all right. You sleep on it, dearie."

"I don't need to, Grannie; I want to!" A wholehearted reply.

Grannie dismissed her to go see the new foal. She leaned back in her rocker and allowed quiet elation to rise in her.

The lessons began auspiciously, a fancy word Grannie rarely used; it was simply another way to say, "in the right time," she told her granddaughter, corresponding as it did with the girl's first menses.

She began with properties of familiar herbs, one at a time, until the girl knew them cold. *Taraxacum officinale* or the common dandelion came first. This time of year, the bright yellow flower heads grew profusely in fields, roadsides and yards. As a source of pollen, they drew honey bees. Leaves and roots were considered diuretic, thus contributing to one name: in French, *pissenlit*, or piss in bed. *Dents* (teeth) *de lion*, for toothy leaves. Dandelion strengthened and nourished the urinary and liver systems, relieved abscesses, swellings and snakebite.

Since she could walk, Agnes had accompanied her grandmother in picking young shoots to eat as greens. They were allowed to proliferate in the small front yard every year, and Agnes formed daisy-chains from the flowers and stems, later blowing the puff-ball seeds away as had countless children for eons. Ever since she was old enough to sit still, or more likely as a means to teach her to do just that, Grannie had taught her to sit and breathe with plants, and to show respect. "One dandelion stands for all dandelions."

Her granddaughter had narrowed her eyes at this assertion, wondering if her grandmother were pulling her leg.

"My Grannie was Cherokee," she once told Agnes, "your great-great grandmother," she explained with a kind of, "so this is why" reasoning. She didn't elaborate. Respect and power, she added, hold great importance in making good medicine—respect being the greater factor. And always, in anything ventured. She'd looked the girl squarely in the eye, reckoning this an absolute matter—no exceptions. Power referred to the good a medicine could do.

"What was her name, Grannie?"

"Whose name, dearie?"

"My great-great grandmother—do you know?"

"Well of course, dearie. Grandfather Hugh called her *Junee*, but her name was Tall Juniper."

"Oh—so she must've been tall?"

"I reckon, dearie."

Grannie spoke fiercely when she needed to convey intents and purposes clearly but quickly. The girl had inherited a natural predisposition for parsing grave matters, compared with those of less serious consequence. Grannie had long trusted her to gather herbs, one kind at a time, heeding the rule and passing the test.

How it had rained that spring! The earth bounced with moisture. Skies meted out gust and gale for three weeks, more than typical spring squalls, and newly planted tobacco starts threatened to drown, the leaves flat on the soil in near abdication. Papa had managed to drain off some of the standing water in the field by carving narrow canals and turning the water from the rows. Rain weary, Grannie longed to hang sheets and pillows in sunshine.

At last, the household woke to bright light streaming into the house. A good day to strip the beds, air the mattresses and pillows outdoors and open windows against musty air. Papa's brother and sister-in-law were expected from Winston-Salem for a short visit, so Grannie was up early with baking and washing.

The heat of the morning sun coaxed a crop of dandelion flowers. Grannie coaxed four-year-old Agnes to gather enough of the yellow heads to fill three quart jars, warning her against bees. Squatting beside a plant, dimpled elbows resting on thighs, Agnes learned to say, "Hello," then, "May I?", wait for a sign, then snap off the flower head and drop it in the jar. Grannie told her she needn't ask each time if the first flower indicated, "Yes, you may." Little Agnes giggled and took up her task.

Papa fermented a yearly batch of dandelion wine, his and Grannie's traditional Christmas gift to neighbors. The wine required six months to work.

Lucy appeared with the clothes basket, and with her mother's help they lifted each heavy, wet sheet and stretched it over the clothesline. Grannie watched Lucy for signs of disquiet and instability. Andy had been away in Viet Nam for two months, serving his first tour as a helicopter mechanic.

For some time, Lucy had exhibited strange behavior; days or weeks, *like she's drunk too many cups of coffee,* thought Grannie. Bouncing from one subject to the next, her responses often sounded inappropriate to the situation. Utter sadness and despair would follow for another few weeks. Calmatives treated the nervous energy, and St. John's Wort (coupled with long walks) eased the melancholy.

Andy Munro was acquainted with his wife's temperament. His own mother, an Italian immigrant, was moody herself, he once told Grannie; "I'm used to it," his doleful brown eyes said. She wondered if Andy had merely joined the Army and accepted the prospect of battle as means of escape—a desperate solution she brushed off as foolish thinking.

As long as Lucy felt sufficiently engaged in an activity—cooking, cleaning, doing laundry—she managed well enough and Grannie's apprehensions eased. But come late afternoon, the *gloaming*—what she and Papa called dusk—and Lucy's face would reflect an expression of blank absence, as if an invisible hand had waved and wiped her daughter clean away. During this time, Grannie would nudge Lucy to read to her little girl, *to waylay the inevitable*, she hoped, and Lucy usually acceded by having Agnes pick out a book. Both on the sofa, Lucy would read in a monotone. Agnes would interject what came next in her small voice, brighter than necessary, in a valiant effort to lift her mother's spirit.

Heartbroken, Grannie would turn back to a task.

Agnes marched back and forth from the yard, carrying flower-filled quart jars. One at a time, she pressed her treasure to her chest against any and all dangers, to pour out the contents into a large rubber dish tub Papa had placed on the linoleum floor.

"Now look at that!" Papa crooned as his granddaughter hoisted the tub to the kitchen table. He'd built a wooden step stool for her and on this she now stood, proudly displaying her bounty, her two chubby hands outstretched to the sunny petals. She beamed, "*Wook!* See?"

"You picked *all* these, girlie? All by yourself?"

"Yep, Pawpaw, ah by masef!" she said, raising her arms and holding up her palms.

"They are just beautiful, and Papa thanks you *so* much, do you hear?" he added, squatting to pull the girl into his arms.

Grannie glanced at Lucy, who stared as if looking through a window from far away. Grannie held out an arm to pull her through and, moving into her mother's embrace, Lucy melted into a puddle of tears. They passed through the hall and into the front room where they sank onto the sofa, Grannie mumbling endearments and shushes.

Papa told Agnes that they were going to the front porch to pull off the pesky green stems from the flowers, and that it'd take until supper time.

"Can you say 'pesky,' girlie?" he asked.

"Peth-ky . . . *nooo*—pess-ky!" the child corrected.

Grannie heard their granddaughter ask about her mommy, and Papa's reply that she'd be all right, that her mommy was just missing her daddy.

"*Oooh*," the child said with empathy, as the screen door clicked shut. The mantel clock chimed six times, and in-between came Lucy's muffled breathing and intermittent sobs. Grannie held her as deliberately as the child had carried her jars of flowers—for all their worth. And the gloaming entered them, the betwixt time when memories surface, either like dandelion flowers after sunshine, or cruelly, and announced unawares.

CHAPTER 6~PEEPS

Agnes leaned against the headboard with sharpened pencil poised, and turned to the first page of her new diary. She laid the pencil down, tucked a pillow behind her, then sat a moment, wondering how to begin. Six months had passed since the cruel night. "Time is the Great Healer," Papa reminded her when he'd come in to say goodnight.

> My name is Agnes Maria Munro and this is the first page of my diary. Two things have happened. Well—a lot has happened, but two lately. First I want to record (this is how a diarist writes) that I was born on August 24, 1966, here in this house—in this bedroom, in fact. My Grannie Cowry delivered me here in Mommy's room—"She-Who-is-Away." I'll write about that later. . .
> So I started my period, or my "courses," as Grannie calls it, and I'm learning about herbs.
> I can't call my period "the curse," like they do at school. Grannie liked to slap me when I started to say it. We aren't supposed to call something a curse if it's actually a blessing, Grannie says. That's the worst of the worst, calling something evil when it's good. So, here I am with this ~~dumb~~ pad stuck to my underwear. Yesterday, she hauled me outside to squat over the ground in the woods first thing in the morning, "to bless the Earth," she called it. At least she turned her back. It felt weird, but somehow special.

I'm getting to rest up here in my room, skip chores and write in this new diary she gave me as a kind of, "Congratulations, You're a Woman Now!" gift. She also told me that actually having your cheeks slapped used to be normal, but she'd forgotten the reason for it, so didn't. I guess I'm glad. Yes—I surely am. Grannie's got large hands, and I've seen the way she chops kindling. Says the size of her hands makes it easier to catch babies, too.

Oh, and I'm not supposed to talk about her being a midwife. I mean, folks around here know, and it's not exactly against the law, but not exactly legal, either. She told me this a long old time ago, after I turned seven, and I think I've known this secret forever.

Guess I'll be careful with this diary. That's half the fun of keeping one, what my English teacher told us when she talked about famous diarists, like Pepys in England. His name is pronounced "Peeps," so that's almost a secret code by itself. It's a fun name. Not like mine, ugh, Agnes. . . I may change it someday.

The notion of changing her name dropped like a ripe apple from one of Papa's trees. *Where'd that come from?* she wondered, then resumed, carefully forming her letters and, taking pride in her strokes.

So I guess—*no*—I know I can have a baby now (Grannie says I must be precise with language, that one day it could be a matter of life and death. She's pretty strict with this).

The Other Thing that Grannie asked (all serious and everything) was do I want to learn about healing herbs and all. I didn't know what to say at first, it seemed like such a Big Question. She said, "That's all right; you just

sleep on it, dearie," (what she calls me), but I
didn't need to—I already knew.

Does it mean I'll grow up to be a midwife
like her and live in the mountains?

She wants me to start drawing the plants
we study. In every season. I like to draw, so
that will be fun. I have colored pencils and a
notebook, different than this one—which has
lines. I'm supposed to write down what she
says, so I don't forget it. And I can't get
behind with my school work just because I'm
doing this. It's my work now too (besides
school, she says). I'll be helping her gather
and make medicine. Earn my keep. . .

Agnes wrote about Papa's happiness that Grannie had a helper,
especially with the gathering and garbling (*where you pick away the
useful plant parts and leave the stems*), and his telling her to always
do exactly what Grannie says, "Cause you wouldn't want to
hurt nobody somehow." Papa told her about the girl up the
road who gathered mushrooms one day and wound up
poisoning her whole family. *They didn't die, just got sicker than snot*
(she wrote), while Grannie did the best she could to ease their
suffering, but *law*—(Papa had said), the littlest girl was in a
poor way for days; *she liked to died.* He warned her that Grannie
wasn't one to cross either (this she already knew of course),
and to just keep her mouth shut and her bowels open during a
lesson and wait until she finished before asking to ask a
question. That's how he put it; *ask to ask a question.*

In English class we're learning how to
describe someone in writing, so I'll describe
my grandparents here:

Grannie is tall for a woman, I hear. She has
long, turning-white hair that she braids and
wraps around her head, like a crown, every
blessèd morning. (I'm allowed to say
"blessèd." I may not say the opposite.) I used
to brush her hair when I was younger, and she
let me braid it. (I wear mine long too, just

because it's easier.) She's stout (she says); not fat—just strong. Good bones, she told me, from her daddy's side.

Her Great Grandfather Hugh Mac Kay came from northern Scotland, in Sutherland. His hair was black, cut short to his collar, and brushed straight back to show a high forehead. It's a black and white photo, so, hard to tell. In the picture he looks dead serious—like he's looking straight through whatever he's looking at.

I see where Grannie gets her way of looking at you when she's trying to drill something important into your skull. But when she smiles, oh, that's THE BEST. She and Papa have wonderful faces when they smile. I'm lucky to be their grandkid—I mean, I feel sad for Mommy—oh, I wasn't going to talk about that, not yet, anyway. "All things in their right time," Grannie says.

I like what she says about looking at something in their "proper phase of the moon"; in other words, "If you're pitiful sad, dearie, don't be trying to do something that's needin' more light—meaning, more information, do you know? Like what you'd have in a brighter phase of the moon. 'Course, we don't always have that 'perticaler' luxury," she said, "But if you can wait, then do." It makes sense. She also says it's just plain logical.

A distinguishing characteristic of her Papa, she decided, was his hat. He always wore it. Except indoors. He had learned from his older brother that a man may wear a hat if he's sitting at the counter, *but it doesn't sit well with him, haha,* wrote Agnes. He never fussed over some man wearing his hat inside, but she could tell it was "stirring him up real bad."

Papa was raised in these parts, too. I like the way he talks, sooo slowww. "Mountain Talk," Grannie calls it. He has kind eyes, hazel-colored, and a red tinge or glow to his skin. It's like his blood shines through it—and it feels like the papery shells of ground cherries. I heard him tell Grannie, "Ever' knock's a new bruise!" She told him to quit visiting the moonshiners, and I don't know what that's got to do with it.

On his forearm he's got a real bad scar. "That's what happens when you don't use your head, girlie," he told me, but only that.

He's tall too, over six-feet-something. And wiry. I hear I take after him—and some my own Daddy.

Daddy. I have an album of pictures. He wasn't tall, so I probably won't be either. He died in "that stinking war," (Grannie says). I'm not going to cross this out just because it has nothing to do with Papa—it would seem disrespectful, or might hurt Daddy's feelings. I know he's watching over me; he's somewhere peaceful and beautiful. Like Mommy. And that's just something I know, like the back of my hand (Grannie also says). But Papa is, in a word (or two), just great. And this is all for now.

CHAPTER 7~REMEDY

Her Grannie Cowry proved her mettle. Daily. Agnes ferreted out the quality by observation: Grannie stood up straight, with shoulders back; she never smiled simply to be smiling; and she never hesitated when lancing a boil. On the occasions Agnes attended her on calls, she marveled at how her Grannie marshaled the situation and made herself immediately *useful;* "a handy trait to possess," she'd once quipped.

Whether her grandmother was examining an effacing cervix (and giving her a needful lesson), or listening to a widower's description of chronic constipation and scribbling her remedy (*eat more greens*), usefulness was her driving motivation, though Agnes—at that time—merely accepted it as who her grandmother was.

Grannie made nearly daily decisions regarding the underfunded and under-addressed health care of her rural neighbors—a complaint Agnes often heard. If the more obvious practices of proper diet and daily exercise were ignored, then Grannie left her clients the appropriate herb to be infused and drunk, or to be administered as a wash. Agnes recorded:

> With dog bite, a handful of yarrow flowers and leaves—astringent and anti-septic—are infused in boiled water for several minutes, allowed to cool and the liquid used to soak the site—repeat over the course of a day.
>
> A "wound" herb, yarrow lessens bleeding. Chewing the fresh leaves relieves toothache.

Often, Grannie left behind a small bottle of an herbal tincture with simple directions, calling these "remedies"— never "prescriptions." She understood and appreciated well the limit of her knowledge. One late afternoon she spoke (gravely) with Agnes about this, as they sat on the porch drinking iced peppermint tea. Grannie shelled peas, Agnes took notes, and both admired the hazy view of distant ranges.

Green stillness lay over the land. Ambient sounds of buzzing bees, flies and cicadas defined Agnes' "quiet". The neighbor's tractor down the hill had ceased its noisy work.

Grannie's teas seldom failed to achieve their purpose, whether to stimulate, sedate or simply to please. For Agnes, peppermint belonged to the third category, but she'd learned it was good for stomach upset too.

Her grandmother resumed her discussion:

"A case of trauma, an acute circumstance, for example— appendicitis—is sent or taken to the hospital as soon as possible, though *we* may have to determine the necessity. I might give them a nervine, you know—something to calm them—then get them help real soon." She continued: "I might wish they wouldn't come here at all if it's something that bad, 'cause that wastes precious time. But it's what they know, and sometimes I *can* help, at least to stop the bleeding, or steady a broken bone and the like. They just don't know what to do a lot of the time, and I guess I just have to accept that if I can help even a little bit, even if they should have gone straight to town, then what else can I do? I can't tell them *not* to come, now can I?"

This was a long speech for Grannie, but Agnes guessed she'd needed to convey the importance of recognizing limits. The nearest clinic lay more than thirty miles away, mostly by unpaved rough road, and even then someone might have to be transported to the hospital another ninety minutes away. Grannie dumped her shelled peas into her bowl and reached into the basket at her feet for two more handfuls.

She was well-regarded and respected in at least three counties, all having to do with this penchant for "usefulness," Agnes surmised.

That evening at supper—which included mashed peas served with butter—Grannie turned to Papa and pronounced a kindred spirit in her granddaughter. The flagging spirits of Agnes lifted.

"It skips a generation, you know," Grannie spoke of courage, but Agnes thought it referred to healing work as well—*that* required a kind of courage, she thought; the nerve to effect a change—not the everyday, nurturing variety of mothers with their families.

"But mothers are the *first* healers, mind," Grannie was quick to amend, and a shiver ran down Agnes' back.

She's in my head, shaking her head once as if she were trying to whip an errant lock of hair out of the way. Grannie continued, reading her granddaughter, and she chortled, "Ha! We have to heal you from that business of gettin' born, and we do that by feeding you *first* thing!"

After breakfast the following morning, with Papa off to hoe his field, Grannie sat in her rocker once again to shell the last of the peas. Agnes sat on a step, using the next riser to hold her notebook. Continuing her introduction, Grannie raised a bent forefinger to the humid, still air.

"First, n'er do no harm, dearie, like it says in the doctors' oath. No harm to the body, an' in *perticaler*," she added in her soft mountain speech, "n'er do no harm to the spirit of a person. That's real important. Folk can sometimes live with awful bad aches and pains, but if they got 'em a soul-sickness, well, that's not the easiest to heal."

Her Grannie often spoke in negatives, emphasizing the opposite.

Agnes thought of her mother and frowned. It hurt so, this *thing*, this knowledge of her mother's pain. Agnes shut her eyes and turned her head slowly this time, from right to left to nudge the thought, then returned her attention.

Grannie bent to her bowl of shelled peas. Agnes watched her sink one of her large, strong hands into the mess of green to bring up a handful, letting them fall through her gnarled, chapped fingers. She repeated the gesture with the other hand, as if it were a form of play and discovery. (In later years, Senga would discover for herself the soothing benefits of frozen peas on arthritic hands.)

Grannie wouldn't elaborate and Agnes didn't ask, but she learned their healing skills had been passed down with a version of the Hippocratic Oath, one that included, "no cutting for stone," (recompense) and discretion. A taciturn nature was bred into mountain-folk, along with an abiding sense of reserve in both good fortune and adversity. The origin of the oath's introduction in their ancestry was lost, but Grannie told Agnes, "No matter; what's important is the doing," and Why's weren't as important as the How's. Agnes allowed the words to steep. . .

Often compensated in the old way, by barter, Grannie and Papa seldom wanted for anything, but neither would they have felt right if they'd somehow avoided the usual hard parts of everyday living their neighbors endured.

"In life, there are those heavy ole rocks needing dug out of the garden," Papa told her last June. One had been her mother's illness. By then, Lucy had been under the care of the white-coated psychiatrists for thirteen months.

She marveled now at this knowledge of her mother, standing *plain* at the bottom of the porch steps, patiently waiting to be invited to join their tea party, and she wondered further if her mother could hear everything she and her grandmother discussed when she was in "that place,"—or the place the doctors' medicines took her. . .

Grannie dreaded seeing her daughter sedated when they visited; Lucy would be wheeled in by the same joyless orderly, to the same cheerless visiting area, where they sat at the same graceless table. The place smelled of urine and rubbing alcohol.

"What's wrong with her that she can't walk?" Papa would ask no one in particular, his voice wrung out, betraying anger tinged with sorrow. Grannie knew he felt helpless and utterly useless on these visits. If she hated the chlorpromazine—their daughter's sedative—she loathed even more her husband's sense of powerlessness. It walked beside him and behind him like a haint.

"Oh my Lord, what if this thing is catchin'?" she muttered to herself, as Lucy's eyes lifted from hands that lay folded in her lap. Her brows furrowed with recognition and concentration as she attempted a smile. Grannie meant *catching* in the spiritual sense, knowing the mind could persuade the body to do unspeakable things.

Upon leaving, Agnes and her grandparents would rise from the graceless table and in turn do their best to administer proper hugs to Lucy, whose vacant eyes flashed in quick fear, like a cowed, frightened creature. Agnes remembered this when she lay down at night; not the sticky-sweet, chocolate sheet cake with cream cheese frosting and tepid lemonade.

On the drive home the last time, Agnes heard Grannie speaking quietly to Papa in the front seat of the old Buick.

"She needs to come home, do you *hear?* Where she belongs. . ." This spoken with a pleading urgency she'd rarely heard from her grandmother.

When Lucy left was how Grannie and Papa described their daughter's abrupt committal to the state hospital and, privately (but overheard by Agnes), Grannie telling her husband, "The girl's been leaving this ole world for years and years."

The cloak may have been invisible, but Agnes could sense when Grannie donned her *Glory Robe.* Papa's deep sighs would follow, with bold efforts to hold back a biblical flood of emotion, to be forever lost to rushing waters if he uttered as much as one, single word.

When Grannie first read the *Glory Robe* passage in her Bible, her soul lit up, as though presented an unexpected gift. Intended to signify a robe of wisdom, Grannie read the phrase as euphemism, to describe a way of thinking, or holding information.

All five senses functioned as one when she wore the garment, she explained to Agnes.

"Several years gone by now, a good, *good* friend died sudden and unexpected-like," she began, ". . . a brain bleed. It was a real bad turn, dearie. Old Myron—her poor husband—finding her there that morning lying dead next to him . . . there'd been no signs, but I failed her, I do believe. . ."

Here, Grannie had paused in her telling and looked away for several moments, waiting for the words, and permission. Certain stories were held sacred to her way of thinking.

"I couldn't help but wonder if I should have seen *something;* I mean she and Myron had just been by for supper. Two nights after the funeral I dreamt of her, and you know how I set great store by dreams, dearie. 'Mary Jo' was her name—and in the dream I was a' knowin' she had passed, so I asks her, 'It's not like here, is it? Are you all right, Mary Jo?'

"'Oh, Aggie!' she says to me, just a-beaming, 'You know how *there* you have five senses?' She meant here, dearie, on this ole Earth; 'Why yes, Mary Jo, I know,' I say to her, 'Well, *here*,' she says—sorta matter-of-fact, you know? 'Here, it's like all your senses are just a one *big* one!' And then she was gone."

Grannie had paused—a sad half-smile forming in the corner of her mouth in Agnes' direction, but gazing beyond her granddaughter, dream-like.

She pondered the significance of the dream every day, so sincere had been her departed friend's response, until one day, with succinct deliberateness, Grannie set her mind to live Mary Jo's message as though it were A True Thing—which it could only have been, coming from love, as Grannie believed. She'd been given *A Big Dream*, she declared to her granddaughter. Then, turning to her, she said, "Look at me" and asked if she understood what she'd just told her. The girl nodded yes, her eyes wide in wonderment.

Agnes understood perfectly what her senses were, from a passed-down childhood game. "What do you see? I see. . . What do you hear? I hear. . . What do you smell? What do you taste? What does it *feel* like? But Grannie introduced a sixth, if tacitly.

This potent new sense—usefulness—came with a liberty to enjoy it, and to feel loved and nurtured. These combined provided Agnes with a Most Powerful Remedy (capitalizing the phrase in her notebook); a healing balm for wholeness, from the same root, hale; *robust, vigorous, sane,* and—her favorite healing word, because it was how she'd heard healthy horses described—*sound.*

"The child's a sponge," Grannie told her husband one night in bed.

"Ain't 'em all?" Papa replied, in his usual understated manner.

Agnes overheard this murmured pillow talk and turned over in her bed, able to fall asleep easily. Buzzing springtime noises of the mountain night lulled her gently away.

The previous fall, Papa had fetched Lucy from the hospital. School was in session. But this was a Saturday and Agnes was home. She rose from the porch rocker, calling to Grannie, "They're here!" Her grandmother wiped her palms on her blue apron, reached up to smooth her hair and pushed open the screen door.

They watched the Buick turn off the road below and begin the climb up the drive. It was late afternoon and the valley had begun its kaleidoscopic change from cool greens to fiery colors. A lowering sun cast an intense quality of light beneath clouds hanging dark with promise of rain. A wet chill punctuated the air. Grannie and Agnes turned to look at one another, to borrow—or lend—encouragement.

"Your Mama's come home," Grannie stated simply and turned to step down to the gravel walk.

"How's she going to be, Grannie?"

Looking back over her shoulder, Grannie said, "Don't know, child," and Agnes knew she didn't—by her use of "child" instead of *dearie*.

Papa pulled up, opened his door, stood and looked to Grannie with an illegible expression, conveying nothing to Agnes, but Grannie must've picked up a subtle cue, as she walked around to the passenger side to open the door.

"Lucy dear, you're here," she said with a smile, and leaning in to help her daughter up and out of the car.

Agnes watched from the porch, then stepped down slowly and quietly stood, hands clasped in front of her. Inspired, she bent to the flower border and quickly pulled up five or six fall-blooming white mums, snapping off the dirty end of each stem. She arranged the flowers quickly and neatly in her fist and crossed to her mother, just rising into Grannie's arms.

Presenting the hasty bouquet, she smiled into her mother's face. Lucy radiated something like delight on her features, but only for an instant, Agnes noted, before her face melted to an impassive mask, the flowers forgotten.

"How pretty, dearie—and how sweet of you to do that for your mama!" Grannie spoke with some enthusiasm, as much to Lucy as to Agnes. "Better you go put them in some water now, will you? Before they wilt?" she added. "We'll just get your mama's things and her inside, and then we'll have supper . . . all right, dear?" This to Lucy, who still regarded all as though a dream.

Papa had said not a word, but set about gathering Lucy's things from the trunk: a medium-size suitcase and a train case, a large manila envelope and another paper bag that looked to contain something.

"Didn't she have a purse?" Grannie asked Papa.

"Uh, I . . . I never saw one," he said, reaching for the suitcase and train case. "Here, girlie, you take these in. Can you manage?" he asked, referring to the envelope and paper bag.

Agnes took both, still grasping the flowers in her right hand.

She badly wanted her mother to reach out and take her in her arms, but her mother was not here, she realized with profound sadness; she was still *away*. Could Grannie bring her back? What was the remedy? Agnes turned toward the house, but waited for her mother and Grannie who were making their slow, crunching way over the gravel to the steps.

Her mother looked shrunken, curled up and dry, *like a leaf*, she thought, and she shook her head in her fashion, to banish the thought.

"How long ago did they give her something?" Grannie asked Papa, "Do you know?"

"Right before we left, Aggie. . . They said she'd be more comfortable riding in the car for that long. I thought it best."

Agnes noticed the troubled look on his face.

"Well. We'll see," Grannie said. And nothing more was mentioned about those medicines, at least in Agnes's hearing.

Grannie had cooked Lucy's favorite meal for her homecoming: fried chicken, mashed potatoes and gravy; carrot, raisin and pineapple salad, with sorghum syrup on biscuits for dessert. No one showed much appetite, but valiant efforts were made to encourage one another. Lucy sat quietly, barely touching her food. She ate three bites of Jell-O salad and a half-biscuit with syrup. *The sweet things*. As she watched her mother, her Grannie and her Papa, Agnes wondered, *What's going to happen now?*

A pallet on the floor lay against the far wall in Lucy's childhood bedroom where Agnes had been sleeping. Lucy would sleep in her own bed and Agnes move to the pallet. She didn't mind. Grannie mentioned that, if need be, she could always sleep on the couch.

"I'll be all right, Grannie."

She turned her face to the wall after bidding goodnight to her mother, who remained mute.

A heavy rainfall kept her company, the rusty metal roof amplifying the drone, until her neighbor's rooster crowed; then, as if granted permission, Agnes fell asleep from exhaustion.

Grannie set about finding a way for Lucy to rediscover her own brand of usefulness, as she settled into her family's rhythms. Lucy must break some habits—and they were merely that, habits. The hospital's basket-weaving activities had not interested her; they had meant nothing—*less than nothing*— Grannie believed. Lucy needed something that was hers alone to lift her from her hell-hole, she told Papa.

The girl is hers alone. . .

The days passed. Harvested tobacco hung like becalmed ocher flags in the barn, waiting to be graded and sold. Papa plowed the field, cut winter firewood and hunted. Agnes, ever the tomboy, accompanied him when possible. "The girl's got good aim," Papa informed his wife proudly after Agnes brought down several doves with the 4-10 shotgun. Between her and Papa, they dressed enough for a large casserole dish, smothered with mushroom gravy and served on rice.

Grannie continued her healing calls and put up the garden with help from Agnes and Lucy. The girl attended school, dried herbs and made tinctures. Grannie Cowry watched life on the mountain swell for them all, to reflect a certain ripeness.

CHAPTER 8~REMEMBER

In 1976, the country celebrated the bi-centenary of the Declaration of Independence. That fall, Agnes's fifth grade class busily prepared for a celebratory Thanksgiving program—Indians and Pilgrims having their say and their feast—never mind the legendary event had taken place more than a century and a half before the war for independence.

Agnes was surprised to learn she'd been chosen to play "The Indian Princess Who Presents the Platter"—one laden with turkey. "A girl who habitually wears her hair in two long braids doubtless fits the role," affirmed her teacher. At home, Agnes voiced awe and trepidation at the prospect. Her news was greatly touted at the dinner table and she noticed her mother did more than just pick at her food. She seemed happier. *Maybe because everybody's not staring at her for once.*

Grannie's mind flew to her patterns box and a suitable style. She'd taught Lucy to sew when her daughter was old enough to stitch a straight line; it was normal for mountain folk to sew their own clothes. Hereby her *dearie* would again recognize her mother and her mother *dearie* in the weeks to follow: through this simple magic of making a costume for a play, and—*May it be, Lord*—Lucy's desire to help her daughter with her lines. This could lead to interest in her homework. And finally, to all other tasks of mothering a ten-year-old girl.

The constant monitoring, the difficult conversations with Lucy's doctor (who believed his patient had been removed to a primitive back of beyond), her own practice and keeping a household together; somehow all had to be borne, and borne well. She felt the burden of strain, but Papa's resolve to give up drinking had remained strong and he'd never wavered. It lent her strength. *Sixteen years have passed since*—she realized with a start. *It feels like a lifetime ago—and only yesterday.* She sighed as she slid the box of patterns from under the bed.

Lucy was encouraged to make as many decisions as possible about the costume, with the girl's opinion considered. Grannie thought they might have to go to town for another pattern altogether, as she riffled through her box.

Which they did. Only her and Lucy; Agnes had school.

At the fabric store, they found the perfect Indian Princess pattern, complete with fringe. They chose a light-brown fabric and lengths of colored ribbon to embellish the dress. After, Lucy and her mother treated themselves to hamburgers, French fries, and vanilla milkshakes at a café. On a whim, as she paid the check, Grannie asked Lucy if she'd like her hair trimmed and her daughter's eyes lit up. They crossed the street to the hairdresser, where Lucy chose a haircut from an array of photographs framed on the wall. She clearly enjoyed having her hair washed. *I wish this is all it took*, Grannie lamented as she picked up a magazine and idly leafed through it.

Agnes liked her mother's new hairstyle—a shoulder-length shag with bangs. After circling the straight-backed kitchen chair her mother sat in, holding her head high like a queen, Agnes exclaimed, "You look beautiful, Mommy!"

Lucy grinned. Then, as though she had forgotten herself, she clamped her mouth shut and stared down into her hands, but Grannie wouldn't have it. "Oh no you don't, Lucy dear—your daughter just called you *beautiful*, and you *are*, do you *hear?*"

Lucy—head still bowed—peeked from under her new bangs and smiled, then held out her arms. Agnes eased down on her mother's lap and embraced her. Lucy held her close for several moments, then released her with the words, "Thank you, sweetie."

The pattern and fabric passed muster with Agnes and, after supper, the crisp, new fabric covered the wide dining room table. Agnes carefully pinned the pattern—following her mother's halting directions—then Lucy cut it out with precision and care. Papa, watching a western on television (large glass of iced tea at his elbow), was informed they needed a turkey feather and he suggested they go hunting Saturday morning.

"Piece of cake!" he called over the din of the TV, the optimistic phrase forever linked with simple joy. A charm.

Within a week's time, her costume was conjured, sown and modeled one evening after supper. Agnes had two lines, and these she rehearsed, at first shyly—Papa's scrutiny unnerving her. Her mother spoke in a voice like butter:

"Just say it like you were talking with your daddy, sweetie; pretend he's sitting right here, 'cause *he is*, you know, and he knows you can do this thing. . . Now, go out of the room, turn around—here, carry this . . . pretend it's the turkey platter."

Lucy handed her a seed catalogue from the coffee table and guided her toward the door into the hallway. Agnes drew herself up to her full height, squared her shoulders and turned around, holding out the catalogue like the sacrificial victim and saving grace it represented. She began:

"Oh, mighty Massasoit, our great and powerful chief, we bring to you and to our new friends, the Pilgrims from far-away England, a feast on this day. You, who have suffered from hunger these many months, long may you remember our mercy and kindness."

She rehearsed her lines perfectly while concentrating on the wall to the left of the front window, then bowed. If there'd been a turkey on the catalogue it would've slipped to the ground.

"Wonderful!" Papa said and clapped. Lucy and her mother beamed and applauded.

"Do you want to do it again, dearie?" Grannie asked.

"No, it's all right," she replied timidly, adding, "Could y'all help me take this off? I don't want to tear anything." Off came the headband (complete with noble turkey feather) and placed on the credenza.

The pageant came off beautifully. Her granddaughter delivered her lines fearlessly, with no hesitation. Agnes made a bow. *She is a princess*, thought Grannie, Papa sat on her right, Lucy to her left, and all three grinned, matching the enthusiasm of their neighbors.

After, all gathered in the lunchroom to sample "First Thanksgiving Foods," Grannie and Lucy having contributed Tall Juniper's cornbread recipe. Agnes and her classmates paraded their costumes.

"I don't think I've *ever* seen our little girl quite so—" Papa searched for a word.

"Princess-y?" Grannie provided, with a wink to Lucy.

"Well, she's certainly behaving less—" Papa began, as he watched his granddaughter. "Like a savage?" Lucy made the joke, knew it and laughed.

Grannie and Papa grinned. They hadn't heard Lucy's laugh—a throaty, full-on guffaw—in so very long. It occurred to them in the same moment and they turned to one another. Papa inclined his head to touch Grannie's.

Grannie engaged Lucy in activities that seemed to interest her: *a simple provision,* she decided. If one morning Lucy seemed distant, Grannie would let her be, doing so with kindness and love. Giving someone time to feel bored, to feel sadness or be "blue," as she called it, was just fine.

To Papa one night, she whispered, "When did people all 'a sudden believe it's wrong or unnatural to feel sadness? I declare, *feel* sad, get it over with! Seems like we're not allowed to feel nothing but happy happy happy all the time. Tain't natural. Can't feel glad without knowing what it's like to feel sad. . .

"I believe we *trade* one for the other . . . that it's a kind of barter, don't you know? When we're sad we mope and rest, and get ready for the next time we'll be feeling happy—or, we'd just burn out quick as a birthday candle!"

She'd been sitting against the headboard and her pillow, but now shrugged down into her sheets and blanket, reached up and turned off her light. She was finished; she'd said her piece.

Papa heaved a sigh, then said quietly, "You're probably right, Aggie . . . goodnight." He leaned over, pecked her forehead and turned out his bedside lamp.

The year's tobacco crop had been stripped off the stalks, hung, graded, tied into hands, packed and hauled to auction where it'd brought a good price. Papa whistled tunelessly as he replaced a hoe on its hook in the garage.

His thoughts turned to his daughter.

Two weeks after the pageant, Lucy showed a renewed interest in sewing. She wanted to make a *proper* dress for Agnes, and this had to be carefully considered. The girl had taken to wearing her costume to school, daring anyone to tease her.

Lucy told her father she wanted to drive into town to look for a pattern, and buy the fabric. Grannie was away on a call to *Mrs. Whatshername;* he couldn't recall.

The late afternoon temperature showed a drop on the gauge. Rain was changing to snow when Papa looked out a garage window. The school bus, he noted, was just rolling to a stop at the bottom of the hill to let the girl off. A niggling pulled in his chest, as if a large fish were tugging at a line hooked to his heart.

He turned to gather the rags he'd used to wipe down garden tools after sharpening and oiling them for the winter. These he placed in a muslin bag and set it under his workbench on a shelf. Daylight was fading quickly as a bank of clouds rolled overhead from the northwest.

"Y'all get on home now," he whispered. After pushing the door closed, he crossed to the edge of the gravel to wait for his granddaughter, pulling his hat down over his brow. Sniffing the air, he smelled the cold scent of snow.

"Hey, girlie," he called, and when she finally reached him, breathing hard from stepping up her pace, he pulled her under his arm and together they walked the last few feet to the house.

Inside, he struck a match to the ready paper and kindling in the fireplace.

"Where is everybody?" Agnes asked as she set her backpack on a chair.

"Oh, your mama drove into town for something and your Grannie's seeing old Mrs. Percy (*That's it*)—her stomach again," he explained. "She needed some *Sweet Annie*."

Agnes' after-school routine was to make a snack—usually peanut butter on crackers with a glass of milk. Then she might watch thirty minutes of television; or attend to some dried herbs as Grannie had shown her; or help Papa with anything he might need. Today, a note asked her to please fold the clothes from the drier and put them away and this she did.

Grannie returned shortly and mentioned the roads were slick. She'd taken Papa's truck, but learning that Lucy had the Buick, she observed aloud that it wasn't good on icy roads.

"Do you want me to start driving toward town?" Papa asked, sensing her worry.

"I think you'd better."

Papa wished she'd mask the concern on her face, for the sake of their granddaughter. *Fear's catchin'*, he'd heard. He pulled on his coat and hat, then leaned down to place another log on the fire. When it caught, he drew the screen together. Then he went out the door. Fear scurried behind.

The truck tires gripped the road well enough. He was glad he'd replaced them during the summer. Snow was falling harder and visibility poor. It was the time of evening, between day and night, when vision is typically tricked by shadow and light.

He switched his lights to low beam, to better see through the snowfall, hoping he'd recognize the Buick if and when he saw it. A car passed, headed in the opposite direction, but it wasn't Lucy. The slick patches of black ice acted like tablecloths being whipped out from under table settings, and even with new tires he had to pay strict attention. He wished for all the world that Lucy was home, safe and sitting in front of the fire with Aggie and the girl. At the end of this reverie, he heard a loud *pop!* as though a transformer had burst—as they often did in ice storms.

Normally, the drive to town took long enough but, during a storm, even a simple rain storm, distance was magnified. He switched on the radio just as a bulletin was being read:

"If you are traveling tonight—and you shouldn't be—watch for an accident on the highway going west, near mile-marker ten, across from the old McAmis nursery. This area has been blocked off, so slow down and let them work, folks."

He slowed to negotiate a curve and then saw it.

Lights from a patrol car blinked on and off; a rescue vehicle, and an ambulance. An eerie orange glow lit darkening, snowy air down the slope to the left of the road. A patrolman stood in the highway, in hat and fluorescent-orange vest over his jacket, directing what little traffic appeared. The niggling in Papa's chest yanked more sharply as he eased on past. He found a place to park, turned off the engine, and began to step out.

"You need to keep moving, sir," said a voice behind a flashlight beam aimed in his direction.

"I . . . I think it's my daughter." The patrolman stepped out of his way and spoke into a hand-held radio. He then told Papa that a fireman would meet him by the rescue truck.

There, below the highway at the bottom of the slope, Papa recognized the Buick, even now, as it lay overturned and blackened from fire. A few persistent flames still burned. It had likely skidded off the steep curve and rolled several times before slamming into a boulder. An apparent explosion ensued. The muffled bang. No transformer, then; he'd also likened the sound to a shotgun going off in a tunnel, pleading with any number of causes. . .

Another man stood beside the fireman. *First on the scene?* Papa wondered; he introduced himself and told them it was his car down there—that his daughter had been driving it.

"Where is she?" he asked, starting for the ambulance, a hopeful note in his voice. And then he knew. By their faces. He knew she'd been trapped in the car and the hook sunk in deeply. Papa brought a hand up to his heart. *Nooo—my Lucy.*

"Sir—*sir?* Come sit down, please. . . We couldn't get the hose to it. I'm sorry. We've got men down there using portable units now, but it was just too hot at first. And sir, the rolling and impact would have—"

Papa understood what the man wanted to convey, and it all became a sickening noise in his ears. He staggered backward into the rescue truck and slid to the ground, his back against the cold and wet side panel and, cradling his face in his hands, he wept—for Lucy, for her mother, for her daughter, and for himself; twin daggers of regret and guilt pinning him now to the earth.

"I'm sorry!" An apology he'd never offered his daughter when alive he cried aloud now, then silently: *Forgive me. . .* His heart burned, and as the pain undid him he fell over on his side. The man asked him if he could help in any way, and Papa shook his head and finally lay still.

Why? What was it all for? He begged the falling snow, the moonless sky, the hard, cold ground he lay upon and, finally, the flames, most extinguished now, whose orange glow had dimmed, sated—having consumed the rest of his daughter's life. And, in his misery, Papa sensed (rather than heard) his daughter say to him, *"I love you, Papa; I forgave you long ago, and everything's all right. I love you. Love my sweetie and mama."*

This thing he would do, and three years later he died. It was his heart.

CHAPTER 9~THE MINSTREL

Grannie followed Papa almost a year later, in June of 1981. A peaceful, "Well, goodnight, dearie," was all she said. The funeral was well-attended. Considered a woman of worth, Grannie was beloved.

Agnes changed her name to Senga.

From a round toddler, she had grown to gangly, pre-adolescent tomboy, to lithe teenager. Still wearing her chestnut hair in two braids, she might've been considered "pretty," but in a purely feral way. Like a mink in the wild. She lived on her own, deftly avoiding the social worker whose case she might become, given she'd still be a minor at fifteen that August. Uncle and Aunt offered a home with them in Winston-Salem, but Senga insisted she would do for herself on the mountain. "Piece of cake," she'd intoned the charm like a mantra.

Always the serious student, she'd be a senior in the fall due to an advanced curriculum.

Persisting in her habits of foraging for wild greens, wildcrafting herbs and roots, she continued making tinctures and tea blends. Grannie's clients had grown accustomed to the girl delivering their remedies, and most were recurrent—insuring a steady income—even if it amounted to a bag of fresh pole beans, or a basket heaped with crisp apples. Senga could eat beans, apples and lambs-quarter all week. Papa had taught her to hunt rabbits, squirrels and doves, and neighbors shared venison and other meat on occasion.

The closest neighbor asked if he could plant Papa's tobacco field, almost an acre, and use the barn to cure it. He'd share the price with her if she'd help with some of the chores. No, she'd told him; he had kids to help, though she'd expect payment for use of the field and barn anyway, ". . . and thank you, Mr. Mac."

It became her habit in the early evening, after filling herbal orders but before completing her homework, to sit in her grandmother's rocker on the front porch and smoke a cigarette. She liked to remember walking behind the hand setter in spring: Papa running it; Grannie dropping in her young *baccer* plants; Lucy and Senga covering then watering them.

Planting days were good days.

A counterpoint rhythm composed her hours, an energy of "making do," thanks to a fierce pride instilled by her grandparents. This, or sheer stubbornness. She seldom experienced awareness of her bereft state, choosing instead (unconsciously) a personal pragmatism; *courage*, her Grannie would've said. It led Senga through the days, and the long, often lonely, evenings.

Uncle mailed her a little money every month, and bus fare to visit them during the holidays. Aunt had grown feeble and travel was difficult; the girl's visits meant a great deal—a tonic.

Oddly enough, her solitude remained a secret, and one she guarded well. She had a gift for misdirection, if casual conversation (it was all utterly casual to her) pressed too close.

One day, following her grandmother's death, a favorite teacher asked Senga to come by at lunch time. Of all the people who may have guessed her circumstances, it was he, yet she chose to mislead him for fear of being removed to a foster home. She reminded him that her uncle and aunt lived nearby and they'd be regularly looking in on her. This was pronounced in such a way as to brook no opposition or further concern. That *nearby* and *regularly* could be misconstrued didn't enter the question. She found that timing—and changing the subject to one important to her interlocutor—usually moved the conversation in her favor. She'd learn to bide her time and to not show impatience, which could raise suspicion.

Seven months passed and Senga abided. Then, she made the acquaintance of Rob McGhee.

Two days before a Trailways bus would take her to Winston-Salem to spend Christmas with her aunt and uncle, two classmates invited Senga to go hear a folksinger at a newly-opened coffee house in Blowing Rock. Having packed her suitcase and arranged to have the cats fed by her neighbor, Senga accepted this unusual (for her) invitation.

Classmates thought her strange, but this awareness lay holed up in a remote and mostly ignored region of her mind, like a fox waiting out a hard rain with little concern. A certain shrewdness in Senga's responses led to raised eyebrows, side-long glances and the occasional eye roll. While she didn't quite dismiss a scrap of conversation aimed at her, she might pause before replying, for an awkward moment.

Several groups stood bundled against the humid, December cold snap, waiting for Crazy Jane's Coffee Emporium to open its doors. Colored lights swung in erratic strands across the top of the old store front's façade. The girls spotted a space and parked, climbed out, grabbed their bags and crossed the street laughing, visibly pleased to be doing something more exciting than their usual nights out—*Or nights in. . .* Senga wryly reflected.

A sandwich board stood on the sidewalk with a hastily scrawled *Grand Opening Tonight!* Stapled beneath, a poster showed a young man, possibly in his twenties, with longish, white-blond hair tucked behind his ears. He leaned against a rock wall, one foot casually lifted back against it, an acoustic guitar propped in front of him. *Like a shield*, Senga thought.

Rob McGhee Sings Some Folks' Songs, it read. Time and place filled in.

She would become familiar with the details of the photograph, having carefully rolled up the nine-by-eleven poster and secreted it into her bag. This sleight of hand occurred later in the evening, after the publicity had served its purpose.

CHAPTER 10~JOURNAL

I have met someone. His name is Rob McGhee. He's a folksinger—and a writer of songs. Anyone reading these entries might wonder at how few mentions of boys they contain. I haven't been inclined, I guess. But I want to describe this evening before I forget something. Just so I'll have something to compare it with someday, IF this happens again.

Some girls asked me to go to a new coffee house in Blowing Rock tonight and, since I rarely do anything outside of my usual routines, I agreed—with apprehension. I become tongue-tied in social situations. Anyway, I have the flyer with his picture and name, announcing his appearance. I never thought I'd be one of those girls who tape pictures of movie stars on their walls—guess Rob isn't exactly that. And besides, it's tucked in one of my dresser drawers.

We found a table and I ordered a cup of chamomile tea; maybe it's true that there's a sense of safety in the familiar. Grannie told me the herb is one of my allies and she (the chamomile) knows what I need better than I do sometimes.

All right, I digress. . .

Senga laid down her pencil and crossed to the front door to let the cat out for the night. Stepping to the end of the porch, she gazed up to Orion and a winter sky awash with brilliant stars. The constellation had already ascended high above the rolling eastern horizon of darkened hills. It was late. She picked up her pencil to continue.

> T and G bought coffees. I expect both had trouble falling asleep last night. We (they) made small talk until a man got everyone's attention, then he introduced Rob. The lights dimmed and a spotlight shone blue. He picked up his guitar, smiled at us and sat down on a stool. Then, he spent a few moments tuning.
>
> I studied him like a new plant before sketching it. He wore dark clothing; a gray button-down shirt, tucked in, and blue jeans. Boots, too. He's more beautiful than the photograph shows, if that's possible. Tall, probably over six feet, thin as a rail, he wears his white-blond hair to his shoulders. His eyes shine like the stark, light blue of an aquamarine. They're sparkly, like our cat's eyes.
>
> I just sat there and stared.
>
> And his voice and guitar? God could not have created a more perfect effect—which isn't to say God literally couldn't have, because obviously God could—well, I know what I mean. Language is such a puzzle sometimes.
>
> Papa and Grannie loved old mountain music. To me it sounds haunting and dark, but lovely. Rob's music is like that. He was born knowing what he is.
>
> The first song was *The Great Silkie*, about a seal that becomes a man, fathers a child, and later returns to claim it. As I say, haunting music. I've heard it many times. In English

class we had to write a paper on some aspect of the performing arts, and I learned about "stage presence." Rob has powerful stage presence. He "establishes rapport with his audience" and relaxes between songs.

Here's "The Marionette and the Lady,"—what I remember. We laughed out loud.

> *I would gladly pull your string, said she,*
> *But Madam, it's attached to me,*
> *And leaning o'er, the Lady gasped,*
> *To find the puppet on her—*
> *Jingle-la-roo and a ty-re-oh,*
> *Jingle-la-roo and a ty-re-ay.*

During the applause, he stared at me for a long time, but it may have been wishful thinking. It seemed to have worked though, because at his break he came to our table and asked if we were enjoying ourselves.

I lost all power of speech. . .

My companions—I pretty much ignored them all night and apologized on the way home, but they laughed, saying I was "done for." I probably looked silly—like one of Shakespeare's "mooning maidens." I'm returning tomorrow to listen to him again.

One evening before Grannie died, she called Senga to her bedside, and held out a hand. It felt cold and light, *as if it was already on the other side just waiting for the rest to catch up*, she wrote. Her grandmother told her she only wished she could've stayed long enough to see her through her first heartache. *I wish she would've chosen something happier, like first love. Maybe like now.*

> . . . I don't think we can miss what we've never had, but I have felt such a longing, a terrible and mighty yearning to belong to something or someone, to be moving *toward*

something. I do believe, and *ardently* (thank you, Miss Austen), that it will come—like a star bursting right over my head one day—and all these twinkling, bright lights of recognition, belonging and triumph will sparkle down all around me. And—this—shall be my very own Glory Robe.

CHAPTER 11
~DREAMCATCHER

After Rob's second performance in Blowing Rock, Senga offered to help pack up his gear, and he called her his "roadie." Leaving his van at the coffee house, she drove them to an all-night café. They agreed that breakfast foods comfort the best.

"My Papa made the best oatmeal," she said, and named the condiments.

"Wait, your dad? Didn't he die when you were—?"

"No, Papa's my grandfather—*was* my grandfather—that's what everyone called him—Papa—including my Grannie. He'd soak the oats overnight in milk and water, so it'd be creamier . . . said he learned it from his mother who learned it from hers, you know, tradition. Did you know the Scots used to make a meal from raw oatmeal and a little water? I guess it'd be like eating raw rice, where it expands in your stomach and keeps you from feeling hungry. I think it'd feel uncomfortable."

Rob told her he'd earned an Associate Degree at a small college near his home town in Georgia, but, "I ran out of steam . . . couldn't earn enough money playing local gigs to cover expenses, so I decided to tour. At least for a while. Which has turned into several years." Confessing little patience for jumping through all the hoops the financial aid office demanded, he added ruefully that, as it was, an associate degree in history wasn't lucrative.

"But I do remember reading about the Scots. . ." he brightened, ". . . riveting stuff, and with my name and all, I felt a kind of—tribal thing—you know? They wound up having to eat much worse than raw oatmeal and water; I'll tell you about it sometime if you like," he said, as he lifted the last of the grits to his mouth.

"Hmm, this name of yours . . . you could be Bobby McGee, ha!" she teased, continuing, "Bobby's just a nickname for Robert. Or were you called "Bobby" and changed it when the song came out?"

She sat back in the booth.

He looked at her long, then stood up, indicating he'd be right back. She wondered if she'd offended him. The waitress came by to refill the brown mugs, and Senga added two containers of cream, squirreling away the remaining five from the bowl into her jacket pocket. She wanted the caffeine, to keep her alert for the drive home. Then she wrapped the uneaten slice of toast on her plate into her paper napkin, adding it to her loot, including six little jams, grinning as she did so to one of the waiters, who observed her from behind the counter, gamely returning her smile.

Rob returned and slid back into the booth opposite her. She looked at him in question, and he mumbled something about coffee. "So do you want to hear about *Me and Bobby McGee?*" he asked, a slight edge in his voice.

"Okay. . ." Senga felt a nudge—of what, she wasn't sure. She felt weary. *Wary?* It'd been a long day, but she made her face look engaged and nodded to him.

"All right then, and no—to your question—I didn't change my name, and anyway, it's spelled Mc—G-h-e-e. The story is that some guy suggested a song title to Kris Kristofferson, 'Me and Bobby McKee,' but he misheard McGee. And get this; the original Bobby was a girl—yeah, no kiddin'," This to Senga's owl eyes. "Remember Roger Miller's version? Then Gordon Lightfoot's? Actually, several folks covered it, then Janis Joplin released it on her album *Pearl*, you know the one that came out right before she died?"

"Wow," was all Senga could think to say, quickly regretting the banal response. "I like Gordon Lightfoot's the best," she said, "And yes, I remember now he was singing about a girl." Then came the dreaded lull in conversation.

"So how long have you been playing gigs, and where all have you been?"

"Oh, after I received that degree I knew I had to go do something, and soon. My parents couldn't help me out any longer—they had their own issues—so one day I called this booking agent, and, well—I guess I've been doing it ever since. Sherry's really good at what she does, finding me work, and . . . she's not a pain in the ass," he added, almost as an afterthought.

"It gets old having to lug all the equipment myself, but some venues have their own sound systems, so . . . oh, yeah, and where? Well, I've driven across the country at least three times in three years. It's an exhausting life, I won't lie, but there's *something* about it that feeds my soul, so I keep doing it."

He admitted he was talking more than necessary. She told him she was genuinely interested, so he continued, confiding that he hoped to make an album one day, that he was waiting for the proverbial "break."

"Mm. 'The Minstrel Boy,' she said quietly when he finished. "I've listened to that since I can remember. That's what you are . . . do you know it? The song, I mean."

"Um, no, not by heart, anyway; I know what song you mean. I'll have to learn it now, just for you." He smiled at her, and she felt it down to her toes.

At 2 a.m., a stifled yawn reminded Senga of her bus trip to Winston-Salem later that morning.

"I have to go," she told him. "I'll drive you back to your van, and thank you, this has been . . . wonderful, and you, um, are a wonderful musician. I'll buy your album when it comes out, and it will, I—I know it . . . and I'm talking a lot. Sorry." She felt mild surprise at this flood of words.

"Would you write to me, Senga Munro?" he asked, as he held the café door open for her, adding that he received mail by general delivery in the places where a gig lasted several days.

"I would. Absolutely."

"Ever heard of 'munro-bagging'?"

"No. Sounds, ah, intriguing."

"A 'munro' is a peak 3,000 feet or higher in Scotland . . . they make a sport of climbing them, I guess," he explained.

"Well, fancy that," was all she said.

Feeling a tingle of joy, she repeated *absolutely*, in her mind; it presaged feelings of certainty and anticipation, all at once. *And stifled the truth sometimes*, she heard from a far corner of her mind.

Back in Papa's old truck, Rob reached into his wallet and extracted a folded paper, then he quickly copied the names of venues, towns and dates for the next few weeks on a page torn from one of Senga's school notebooks. In turn, she wrote down her telephone number and address, handed it to him, then leaned over and kissed him on the cheek. A tentative brush. He reached for her face, held her gaze for a moment, and closing his eyes, he moved to kiss her mouth, gently but deliberately.

When they parted, each took a breath and smiled into the other's eyes. Senga leaned into Rob and he held her long. His smell reminded her of a sticky August afternoon. They inhaled each other's dreams. *Does this work like a dream catcher?* she wondered. Dream catchers, where bad dreams are snared by a carefully woven web, encircled by a round hoop, like the small one hanging on her bed post at home.

In the months prior to Senga's graduation, she and Rob engaged in a two-step of literary efforts, frequent, short phone calls and three occasions of meeting for a tryst, once in Senga's home on the mountain, and twice when she traveled to meet him. *A Minstrel Boy, indeed*, she mused, *ever going off to war, real or imagined.*

They made love for the first time while picnicking in the woods on the mountain. She was disappointed by the perfunctory nature on her lover's part. Rob simply rolled over on top of her, fiddled a bit and *Bob's your uncle*, a strange phrase her Papa used to say, its meaning suddenly clear.

And . . . it hurt.

Where do feelings, versus the truth, apply here, she wondered afterwards. Subsequently, whenever they "made love" (she thought of it, sadly, in quotes), she had to remind Rob to use protection. She'd also begun to ingest Wild Carrot seeds daily as another preventative measure, aware they weren't always effective.

One night, Rob simply refused to comply.

They had sat down by a gurgling stream that flowed just below the motel room. Surrounded by darkness, save light shining from their room's window behind them, Senga watched as he reached into his front shirt pocket and drew out a tightly rolled joint. He lit it and inhaled deeply, holding the smoke in his lungs for several moments while looking over at her. She stared back. He held up the joint, raising his eyebrows in question. She shook her head and looked away, toward the stream.

Glinting black water flowed by and she watched tiny bobbing sailboats, carrying a precious cargo of trust, disappear over the next ripple. A few laden vessels still lay in harbor though—she hoped. Senga had detected the smell of grass on his breath before, and if there was one smell she couldn't abide, it was this. Her mother's demise was thickly woven into it, like a newborn fawn caught in a tractor baler and kicked out behind, unbeknownst, mangled and dead. *Well, it's all over but the shouting,* came the phrase. From where?

Senga knew cannabis wasn't the evil weed it was portrayed in films like *Reefer Madness*, but she couldn't help her own associations with it. Her mother had been gone five years now, and Grannie had told Senga how it was a gift of amazing grace that Lucy's last several weeks had been happy ones. Senga heard *sober, and not wasted* (in both senses), either on the psychiatrist's prescribed drugs or, on the grass and whiskey. The smoking of tobacco was discounted, strangely enough. "We're *baccer* farmers, after all," Grannie had reasoned, though Senga never saw her smoke anything but pork.

At her graduation ceremony, Senga was recognized as the county's youngest graduate in recent history. She accepted the distinction with equanimity, if not a little mortification, as she glanced over to her uncle and two cousins. Senga hadn't seen the boys since Papa's funeral three years earlier. Her guests sat up proudly in their too-hard reserved seats in the audience.

Rob didn't attend, but she understood—or so she told him. And it was here on the journey of their relationship that she detected a pattern—her habit of glossing over things for his benefit—which, in truth, confirmed, at least reflected, his own lack of consideration toward her or her sensibilities. *It's a bit like* . . . she cringed, deciding whether to complete the thought, then realized, *Oh God, I'm doing it!—the bloodied wife comforting the husband who has just beat her senseless.* An overstated metaphor, to be sure, but she determined to pay better attention to this—notion. All she could think to name it.

Another year passed. School studies behind, Senga inventoried and reorganized her store of herbs, books and notebooks. A new interest, prenatal care, engaged her evenings. Her days were full while she and Rob managed their distances, literally and figuratively.

One afternoon, he reached her by phone from his motel room. "Why don't you come on the road with me?"

He'd called to see how she was feeling, adding that it was a really *nice* room this time, trying to sweeten the deal. He was working a two-week gig in Asheville, not far away. June in the Appalachians brought with it a sweet beauty, if tourists—like flies—as well.

"Are you in*sane*?" countered Senga, "Or just stoned? I'm having a baby in four months, or have you forgotten?" She checked her temper; *Hunh, I'm railing; is this hormonal? Or am I just angry a lot of the time?*

Rob had yet again dismissed the condom and Senga her senses, but she'd kept her fingers crossed. *Should have kept your legs crossed, dearie,* came the thought.

After hearing Senga's news three weeks ago during a phone call, Rob had asked her if she *really* wanted to have the baby, alluding to alternatives. She became very quiet, and then told him to *go on then,* that she'd have the baby with or without him.

"We'll manage, Senga. You can just hang out; you know—read, um, relax . . . it'll be good for you and the baby, and cheaper in the long run."

"Food on the road is *not* good, and besides, I've got my clients."

Ignoring the latter assertion, Rob continued, "We'll pay attention, that's all. Soup's always good. And you can bring your herbs. At least think about it, will you? I miss you, Senga, and I don't like it that you're alone up there."

Safer here than there, Senga thought later, as she looked out over the burgeoning summer foliage from the front porch swing—the frog song, *ribbit*, like her heart beat. Rob had said "cheaper in the long run," she remembered. *Hunh. Well, that boy needs to choose his words more carefully. Cheap. Cheap is a* cheap *word*. But a change of scenery and pace sorely tempted her, and she acquiesced, finally, in favor of a little adventure in her life.

The next morning she informed her herbal clients that she'd be out of town for a while and dutifully reminded them of the home health care program that would answer any questions they might have, and offer assistance. By virtue of her Grannie's dedication and clout, Senga enjoyed a certain standing among the health care workers, and she tried to respect this. The public health nurse relied on her from time to time to be her legs if she couldn't travel the distance to a non-emergency case. Some back-country folk still eschewed the telephone. But Senga would break the family tradition of catching babies—at least for now, she thought. *Times are different, is all*, Grannie would have said. Care was better available now, if not perfectly. She could always be useful here if she so chose.

That evening at the kitchen table, hot cup of peppermint tea at hand, she began a list for the road. Oddly, the first two items called to mind were her Papa's twenty-gauge shotgun and his .22 rifle. *You never know; might need to shoot dinner*. Next, his felt hat she'd taken to. She didn't know how long she'd be away, so she packed with all possible weathers in mind.

The neighbor lady had given her a baby shower and several clients had knitted blankets, sweaters, tiny caps and booties. She'd found other layette pieces here and there, including a used travel bassinet. She jotted, "regular clothes," for when she could finally give up maternity wear.

Reading materials, including herbals went in, as well as Grannie's childbirth manual; also, a comprehensive assortment of herbs and tinctures and other first-aid necessities, well-organized. Into a satchel went toiletries. Foodstuffs in a cooler and box.

Cramped as the van was, she'd be able to lie down if necessary, to her great relief. Her ankles swelled by evening. *Drink more water*, she heard.

Senga composed a quick note to Uncle to say she'd be gone for a while, and to not worry if she didn't answer the phone. She again conveyed her sorrow about her aunt's passing. Grannie had been firm about expressing thanks (that, and greeting people).

She'd pay a visit to the neighbor who leased the tobacco field to say she'd be away for a time. The cat could survive on mice and she didn't think Uncle would turn her away when next she arrived on his stoop, holding his surprise great-great niece or nephew.

Emily was literally born "on the road," in two senses: Rob was playing gigs through the Plains states, Senga in tow, growing larger, and stopping by medical clinics bi-weekly. She was never turned away. Her gift of presence—*Whose?* she asked. Grannie (and now Senga) always gathered and dried raspberry leaves to have on hand for childbirth and the preceding months. Drinking daily cups of the tea toned the uterus, and this she did without fail.

Her time arrived at 2 a.m., in early October, after Rob's performance in South Dakota. They were traveling to Gillette, Wyoming, two hours away. The plan—to sleep in the next morning.

Rob pulled over on Interstate 90 several miles inside the Wyoming border to his passenger's insistent cries that her water had just broken. Senga climbed out of the car, cradling her belly, and told Rob to begin timing the contractions. She returned for her coat against the chill and stepped onto the wide borrow ditch.

Weaving back and forth, walking up and back, practicing her Lamaze breathing, she listened for Grannie Cowry's clear but soothing instructions—calling from the soil; waving in the grasses and the breeze; seen in the ghostly far-off hills, in the moon and stars above. Familiar voices spoke now as one, and

Senga slowed her breathing. She panted when contractions squeezed like an angry fist. An object in the grass glinted, offering focus for her concentration. Then she stopped, clutched her belly again, and groaned loudly.

Another phase of the moon could've left them in darkness, save glaring headlights. As it was, its brilliance on this night illuminated an otherworldly terrain. *We could be on Mars.* Sandstone formations in surrounding hills glowed with eerie incandescence.

All Rob's attention lay with her and he remained as solicitous as she'd permit him to be.

Presently, a Wyoming State Trooper pulled up behind the van. Grasping the situation, he radioed for the nearest ambulance, but the birth was imminent. She squeezed one of Rob's shoulders for support as he worked to pull off her underwear, then she held up the hem of her long skirt, using both hands and began circling a spot, then back on itself—like a beast before settling.

With cries, grunts and groans, she squatted over a patch of soft, deep grass. Rob rushed to support her, voicing complaint that his back was threatening to go out. Ignoring this and, feeling an urge to bear down, hard, Senga learned that birth sometimes meant a slippery baby squeezing herself into the world, not to be caught by a Grannie, but by the earth's own ample lap.

The trooper hurriedly handed over the blanket from his cruiser's trunk after Rob tearfully and gently wiped down the infant's vernix-covered skin with a fistful of grasses. Senga, now reposing on the ground, told Rob to clear the baby's mouth and nose; then, as she'd watched Grannie do on calls she'd attended, she told him to hold one of the baby's feet up to her and she flicked her thumb and forefinger to it several times, to initiate the baby's gasp reflex,.

"Please, *whenever* you can," entreated the trooper, "Get in the car and I'll have you to Sundance fast."

The umbilical cord and placenta, Senga thought, but the lights of the ambulance shone visibly in the near distance and they all quieted, this profound quartet, each smiling (one, somewhat) at the other in gratitude for their good fortune. Emily lay on Senga's belly, breathing evenly, her eyes open.

Thank you, sighed Senga. October. Anything can happen, weather-wise, in Wyoming, especially in October, she'd learn.

Rob followed the ambulance, wherein she delivered the placenta and the cord was cut. In Sundance, Senga was admitted to the hospital and Rob telephoned his booking agent to tell her to cancel his gigs for the next few weeks. She ranted for only a moment before he informed her of his new baby. The woman capitulated immediately, "Unbelievable," he told Senga. Sherry congratulated him and asked him to get in touch when he could return to work.

Senga and Emily were declared healthy and released from the Sundance Hospital in the morning, after only a few hours. Arrangements for payments had been discussed and confirmed. The feisty charge nurse asked Rob—with steely-eyed glare—what he planned to do *now*. (Senga had intimated their gypsy-like existence.)

He looked at the nurse—and Senga—with a most amazed, blank look, adding that he'd been so caught up in the next gig and in taking things as they came, that the notion of a plan, and executing that plan, had never occurred to him.

In truth, Rob led, and had led, a most cavalier life, as in "casual."

Senga remembered a phrase; *not only did he not know, he did not even suspect.* On the heels of this epiphany arrived a quote about carelessness from *The Great Gatsby*, bearing fair witness to the first observation. Had Fitzgerald meant it in passing via his novel's narrator? No. She had *read* it in passing, not fully present to its significance at the time, sitting blissfully ensconced in honors English. Ah, but *literature abides and prevails,* her teacher had repeated—another mantra Senga used, as a charm against despair.

He's careless . . . the father of my baby is a careless person, Senga admitted, while holding her newborn daughter to her breast. *And here I came with him . . .* Then, setting aside the sad observation, she allowed herself to wholly sense the inexorable life force exchange between Emily and herself, *the ineffable,* and both learned to love the life they lived together, as binary stars; to savor it, through the force of shared wills.

They settled nearby in a small town called Sara's Spring, for its hopeful sound, for its friendly residents and for its simplicity. Moreover, it boasted a library, where Senga, in time, found a job and availed herself to its stacks of knowledge, beyond what raising a daughter required. Rob McGhee came and went like a will-o-the-wisp.

PART TWO

The steely crow dipped and cawed as it approached the coming chasm, having followed the silver snake of moving water. A conifer near the lip of the falls caught its eye for the colorful ribbons, and the bird marked the tree for nesting material. Falling water gave way to thundering spray, as the bird swooped into the wide, red-to-violet rainbow, sparkling in the mist. Humidity dampened the bright resin scent of the forest.

A figure below startled the crow. Upon closer inspection, a man sat hunched over a child folded in his arms. Both appeared carved of stone—one with the slab whereon they sat. Coltish blue legs skirted the muddy ground, unmoving, and the bird sensed death. The man, facing the shallow, rock-strewn pool before him, would glance away, as though expecting someone.

Motion at the base of the cliff revealed another figure. Black, greasy mud stained clothing, hands and jaw; the face mostly hidden beneath a green hat, the color of ponderosa pine needles. A long braid, the color of woven autumn grasses, momentarily piqued the bird's interest, then, with another *Caw!,* it pumped its wings to climb higher.

CHAPTER 12~WEAK TEA

Wyoming Black Hills

October, 2013

Cursing Morpheus, she rose from her solitary bed, pulled on a raggedy blue robe and worn-out slippers and padded to the cabin sitting room. After opening the woodstove door, she laid a split log onto still-glowing coals, blew to coax a flame and sat down to gaze into the fire.

It didn't take long.

The wave of grief began in her lower back, traveled up and over her shoulders to her heart, where it paused. Then it sank into her gut to mock her carefully chosen, nightly nervine. A remedy. *Brew the tea longer*, came the thought—ridiculous in its timing. Tears held back, as usual.

A second wave swept her onto a beach of dry desolation, where nothing but sand and visible absence abided—a wasteland of bitterness and despair, the lonely, lapping water serving as a cruel, elemental reminder. Clutching her abdomen, she rocked herself, humming tunelessly to shortened breaths. In time, her breathing slowed and flattened to a dull fatigue.

The image of her daughter rose in her mind, and she detected a question in the girl's expression. *There,* she remarked. *Just—there. Your brow . . . I'm here, sweetheart.* She realized with quick regret she'd overlooked her nightly recollection, a practice of quieting herself and remembering her daughter, Emily, standing by the berry-laden juniper tree. Her guardian.

For nineteen long years Senga had observed the ritual.

From a blue-green branch their prayer cloths waved; Emily's, a length of blue ribbon, and hers, green—their respective prayers left private.

A prayer is something you feel with your whole being. . . Is this a prayer?

Emily, ever nine years old, "of the white-blonde-wispy-hair and crystalline blue eyes," her father had sung; her lanky young limbs promising height and grace. The girl often wore an expression of utter sweetness—a love that continued to spill and tumble through her phantom being. Caught evermore on the wingspread of a passing bird . . .

CHAPTER 13~UNBIDDEN

In the hour before dusk, when woods sound either busy or eerily quiet, the long-haired man stepped mindfully on the wet forest floor, careful not to muddy his new moccasins. His wife, She Who Bathes Her Knees, had sewn them only recently—her parting words ringing in his ear, to not wear them home caked in mud.

From the crest of the ridge, he'd spotted the large whitetail buck below and shadowed the animal to this hillside vantage point. With care, he crossed to a pine for cover, drawing an arrow from his quiver, and dropping to one knee, he sent the arrow flying toward the buck. The man watched the great head swing in his direction.

Following an early supper of chicken soup and toast, Senga cleared the table, washed the few dishes and reached for the can of wax and a cloth. The scent of sealing wax smelled clean. She applied the dark amber to the table top in small circles and rubbed it in, a meditative task.

Glancing through the east window to the hillside as she worked, she was startled by the sight of a man, dressed in buckskins, drawing a bow. She followed his aim to a drop tine buck, and when she looked back, the man was gone; the buck, trotting off to the south, remained unharmed.

Her heart squeezed in alarm.

After investigating and finding nothing, she grabbed her walking stick, locked her door and set out to hike. To calm herself.

Pushing on through thick, wet grasses, she hoped a deer trail might intersect, making the way easier. She preferred the liminal spaces when hiking out, on the cusp between meadow and wood, between day and evening. If the air felt too warm, she could step into the shade and, if too cool, into the sun. But another motive figured. Things happened in the in-between places. A force permeated them: an expectancy, potency and energy. Thoughts enjoyed more freedom.

Adrenaline coursed through her veins a long while, even as she exerted herself, but now it dissipated and calm returned. The image of the Indian behind the cabin pressed against her vision, as did his sudden disappearance. *A wonder.* She held the features of his singular face in mind to later sketch.

It was October. One month past frost date for northeast Wyoming. Senga hiked on, through decaying leaves, resin of pine needles and pungent sagebrush. Recent rains deepened the burgundy color of a bur oaks' bark, particularly during a lowering angle of the sun, such as now. The drone of an aircraft revealed a high-flying jet, chased by a kite-tail of white vapor in a cerulean sky.

Expecting to return home after dark, when the temperature would drop, she'd dressed warmly. Papa's fedora on her head. A pocket held a folded cloth bag, in case she needed to carry something home. Another pocket accommodated a sketchbook, five color pencils and a sharpener.

She cinched the jacket round her waist. Dry creek bed breaks, aptly named, split up the land and provided cover for wildlife. They lent interest to the landscape—if also a degree of strain to a hike. Walking outdoors had become a crucial habit, a needful thing, an essential practice. Her body craved exertion and fresh air; much as a thoroughbred must run, to infuse blood with oxygen, she credited the hikes and nature with keeping her whole.

"Oh, my. . ." She leaned on her walking stick, palms gripping the round wooden end—a *head-knocker*, a friend had once called it. A treasure trove lay before her.

She quietly greeted the congregation of plants by nodding her head. Dark, bristly *Echinacea* flower heads dotted the landscape, their pink petals dropped since August. Hundreds, possibly thousands, stood at attention, diminutive sentinels surveying far-reaching rolling hills and meadows. The greenish-black stalks mingled with sagebrush, in contrast to the softening lavender sky. Low on the horizon, the red sun cast its mellowed light across fields and ponderosa pine-covered Black Hills—that which gave the Hills their *Black*.

Pulling out the sketchbook and pencils, Senga squatted to face a petal-less flower. She smiled and began. Working quickly, switching colors as needed, she pressed harder to deepen the shading on the stem. The sketch was soon completed, and she replaced tablet and pencils to her pocket. She'd return tomorrow, spade and bucket in hand, after speaking with Caroline and Rufus, on whose land she stood. The medicinal roots would be easier to dig now, thanks to fall rains.

Senga was a simpler—an herbalist who mainly uses one herb at a time.

"All right then," she said, adding a whispered breath of gratitude.

She turned away, planted her walking stick before her and hiked back toward the tree breaks to meet a deer trail. A long trek awaited her in the dusk, but a good time of day to be outdoors.

Turkeys commenced their raucous evening flights into the trees on the side of the ridge, wings ruffling like wet sheets being shaken out. A tom gobbled, another answered in the distance. Her soft swishing steps onto wet grass kept time with her breaths, a rhythmic pace. The air smelled clean and sharp in her nostrils: pine sap and ozone. Frogs and crickets sang in unison. *Winter's coming soon.*

Senga wore no watch and couldn't gauge how far she'd hiked. Months had passed since she'd hiked cross-country (by another route) to her neighbors' ranch, instead of driving the long way around on the county road. Hiking cut the distance by half, but not the time.

When she reached the far gate to her property, night had fallen, and she groped for safe stepping. *Dark of the moon tonight,* she remembered, scanning the skies.

Another night as dark as this, years ago, came back. Of gathering cows on horseback, and returning at midnight in velvety darkness. Of extending an invisible hand before her face, blind to the inky black—as if dark had mass. As her horse gamely trod the well-worn path, she'd pondered that which composes reality and the difference between seeing and believing.

What else hides under cover of darkness?

A horse's capacity for sensing its way at night won her approbation in the present scheme of things, and Senga strode carefully, but purposely grasping her walking stick, toward the distant glow.

CHAPTER 14~FAIR ADEQUATE

Cabin steps gained, the stout stick knocked the pine boards; another step, and Senga directed a bold glare behind, to ward off invisible intruders who may have followed. She reached (furtively)for the key and unlocked the hand-made door, then clutched the latch, lifted, pushed and crossed her threshold.

Assessing all quickly, she shut the door, turned the lock, and leaned her stick against the near cabinet, then crouched to light her ready kindling in the woodstove, having laid it earlier. Soon, warming flames shone brightly through its translucent door. She positioned her wing back chair to face the fire after filling the electric kettle with water for her nightly cup of tea. Occasionally she added a splash of brandy or warmed milk.

All was quiet. *The quiet—visitors notice the quiet.* A defining characteristic of her life now, a character she welcomed and recognized. Yet jacketed against the chill, she released the day's cares, rising once to brew the tea. The chamomile's apple fragrance scented the air, conjuring a shy peace. Crackling fire and whirring convection fan on the woodstove defined the silence.

Only human sound, or noise—*how it's often interpreted—disrupts the ambience of silence, which includes all of Nature. Music and laughter (especially a child's)—occupy another realm altogether. . .*

Senga rented from a man who'd inherited the property thirty-five years before. He'd built the two-room cabin and garage himself, with the intention of using it as a hunting retreat. For several years it served him, until poor health prevented travel. The rent check was mailed to an Arizona retirement community.

90

When the cabin and small acreage became available in the fall of 1996 (and offered within her means) Senga did not hesitate.

Her landlord permitted her to improve it however she liked, as long as she paid for it. Building a six-foot-tall fence around the garden and fruit trees had set her back, but fresh produce every summer and fall made up for it. The owner had planted three apple trees, wisely surrounding the trunks with chicken wire. Even so, they'd suffered depredations by deer and raccoon, and the voles had gnawed on the lower trunks in winter. Senga had pruned heavily, and the trees had rallied with good, large fruit. Over the years she planted thirteen more, now in varying stages of productivity, the fencing necessarily extended. So far, the well's always-fragile capacity met watering needs of home, garden and orchard.

The cabin was small, but it suited. She named it Starwallow, for the endless field of suns above her, and, if she were honest, to acknowledge her default mode—wallowing.

Warm now, she removed the jacket and pulled open the slim drawer of the table and lifted out two sheets of blank paper, her pen, an envelope and a stamp, then fished her colored pencils from her jacket pocket. She conjured the image of the hunter and sketched his likeness on one sheet. *Pretty close.* She was struck by his wild beauty and wondered if she'd exaggerated. On the other sheet, she composed a letter. When finished, she left the envelope unsealed, in case she had more to say in the morning.

Sipping her tea, she might have contemplated the mystery, but chose her surroundings, doing so as an artist might study a still life when deciding objects to include in a painting. A meditation in seeing. She'd furnished her meager two rooms in this fashion, making changes seasonally to accommodate a new fancy or a found object.

Little proved superfluous. *Perhaps a few books. . .*

From where she mulled in the cabin's main room, part of the bedroom was visible, where stood her bed, a small table, spinning wheel and dresser. A curtained-off cubby hid sink, medicine cabinet with mirror, toilet, narrow shower stall and a low-volume water heater.

Fair adequate, she liked to think. The cabin's virtues lay in well-insulated walls and, paradoxically, in two expansive, salvaged, thus leaky, windows, each giving onto east and south views. A gain by common sense in one compromised by the other. It mattered little to Senga. Resting her eyes on her spinning wheel in the bedroom, she acknowledged its beautiful usefulness; next, the walnut table and captain's chair.

How is matter so tied to memory? Do cells of beloved and much-used belongings somehow permeate our own by some common membrane? And this wood having once lived as trees; does its DNA—?

She dismissed her wondering at the narrow, five-drawer chest and the two, small cabinets that held provisions and clothing, to review their contents in a quick appraisal for the oncoming winter months. *Two pairs of wool socks*, she jotted on a running mental list.

The kitchen was efficient. The landlord had situated the sink under a tidy French window, with work space on either side. A smaller refrigerator and stove stood by conveniently. Opposite stood a wall, mounted with floor-to-ceiling shelving, storing various dried herbs, roots and tinctures. Books and boxes too. Shelves crowned each large window, for objects routinely circulated below for sake of appreciation.

The present piece was a Spirit Bear. A gift. Glossy black, the pottery figurine fit neatly in her hand. Carved with symbols representing the Sun, Moon, and the bear's footprint, it reminded her to notice signs, whenever they might appear. *Like now?* Beside the bear lay several items; *bright shiny objects*, Senga thought of them, though not all were: a single earring, five red beads, two Lego pieces and two half-inch screws. All gifts from crows, left on the peanut feeder; to thank her, she believed.

A loud pop from the woodstove startled her and she stood to add another piece of pitch-pine before bed. She made her nightly toilette slowly and deliberately. Considering herself middle-aged at forty-seven, her face had weathered, despite the olive oil she persistently used, a habit recommended by her Italian grandmother, or *nonna*, Maria Teresa Barone Munro. *This Wyoming where you live is not kind to face*, she'd once lamented to Senga. *But the oil of the olive—it heals; you will see, bambina.*

Maria Teresa had returned to Italy in 1975. Her American husband and son having both died, the woman sought the comfort of her homeland. For several years, Senga received the occasional letter, written in broken English, touting the oil of the olive for every purpose.

Senga had received no reply after writing her about Emily. Perhaps it was too much.

She resumed her toilette. Aging had once bothered her, but no longer. The oil now merely kept her skin from feeling parched and uncomfortable. She credited St. John's Wort tincture with deliverance from petty concerns, counting it "ally," as well. Her hair was turning prematurely white and in strange fashion: a stark, white streak began at her forehead, and continued in a pattern two inches wide. She wore her hair long, in a single braid. "Easier than messing with," she'd once declared, remembering her mother's efforts to curl it.

Ah, Mama . . . she sighed.

After dispensing five or six drops into her palm, she rubbed her hands together to warm it and massaged her face and body. Thus anointed, against any and all evils, she placed a half-dropper of yarrow tincture on her toothbrush to clean her teeth and gums. After closing down the stove's damper, she shrugged into her robe and unlocked the door. Stepping onto the porch, she bent down to unplug an electric cord and was plunged into darkness.

The cabin roof extended over the narrow porch; enough space to protect two chairs from rain (as long as it fell straight down and not a typical Wyoming sideways downpour). What people failed to realize about the Black Hills (if they weren't residents) was that the sunken lay of the land encouraged fewer blustery days than the rest of the windy state; nevertheless, weather ruled.

Wood smoke sweetened the air. Senga detected ponderosa and sagebrush—the pines' spicy bark; *Artemisia's* pungent scent. Darkness improved olfactory sense.

No moon, indeed, she confirmed. Stars burned brighter. Friend Orion presently ascended behind the ridge to the southeast, invisible. Cocking her head to the side, she listened with expectancy. Rewarded, an owl's hoots issued from the lap of deep woods, below the timbered ridge rising to the east.

Hoohoo—hoo! Thrice called the owl.

In this northern end of the valley, horizons lay narrow and high, but the view to the south, toward Sara's Spring (the nearest town), unfolded long and far, as elevation dropped toward the Belle Fourche River. Senga wondered if the physics could be similar to the phenomenon of being deep in a well at midday, yet able to see stars overhead. She'd dismissed this hypothesis as another fancy. The Milky Way, glorious in its wide, arcing band, stretched expansively on its near north-south axis, mirrored in miniature by the nearby meandering creek that split the valley in two. Senga sensed the immediacy of that which her grandfather called The Great Lonesome.

She turned back toward her door, but not before facing skyward once more, with wonder, and a bitter-sweet resignation. *The company of all these stars, all these trees and all these visiting thoughts—"pale in comparison," they say. But I don't say it. There is no comparison; there can be no comparison.* To Emily.

A word (or glare) often warded off the invisible intruders, her name for doubt and despair. Inside, she locked the door, returned her robe to a peg, pulled on her long johns and climbed into bed. A lamp shone on a framed photograph of her daughter. Her last school photograph. Senga turned out the light and settled into her nightly ritual, to fall asleep in its midst.

Hi, sweetheart. . .

CHAPTER 15 ~NEAR CONNIPTION

A leg of lamb in Safeway can run you fifteen dollars a pound, and selling on the hoof to neighbors gets us less than three dollars a pound—no offense, hon. Makes no kind of sense, Senga. At least the damn things don't have to be sheared, on top of it. I'm telling you, we're gettin' too old for this horseshit, but what are ya gonna do?" her feisty neighbor added, rhetorically, and taking another breath, launched anew.

"We're down to a half-way manageable flock now and, with a hired man, it ain't too bad yet—you still there, Senga?" Caroline asked between breaths.

Senga pictured her neighbor peering into the mouthpiece of the old, black wall phone, against the red and yellow-flowered wallpaper to the left of their kitchen door.

"Yes, yes, Caroline, I'm here. Um, so do you still have one of last year's lambs saved for me . . . I hope?" she asked carefully, hoping the agreed-upon price hadn't changed, her cash flow being, as it was, a trickle by month's end.

"Oh, yeah, hon, of course, but ain't we waitin' 'til late November?"

This ritual assessment of Caroline and Rufus' current state of affairs thus conveyed, and arrangements for her yearly lamb delivery sorted out, Senga ventured to ask if she could come by before noon, to dig some *Echinacea* root, correcting to "coneflower," its common name. She amended the request by assuring Caroline she'd save her some tincture when it was ready in six weeks, her neighbors having learned the herb was, indeed, a good remedy against infection, flu and the like, but mainly when tinctured.

"Hell yeah, hon. Come dig all you want—just fill in them holes, would you? The horses don't need no broken legs—and can you stay for dinner?"

"Thanks—I'd better not this time. Kind of you, Caroline, but the roots need to be tended to right away. Everything else okay?"

"The old coot's fine, if that's what you mean. It still bothers him, but he don't talk about it. Maybe your medicine worked, ha!" she snorted, adding, "See you later, or not, if you gotta get back. Bye now," she said and hung up before Senga could respond. As usual.

Rufus watched his wife hang up the phone and sit down in the ladder-back chair, below. He had been knocked down while wrestling the ram into another pen. The diabolically single-minded beast had determined to remain with the rest of the sheep—his private harem—in the paddock. A bruised pelvis had Rufus laid up for several weeks. Senga had brought over arnica oil and comfrey for compresses, while he preferred his medicinal whiskey and tobacco.

He wouldn't let on to Caro, but he dreaded the physical therapy appointment scheduled for next week in Sundance. Other than that cloud, it was shaping up to be another fine day, weather-wise. October could be tricky.

Rufus and Caroline Strickland lived on the family ranch, originally homesteaded in 1906; as it happened, the same year nearby Devils Tower was declared the nation's first national monument by Theodore Roosevelt. Recorded family history stated that Rufus' grandparents had, "attended most gleefully the ceremonies, and reveled heartily in the festivities which followed." Both in their late seventies now, Rufus and Caroline switched from running cattle to raising sheep in 2006, although they often wondered why when cattle prices improved.

Dorper sheep, a meat breed, originated in South Africa, a cross between the Dorset Horn and Blackheaded Persian sheep. A flock of sixty (give or take a few), two dependable geldings and a mare; a Great Pyrenees dog named "Gus," to guard the sheep; the Guernsey milk cow; and several barn cats comprised the remaining stock. Chickens and guineas too. And Caroline took in strays.

It was just the two of them now, and the hired man. Their daughters had married and left Wyoming, an all-too-common occurrence among the young, who sought careers and relationships—or both—in more populated states.

Rufus sat at the kitchen table, the ubiquitous hand-rolled cigarette dangling from the corner of his mouth. He regarded his wife. A lopsided, wry grin carved a deeper groove into the right side of his face, the left side smooth as glass. He'd once been what was called "Hollywood Handsome," but never knew it, making it all the more so. Rufus remained the self-possessed quiet type. One who chose his humor with care.

His wife had aged less gracefully, a fact she accepted most days.

Grown thick around the middle, and never knowing what to do with her too-thin salt-and-pepper hair, she kept it clipped short. Skincare was ignored and she wore the same jeans and flannel shirts most days in winter, the same white long-sleeved shirt in summer. (Laundered, of course.) But the Stricklands could boast a singular marriage. Together nearly sixty years, they couldn't crack the glib joke, replying, "Eight glorious years!" when someone asked *How long?* Having grown used to and tolerant of the other's frailties, both summoned humor, as if it were a genie, waiting to do their bidding.

"You have time to fix me a sheepherder's breakfast this morning, Caro?" he parried, as he leaned back gingerly in his chair, lifting his arm to her waist to pull her toward him.

"Ha!" she snorted, rising stiffly from the chair. "Haven't heard *that* one in years." She cocked an eyebrow. "And what exactly is your idea of a 'sheepherder's breakfast' these days, old man?" she coyly inquired, batting her mascara-free eyelashes at him.

Rufus hesitated to prolong the banter. "Oh, you know, the um, usual?" he teased, blue eyes wide with hope.

"Ah, well," she considered. "I'll have to run out to the freezer for the bacon, then. Ain't none in here." She started for the kitchen door. "Besides, Gabe'll be here pretty soon for his breakfast. I saw him comin' back from his run."

"That's not—" He took a deep breath. White, beetled brows stitched in consternation. "Damn, Caro, your memory can't be getting this bad—you aren't that old!" And unable to hold a straight face any longer, it broke wide open in a boyish grin, while he struggled to raise himself from the chair, planting both arms on the table for leverage.

"Oh, *hell*. . ." he muttered, ". . . damn son-of-a-bitch. . ."

"Mind over matter, Rufus," Caroline glanced over her shoulder to him as she opened the kitchen door.

"A piece of *ewe!*" he called out as she shuffled onto the back porch toward the freezer. "Remember? E-W-E," he spelled, as Caroline returned, brown eyes rolling, but smiling.

"Aye, *weel*, ye ole sheep shagger. . ." she said in fair imitation of a Scottish accent, "Not sure what you could do with that wee pelvis now any*hoo*, do you? The sheep are safe, I reckon."

"Caro, I'm sure we could figure something out, but all right—*later*," he suggested, adding a pronounced wink.

He hitched over to the coffee pot, refilled his cup, then slowly sat down again to wait for Gabe, the hired man, and for a less adventurous breakfast. Caro leaned over his shock of white hair, one hand wielding a cast-iron frying pan and, in the other, a carton of eggs, then—*mwah*—she planted a noisy kiss on his pale forehead.

"Later, old man," she whispered into his right ear. "Can you hear *that?*" she asked with a smirk, then turned to the stove. A stomping of boots on the door mat announced Gabe. "Here he is. What do we have going today, besides the sorting?"

Gabe Belizaire called out once, "Mornin'?" and waited for the door to be opened to him.

"Gabe. Haven't I told you—just come on in? You don't have to wait out there. Hunh. Wait 'til January—you remember *January*, don't you? You won't be standing there being all polite and all. Coffee?" And before he could answer, she was pouring a mug-full.

Try as he might, he could not simply open their door and let himself in. He always felt welcome, but he supposed it was an unconscious or, maybe, a "mannerly" thing.

After hanging his hat on one of the hooks beside the door, he stood a moment, wondering if he should remove his coat as well. The tack room in the barn could've been warmer, but it'd do just fine, he'd decided long ago. As a result, he sometimes overdressed. With a low huff, he slipped out of the weathered, wool-lined corduroy coat, hung it beside his hat, and sat down at his place.

"Thank you, Miss Caroline . . . and mornin', boss," he beamed then lifted the mug of coffee. *Oh my . . . God bless you, Miss Caroline,* he thought. *Real coffee. Even without the chicory, it tastes like home, and my black-ass is a long-ole way from Louisiana.*

Adding *miss* before Caroline's name, and calling Rufus *boss* or *patron*—pronounced in Cajun French—appealed to his sense of decorum, and he didn't defend their use. Besides, he knew who he was. And what he wasn't.

"Oh, milk and sugar; I'll get it," said Caroline, reaching in the fridge for the half-gallon jar of fresh milk, thick cream resting on top, the lily gilded. She took a tablespoon from a drawer, lifted off four heaping measures and plopped them into a dish.

Gabe's eyes rounded as he remarked, "I am surely going to get fat living here, Miss Caroline. You are spoiling me rotten," he added, with a wink to Rufus, who'd just looked up from his small notebook.

"Mornin', Gabe," Rufus greeted, then returned to his figures.

"Well," noted Caroline, "you Southerners like things sweet, and plenty of it; I'm just glad that cow's milk ain't going to waste." Julia (the cow) was so named after a certain, former lady acquaintance of Rufus' who wouldn't take "no" for an answer. Caroline took perverse delight in pulling and squeezing Julia-the-Cow's teats morning and evening, during the several weeks the cow gave. The insult was not lost on her husband.

Rufus and Gabe tucked into their breakfast, neither speaking a word, until Gabe expressed his appreciation when finished, something he never failed to do.

She loved to cook for good eaters, especially the polite sort.

Rufus reached into his shirt pocket, as Caro cleared the table, for a tin of Prince Albert rolling tobacco, then for his papers. He proceeded to roll an almost perfectly-shaped roll-your-own, put it to his lips and lit it with a match. After inhaling once deeply, and blowing the smoke out with a satisfying exhale, he was ready to discuss the day with his hired man—with whom he got on—*which always makes life more pleasant*, he'd once remarked to his wife.

They would sort ewes from the lambs and wethers, or, castrated males, that would be hauled to the sale barn the next day, culling one out for Senga, and two more for the new folks.

Meanwhile they'd put them all back on grass.

"You hear anything about those people up at the old Berry place?" Rufus addressed his wife, "You know, the ones who want these other two lambs?"

"No. You?"

"Mmph," Rufus stalled, "Well, nothing worth repeating," he said, stealing a quick glance at Gabe, who was gazing out the window. "Is there more coffee, Caro? One more, Gabe?"

The Berry place, up in the "peaks," or, higher elevations, had been a working sawmill a hundred years ago. Logging had provided occupation and materials with which to build; still the case in the area. The bones of former mills and habitations stood shadowed among trees, deep in the timber. On the treeless prairies too, several structures yet swayed, if drunkenly, against the elements, their roof beams sagging or broken in half. All, deserted testaments to dreams, determination or, just plain desperation.

Settlers came and went, dependent on grit and patience. Rufus and Caroline had watched dozens of hopeful, starry-eyed dreamers move into the county in the almost eight decades they'd lived here, both, "born and bred," as the saying went. Settlers included single men, such as Gabe, though few were Black, or "African American" (as their daughters corrected them), and couples—with or without children. They arrived with either a secured, prearranged situation or in search of one. Many a rancher smiled to have a wife with a teaching degree—and it was the wife, seldom ranching "spouse," in the school system.

Saw mills employed a fair number of workers year-round, while in the adjacent county, open-pit coal mines and gas wells tempted small town graduates. In mining everything, from rare earth elements to bentonite clay (if you included logging, which to Rufus had always seemed "a kind of mining"), the notion of living lightly on the land receded further and further away. He and Caroline wouldn't begrudge anyone a living, but it was "too damn bad and a shame we can't make do without those reasons for all the mining," they'd concluded years ago. And—lest they forget, and they did not—all of it provided jobs, occupation and food on the tables.

Newcomers, the Stricklands knew, pretty much remained so forever. It was just the way of it. Unless your forebears had homesteaded a hundred, even seventy-five years ago, you were not a local. Caroline would quip that at least the recent "white settlers," as she nicknamed them, weren't most likely inbred, and more than likely would bring in new blood—and height, for example. This was the tired, old joke in Sara's Spring, where many of the community's inhabitants had descended from two unrelated families: the Heisers and the Wagners, who'd arrived in 1887. Sara, short stout-hearted wife of Jacob Heiser, had happily discovered a spring on a wooded hillside while foraging one day in late summer. Moreover, it proved to flow year-round with sweet water fit for drinking. Not alkali, as some shallow wells had done. Thus, the town had sprung up, so to speak, nearby.

Rufus had asked Caroline nicely (and delicately) to reconsider her penchants for sarcasm and hyperbole when Gabe Belizaire arrived the first time. After eight months, he returned to Louisiana for several years. Realizing he missed the Hills, he asked Rufus if he could use a hand. Yep, he sure could, replied both Stricklands; to Caroline, Gabe was still a "white settler," and always would be.

"Just because he's a dark one ain't no reason for a whole change of vocabulary," she had informed her husband, and, "What was it you called it? *Penchants?*"

CHAPTER 16~FACTORS

*T*rrr . . . *trrr* . . . *trrr*. . ." Waking to persistent tap-tapping of a woodpecker—identified as Downy a week ago—Senga sat up in bed and rapped her knuckles against the wall. The tapping ceased then, resumed, machine-gun-like.

She threw off her covers with a *pfft!,* banged harder on the wall and waited.

Silence.

Planting her feet on the small braided rug, she leaned over to stretch her lower back, an exercise Papa had once practiced against lower back pain. The trick lay in executing it slowly, both the leaning over and the rising again. She stood up carefully, lifted her arms over her head—holding the posture for several moments—and swayed twice, side to side. This constituted her daily regimen, other than walking or hiking. Blizzards earned a day or two off.

She struck a match to pinecones and paper in the woodstove, filled the kettle with water and plugged it in. From the small refrigerator, she lifted out the jar of milk and poured a cup into a pan to heat on the stove.

Meanwhile, she peeled off her long johns, changed her mind and pulled them back on, sprayed her underarms with tincture of yarrow, splashed water on her face, then plucked her jeans and turtleneck sweater from one of five hooks in the bedroom that held her wardrobe. Last, she attached the newly-oiled scabbard for her digging knife, a Japanese Hori Hori, covering it with her sweater.

When she drew back the sitting room curtains, a fleeting pentimento of the hunter appeared, what she had seen; only an impression.

Alerting her, the kettle clicked off, while steam bubbles were just rising around the edge of the pan. Pulling it neatly off the heat, she then set it on a cutting board. Seated, she pulled on thick wool socks, then rose to make the coffee. It would brew while she returned to the bathroom to brush and braid her hair, with, "Well, that's as good as it gets," as amen.

Taped to the mirror and attributed to St. Bonaventure, a quote read, *Enter into yourself, therefore, and observe that your soul loves itself most fervently.* Amen lagging.

A Franciscan priest—and friend—in Montana, Joe Rafaela, had prescribed the words when Senga was lost in self-blame and out of her mind after losing Emily. "For perspective, perhaps?" he'd respectfully proposed when proffering the piece of paper. An on-going thing, she'd wryly conjectured. *And at the end of your life,* she'd hear, *if you are lucid enough, ask your soul if you loved it enough.*

What's enough, anyhow?

"Arghh!" she interjected, "Enough!" This in response to the woodpecker's noisy return, and she hustled from the bathroom to the front door, flung it open, and dashed around the cabin to the gabled end. In time to see the black-and-white bird sail away. Serenely. Peering up, she discovered several holes pecked into the wood. She'd speak with Rufus or Caroline about solutions—barring shooting the bird,—which was how they'd respond, pragmatic, both, to the core.

When she finally sat down to breakfast, she decided *café au lait* remained one of the best things she did for herself in this life. *So how am I doing, old soul?* Dunking a thick slice of buttered toast, with chokecherry jam, into the coffee rounded out her exquisite pleasure.

She'd be away most of the day. After pulling on her old leather jacket, she closed the door and locked it. The one-car garage stood fifty feet away, beside a clump of bur oak trees. Both cabin and garage had been built in the same batten-board style, from local rough-cut pine. Of the five senses, smell is the most evocative. Senga was reminded of this whenever she pulled open the first of two, wide garage doors. On this day, however, her car was parked outside. Inside, several bushel baskets of apples greeted her, their sweet aroma rising to the rafters and mingling with other scent molecules.

Her grandparents' garage in North Carolina had smelled uncannily similar. Was it in some property of the wood? Or a car's gas-combustion engine, trapped, when doors were closed? Likely a combination of factors—her usual explanation for cause. In any case, she equated the scent with comfort and security. *Love?*

Senga had *felt* loved when she lived with Papa and Grannie. More fact than feeling. She'd also felt her mother's love, acutely, in the weeks preceding her death. Making her loss all the more difficult. The sense of smell happened to be her most powerful, one she'd educated, given her herbal studies. It had developed apart from, and beyond the less fragrant companions of her childhood: the acrid smell of her mother's cigarettes and another strong odor that often accompanied it in the evening (when they lived away from Grannie and Papa, she had noticed). Like the reek of dank, burning hay was the smoke of cannabis; then, there were the fumes of whiskey on her mother's breath, when, or if, she came in to say good night and, often, a sickroom stench of diarrhea and a seemingly-constant foul smell from her own recurring strep throat.

But Lucy's last weeks smelled lightly of Lily of the Valley eau de toilette. Scent as antidote.

Senga had learned to surround herself with antidotes: apples stored in her garage and arranged on the counter in the cabin worked their magic, as did the scent of coffee grounds. Strange she'd held this irrational affinity for the smell of cigarette smoke. *Possibly a correspondence with its sedating effect.* She understood, poignantly, its association with her mother's sometime affection. Having enjoyed smoking herself for over twenty years, she at last gave it up in hopes of reducing anxiety and angina, her circling "hungry wolves," shape-shifting to binary stars, circling each other.

Her hatchback was of a size, when garaged, to allow for a small chest freezer, shelving for storage and hooks from which to hang tools; among them, a long-bladed spade. She lifted this from its hook and greeted Hermione, the straw-stuffed, scare crow-crone propped up in the corner. Her wardrobe had undergone several permutations over the years. A colorful scarf covered her head, and a black-and-white checkered duster hid a skirt. Arms stretched forth in the all-embracing stance for joy, with twigs (for hands) peeking from long sleeves.

Senga carried the spade to the vehicle. Next to it she placed a white, five-gallon bucket to hold *Echinacea* roots. Then, she pushed down the rear-door, walked round, slid in and sat a moment.

Emily felt loved. She believed this. An insidious doubt had crept up like a badger inching toward the nearby pond in early morning. Unbidden too, but seeking water. "Feelings aren't necessarily Truth," she spoke aloud. But, feeling loved *still,* Emily would draw comfort from Senga's ability to declare, "Yes, she was certainly loved."

In the end, is one inference simply subjective, and the other objective? Two sides of the same coin? In the end (she closed her eyes to wish), what she wanted—what she longed for— was peace. And a blessèd end to this "knowledge versus feelings" haunting. Was one subject to the other?

She made an exasperated sound and moved to start the Honda, pressed her foot to the accelerator to rev the engine until it sounded normal and sat a moment longer—lost in the engine's hum. Then, looking over her left shoulder, she backed slowly, turned the wheel and rolled forward onto the drive, which soon met the highway. Stopping at her mailbox, she replaced the empty mailbag and added her monthly letter to Joe; then, after settling in, she emptied her mind. To make room for scenery.

The Wyoming Black Hills include the Bear Lodge Mountains, the Bears' Lodge (a.k.a. Devils Tower), the Belle Fourche River Valley, Inyan Kara Mountain, Keyhole Reservoir, several towns and unincorporated communities. Long ago, the Lakota named the landmass, "The Heart of Everything that Is." Mysteriously, a Landsat image taken from space shows a singular shape and color—that of a heart. *The mind boggles,* Senga had quipped.

By contrast, Mount Rushmore generates a steady influx of tourists, but the first time she and Emily visited was the last time. *Was she truly this contrary?* she'd wondered. She couldn't explain her discomfiture to Emily, who, at five, simply stood with mouth agape at the stony faces. The natural beauty of the mountain remained a monument unto itself, enshrining life and all its grandness. They left soon after, to erase the inarticulate upset with chocolate ice cream cones.

Memory makes inroads on quiet roads.

Senga encountered no vehicle on the highway before the turn-off to Strickland's, and followed a twisting, graveled county road. The county was designated "frontier," more isolated than merely rural. She occasionally drove to the Montana border, meeting no one. Available at hardware stores, the county published a land map, showing properties and owners. Where her rented cabin stood simply read "Murphy" (her landlord) and, identified every few inches on a one-inch-one-mile scale, another landowner, and another. She hadn't met half the neighbors within a twenty-mile radius; those with whom she was acquainted had made her feel welcome, and for this she was grateful. Rural living in the West exemplified "live and let live" philosophy.

Maybe too much so . . . sometimes, she speculated.

Tires rumbled across the first car gate, onto Strickland's ranch. Three horses grazed on her left, munching their way up the slope. On occasion, Senga rode the chestnut, named "Sadie." She belonged to Caroline, but required more riding than Caroline had time. Down and off to the right appeared the house, barn and outbuildings, including an old Quonset for a tractor and implements. The house expanded over the decades: another bedroom here, a bath there; finally, a spacious, sunlight-filled family room, embracing a grand fireplace, built from handpicked rock from the river banks.

In the paddocks below, Senga spotted Gabe, waging battle with one stubborn sheep. Gus the Great (her nickname for the massive white dog) wasn't as agile or effective as shepherds at herding, but he earned his keep as guard dog. Coyotes and mountain lions preyed on lambs. As a smaller farm flock, the sheep could be easily herded most nights into one of the ranch's long sheds.

At the fork in the road, Senga veered right, instead of toward the *Echinacea*, to head toward the paddock. Gabe could use a hand, and it was still early.

"Howdy!" she called, stepping from her car. She pushed the door closed and strolled to the enclosure. Bleating sheep greeted her.

"Well, lookie who shows up just in time," Rufus grinned from under his hat. "How're you doing, girl?"

At forty-seven, Senga enjoyed the salutation.

"Good, good—thanks. Yourself?" She glanced at his posture, in order to detect an unnatural stance, more than might be usual at this stage of recovery. When she was satisfied at his progress, she looked over to Gabe. "Hey, Gabe. How's it going? Having fun yet?" she added, rhetorically, and, with a wry chuckle, turned back to her car. Through the window she brought out a pair of leather gloves.

"Mornin,' Senga," Gabe answered, after depositing a complaining lamb into the adjacent paddock. "We're moving lambs and wethers over there—taking them in tomorrow, except yours and a couple others—and the buck's done his business, so back to solitary for him, poor dude."

Stricklands chose to lamb in February—preferring cold and snow to later rains. *Six-of-one*, Senga had always thought, but then, she'd never slogged through spring mud to a lambing shed.

"Y'all eating lamb yet, Rufus?" she teased, knowing the answer would be accompanied by a look of utter distaste. He drew out his tobacco can to roll a cigarette. She pulled on her gloves and waited for instruction. Gabe would catch them if she'd then *kindly* move them into the next pen. He used words such as *kindly*. Rufus was able to help by opening and closing the gate between pens, and Gus stood on guard to dissuade separated lambs from running back.

With one hand grasping a lamb's copious neck wool and her other fist locked onto its rump wool, Senga guided the animal to the gate, waited for Rufus to open it, pushed the lamb forward and turned back for the next—all exuding the frenetic energy of the young.

The thin, fall air vibrated with *baas* and high-pitched *mehs;* Gus joined the din with the occasional deep bark and Gabe's grumbled syllables sounded like far-off, rolling thunder. Sheep can, and do, play hard to get. They suffer bad reputations for several reasons; thick-headedness but one. Rufus offered salty encouragement, as salty as Gabe's sense of decorum around a woman would allow.

"Now as my Uncle John used to say . . ."

"*Aw*, boss," Gabe interjected, gasping, "we appreciate the thought, man, but—*oof!*—we'll pass this time." He heaved a large old ewe backwards as she threatened to break his tenuous hold. "I've never done any bull-dogging, but these old ewes must (*oof!*) run a close second," he declared.

When the chore was done, Rufus had Gabe release the ewes and the three spoken-for lambs into the near pasture, but the sheep chose to remain close to the paddock, hovering.

"They'll figure it out," Rufus mumbled, cigarette clenched tightly between his lips. He jerked his cane off the fence and started toward the house. "Come have cookies and coffee, Senga—you earned it, and thanks," he called to her.

"No. Another time, Rufus, thank *you*, but I need to dig these roots while the ground's still easy. And Caroline already asked. So, when's your next therapy appointment?"

"Next Wednesday, and I am not looking forward to it. They *hurt* me!" he admitted with wide eyes, raised eyebrows and a frown, all for pity's sake.

"Poor Rufus. Will you need a ride? Be happy to," she added, pulling off the gloves and pitching them into her car. She knew physical therapy for a bruised hip could be painful. Essentially a bone bruise, the inflammation rallied "all hands on deck" to counter the injury. Caroline had unearthed an ancient heating pad; now her husband's moans ranged between agony and ecstasy.

"Caro's driving, but thanks for the offer, Senga. Better get to your digging before the weather turns," he said, regaining his usual equilibrium. "And what *the hell* is that you're wearing?" using his cane to point to the sheathed Hori Hori at her side, momentarily losing his balance.

Senga unsnapped the strap and drew the knife with careful reverence. "My new tool. . . See the edge? Good for roots; works great. It's all the way from Japan."

"Is that right? Hunh. Sure is a long thing. Ha! What do you figure Crocodile Dundee would say about that. . ." An oft-viewed film. "And how'd you get it from Japan, anyhow? Christ. First cars, now knives!"

Gabe suggested an online purchase and Senga said yes, exactly so. She used the public computer at the library now and then.

Rufus examined the knife and handed it back with a grunt. "Nice grip, and good steel—that stainless."

She returned it to its scabbard.

"Well, see you later, girl." The warm smile reached his eyes, and he hobbled off, leaving her and Gabe to discuss which of the three lambs she'd prefer.

"Oh, they all look about the same, Gabe; what do you think?" she asked after stepping off the fence in order to examine the sheep, most still complaining.

"That one's older, but the other two've about caught up in weight. You want the older one? I think it'd be better, personally. Gives the meat time to distribute the fat properly. At least that's what they tell me," he added, looking down at his boots.

Ah, modesty, thought Senga; *the endearing quality*.

"You pick one for me, Gabe, would you? I trust you. And I'd better get going. See you Friday," she said, reaching her car.

"I'll be there, Senga, and, hey, thanks again," he said, touching his hat brim to her. The gesture touched *her*. Had he picked up the chivalry from Rufus?

Gabe had returned to the area two years ago. Two weeks ago, he'd told Senga he could still count only five persons as "friend" here: Rufus and Caroline, herself, Earl (an old biker who ran the café up in Alzada, Montana) and "Sweet Francesca," who worked at the nearby Blue Wood Guest Ranch for seven months of the year. Francesca *frustratingly* (Gabe's word) returned home to Italy in winter to drum up business. Western United States guest ranches were wildly popular in Europe, perhaps as much as Tuscan holidays were to Americans, Senga wryly observed.

Gabe reminded Senga that, sometimes, five friends—if they were true—would do.

CHAPTER 17~DIGGIN' IT

Let's keep this to ourselves, shall we, ladies?" Senga whispered as she stepped out of her car and marveled anew, having doubted yesterday's discovery. Her instincts seldom betrayed her, but this represented such an overflowing cup.

In parts of the world (the Appalachians came to mind), a heavy crop of any valuable herb (like *Echinacea*) might be subjected to bull-dozers and other draconian means of over-harvesting. This was not lost on her. American ginseng suffered from such. In Switzerland, it remained illegal to harvest Gentian, an herb used in making bitters formulae. The prevailing question begged: how many cures, hidden in undiscovered sources—animal, vegetable or mineral—were overlooked and destroyed every day, say, in rainforests, due to thoughtless farming, mining and logging practices?

But what is directly in front of you to do at this moment? Senga approached a grouping of six blooms, one an especially tall specimen—The Grandmother. She dropped to her knees and moved to sit down, grasses providing some protection against the damp. She turned her attention to her breathing and to the spiky head of the flower.

With softened gaze, she greeted the plant; a simple courtesy her Grannie Cowry had insisted upon toward persons and plants alike. Her grandmother's sense of urgency had increased, as time to hand over her gleaned seeds of wisdom drew short. *Always greet anyone you meet, dearie, do you hear? It might be the only civil or bright thing a person will hear in a day; why, it could even keep him or her from making a terrible mistake,* she'd added. Strange light had burned in her eyes.

Senga readjusted her posture. "Good morning, dearies," and could she please harvest some roots? She actively listened for any indication—a sign, a sense of permission, or, the converse—refusal on the part of the plant, and Senga would respect it. Nudged to continue by an inward notion, she began to breathe as Grannie had shown her, inhaling oxygen from the plant, while it completed its own miracle of transpiration, "inhaling" carbon dioxide. Trees accomplished the same; great forests were aptly named "the lungs of the Earth."

After several moments, she bowed her head and stood, then walked, stiffly (from having too recently worked with the sheep), to the car for her tools. Oblique rays of sunshine warmed her back as she dug. It was strenuous, and she removed her jacket. Alternating between spade and Hori Hori—its long, serrated edge eased into softened ground, and she was glad of it. Digging inspired contemplation and memory billowed like the proverbial cloud in the sky. . .

She was eleven and digging roots with Grannie in a humid forest. She heard frog song, and the cicadas' constant buzz. The undergrowth grew thick and impenetrable in places. Rich scent of fertile humus below, leafy-green above, activated by the heat of the sun and moisture beneath—these surrounded and embraced her, as if she were theirs.

The green canopy proffered shade against their labor, and their reward? A bounty of useful roots.

Senga returned through a tearful veil. "*A fine day,*" Grannie had declared, "*A fine harvest, and a fine prospect of much good medicine.*"

Using her knife, she sawed a tiny piece of root and placed this in her mouth. After chewing for several moments, her mouth felt numb. The root produced saliva, but also perseverance for her chore, which could take up the better part of the day.

Seed heads buried in the divots, she replaced the soil, heeding Caroline's injunction.

When the bucket would hold no more, she scraped the spade and placed it in the car; the Hori Hori, in its scabbard, rested against her hip. Seldom without it, she regarded it *talisman* against feelings of helplessness, if not the reality. If merely a matter of form, it was also sign that she was "one who dug roots." No one objected (though she suspected talk) to the tool peeking from under a shirt tail or sweater.

Some American Indians called *Echinacea*, "snake root," and, in cases of snake bite, they would chew a small piece of root until well masticated, place it on the site and wrap it until further treatment could be administered. The herb's antibiotic properties often prevented the main evil, infection.

She only began to dig the root for herself after moving to Wyoming. This particular species, *angustifolia*, wasn't prevalent in the South. She sold bottles of the tincture in late fall, to give away as many.

At home, she dumped the roots onto the porch. A stiff brush dislodged clinging dirt and then they were soaked, to remove any residue. As she waited for her sink to fill with water, she mentally hoed tobacco rows with Papa, remembering the sweet smell of earth.

Hungry, she smeared chunky peanut butter and honey on bread. A mainstay—apart from soup. The honey included minced garlic and onions and powdered ginger—a favorite remedy and preventative medicine. She opened the refrigerator for the jar of red clover infusion, and took both sandwich and drink to the porch. Working outdoors improved appetite, a righteous trade and fitting arrangement in the scheme of things. Handling both animals and plants in one day counted as double blessing, never mind seeing friends. Black-capped chickadees, busily harvesting thistle seeds in the pasture, paid scant attention. She swallowed the last bite of sandwich and rose, setting her cup on the flat porch railing, then walked down the steps toward the garage and freezer for her evening meal of beets. Assured no beast had ventured in (like a rattler), she pushed shut the wide garage door.

Most who lived in the country had a rattlesnake story. Hers involved shooting one with her .22 as it crawled across her threshold one afternoon; then, she took a hoe to its head, gagging as she did so. Even dead, a rattlesnake's fangs can deliver a lethal dose of venom. Her philosophy was simple and she hoped fair: rattlers, stay out of my yard and house—or else.

A hand-numbing exercise, Senga used pruners to slice root lengths into quarter-inch sections. Pausing a moment, she switched on the radio for company. Several clean jars sat on the counter, waiting to be filled two-thirds full with the root. She reached for the half-gallon bottle of vodka from the high shelf (decidedly not "top shelf") and refilled the jars with the alcohol. After screwing on the lids, she labeled them *Echinacea angustifolia Tincture, in 100-proof vodka,* adding the date.

Caroline repeatedly joked that the alcohol likely fixed what ailed you. Senga brushed it aside.

Papa once told her, when revenuers in the South all but destroyed the stills (or *thought* they had, *wink-wink*), medicines made from the available alcohol, as well as its disinfecting properties, also ceased to be as available in the back-country. A marked rise in chronic illnesses ensued—the decrease in alcoholism and blindness notwithstanding, of course. He'd spoken only half in jest.

She arranged nine jars on the counter with a note of satisfaction; here she could conveniently shake them daily. The fairies took their share after a few days, and the jars would require topping off with more alcohol. This phenomenon happened in distilleries too, Grannie told her—adding the fairies had been replaced by angels. *Whatever gets you through the night,* Senga shrugged. *And a rose by any other name . . .*

In October she took stock: inventoried supplies, herbs and medicinals; examined the cabin's electrical wires for mouse or pack-rat damage; checked the crawl-space for interlopers. Her first project upon moving in had been a painstaking task and one she never wished to repeat.

Crawling in and out on her belly under the cabin, she'd pulled batts of fiberglass insulation behind her—one after the other—using a staple gun to fasten them to the joists and causing her right hand to ache for days. But first, she'd had to drag out all the wood and detritus that'd lain there for years from the original building project. Her landlord had warned she wait until after first frost, when cooler temperatures might lessen the chance of spider bites. Three days into her residency, she'd discovered two Black Widows among some rags left under the sink. A wave of grue rose from her gut.

There's always a snake in a garden, she'd whistled in the dark.

Taking stock of any presently held philosophies also fell to October's list of *Stuff*. "But not now!" She switched off the radio, having finally heard the weather report: snow predicted for tomorrow night.

In the orchard, crutch-like wooden supports braced heavy-laden limbs, but added weight of wet snow on clinging leaves posed a risk. Senga had learned to wait as long as possible to harvest, as apples needed a good frost to sweeten. Meantime, she'd fetch boxes from the garage and get on with it; one for the "good ones," and one for the seconds—those saved back for pressing. There remained only a few trees to harvest. Rufus told her he'd bring his apple press whenever she was ready. Making hard apple cider had become their shared endeavor.

She worked at the branch library in Sarah's Spring on Tuesdays and Thursdays. Twice a year, she arranged workshops around herbal medicine making. She also conducted local "weed walks," meeting a few clients this way, particularly the elderly, noting their interaction and outdoor walking proved as valuable as any medicinal.

Old timers recognized traditional cures, and Senga noticed it was elderly gentlemen who spoke up first, mainly regarding animal husbandry; linseed oil, turpentine, and a small amount of ether, mixed, worked well against *proud flesh,* or granulated tissue. Linseed from the flax plant, turpentine from the resin of certain pines. *Herbal.* The women would then offer their tips and remedies. In treating human ailments, both genders stood in agreement: medicine nowadays could use some good, old-fashioned bedside manners. Healing involved more than potions. . .

The apple picking went smoothly once she found her rhythm: twist lightly and into the bag. Repeat. When light grew dim, she hauled the boxes into the garage, setting aside seconds, and returned for the ladder. On Friday, it'd go quickly with Gabe's help. If October's weather held.

In the cabin, Senga ladled a hot bowl of soup from the pot. Leftover bean with salt pork. To which she added two tablespoons of dill pickle juice. Whole wheat bread, butter and two teaspoons of garlic-honey for dessert. As water heated for a second cup of tea, she washed the few dishes, then sat down and composed a list: flour, sugar, coffee, lettuce and olive oil. Maybe raisins. And yeast. From Spearfish: vodka for tinctures.

What else while there? The college town's gallery rotated exhibits regularly and she hadn't yet visited this season. Gazing at art as calmative. She jotted *gallery* on the Spearfish list, shivered, and rose to rekindle the fire.

CHAPTER 18~GABE

After supper, Gabe Belizaire stood up from the kitchen table, chair legs skittering on the linoleum as he pushed back. He chose three gumballs from a bowl on the table, then turned to Caroline to thank her once more as he shrugged into his jacket and situated the tired, tan Stetson on his head.

"Thank *you*, Gabe, nice of you to say so—again," Caroline replied, raising her eyebrows to Rufus, with a *why don't you say nice things like that once in a while* look. Rufus made a noise and jotted a note.

"Well—" Gabe began as he reached for the door knob, pausing when Rufus addressed him.

"I'll meet you at the paddock, Gabe, say, in around thirty minutes? It might take me a while, but I'll get there. Why don't you haul the trailer on over? Might as well," added Rufus and, casting about, he spotted his cane, frowned and pursed his lips.

Gabe guessed the man was busy gathering his courage. Rufus lifted the cane off the back of the extra chair, stood and stepped to the hallway, toward the bathroom, muttering an oath under his breath.

"I heard that, old man," Caroline called from the sink, then winked at Gabe. No dishwasher for her, she enjoyed the silken feel of water and soap on her hands; "My *hydro*-therapy!" Gabe had once heard her exclaim sarcastically. She admitted she *loved* her clothes washer, however, having used an old ringer machine for too many years. Still liked a clothes line, however, save in the dead of winter. He and Caroline shared the preference.

Gabe stepped off the porch, popped a gumball into his mouth, and continued toward the barn. He glanced at the sky and sighed. It had been the perfect fall day, when long underwear felt right. He headed for his room in the barn, doubling as the tack room. Good thing he *liked* the smell of horse sweat and leather, he'd joked when first shown his quarters. Between them, Rufus and Gabe had tried to mouse-proof the room, and there *were* all those cats. He continued to set traps—squirrel-tailed pack rats being the worst offenders.

Cheeky-damned-rat-bastards! Rufus cursed them with aplomb.

The homestead's original barn had burned to the ground in the fifties, Rufus told him one day while they mended fence. "A hideous end for several good horses, including a valuable and renowned stud," he'd added, shaking his head. The cause was never discovered. A violent thunderstorm had struck during the night and dry lightning suspected. Plans for the new barn included an indoor water pump (instead of half-way to the house). The tack room was rebuilt larger, with a toilet and sink plumbed in a corner and curtained off for privacy. He could shower at the house.

Gabe was satisfied with the arrangement, *all the way 'round,* he'd written to his parents in Louisiana, and he reminded himself of this fact daily, usually after splashing cold water on his face upon rising.

He headed for the pickup and fifth-wheel stock trailer.

That morning, after pulling on his jeans, he'd crossed to the sink to clean his teeth, a habit he aimed to keep. His image had given him a turn. If only for a split second. The mirror was harshly lit by a naked forty-watt light bulb, dangling from above.

"God-a-mighty, but you are a black, Black man," he remarked dryly to himself. Blue Black, they called it, particularly around Charleston, where his ancestors from the Sudan had disembarked from slave ships.

His surname, Belizaire—his mother explained—belonged to a planter, and slave owner, who once lived in Louisiana. If someone were to paint Gabe, she'd blend indigo with purple to find the shade.

"Not used to seeing your kind, now are you?" he uttered rhetorically, peering at himself; "Or not used to *not* seeing them." He squinted.

His eyes stood out, if a stranger were asked upon being introduced. They were large, round and heavy-lidded, with near-ebony irises. Two long creases framed a ready smile, and his face "cracked wide open," his mother used to say—eyes crinkling in concert. He preferred his hair trimmed short, so his hat might fit consistently well, and frequented a barber at every opportunity. But he grew a prodigious mustache, and left off shaving every day during the colder months.

Leaning just this side of six-foot, his height was ill-suited for a bull rider. "Makes it more difficult to get out of a jam," he'd once admitted to Rufus.

Gabe stayed in shape as a matter of principle, but also because bull riding demanded it. It was true he hadn't entered a rodeo in months, save the one over in Hulett, for its proximity. If another opportunity presented itself, he'd stand a better chance. So he followed a routine of pushups, sit-ups, stretching and running—the latter drawing cat-calls from his employers, who thought their hired man was a mite loco. But then, bull riders grew used to this opinion.

Growing up in southwest Louisiana, near Lake Charles, he had worked cows and had wrangled horses since boyhood. He graduated from riding calves for childhood amusement to bull riding for risk and a little profit. Both parents worked for a rancher who raised rodeo stock bulls and steers; the Belizaires lived on the place, his mother as head cook.

Gabe enjoyed working with animals, and helping where he could, but his younger sister wanted something else and, not knowing what that might be, she moved to New Orleans after graduating high school in 2004. Thought lost after Hurricane Katrina in 2005, the family learned the girl was on her way to Wyoming, to work as a cook herself on a guest ranch located somewhere in the northeastern part of the state. Gabe felt relieved, then disappointed, then furious that she couldn't be bothered to let her family know. *What's the matter with the girl, anyhow?* he'd wondered. He caught up with her in Wyoming.

A truck driver had given her and another girl a lift, when he spotted them standing forlorn in a rain storm outside a truck stop just north of New Orleans. The week before, Hurricane Katrina had created homeless refugees out of thousands, and his sister and her friend must have fit the bill, Gabe reasoned. The man offered the girls a ride to Rapid City, after they told him they had jobs waiting somewhere in the Wyoming Black Hills. Meantime, the trucker telephoned the Belizaires (having demanded their number) and left a message that the girls— *"They be all right."* The next day he reached Gabe's father, explained the circumstances, and promised he'd do what he could to see to the girls' safety once they arrived in Rapid City. He had daughters of his own, he added, hoping "somebody might do the same for us."

"He wants to know if I want them girls put on a bus back to Lake Charles," his father asked, shielding the receiver.

Gabe stayed mute and listened.

"No sir. Let 'em work for a while and see how that goes, but we're obliged to you for helping them out, and say—if they tell you the name of that guest ranch, can you let me know?"

He had. The Blue Wood, off Highway 24, in an area of the Hills called the Bear Lodge Mountains, just north of the interstate. His family agreed that Gabe would travel to Wyoming in late fall and bring his sister home, after she'd tasted a "mite more independence."

His mother experienced a hurricane of emotions. "Of all places—Wyoming! I don't even know where that's at!"

Gabe and his father hatched a plan, praying it'd settle the woman's nerves. He'd need a leave of absence from his job and enter rodeos between home and the Black Hills to earn a little day money. His father insisted on helping with gas, and Gabe would pay for room and board.

He began to look forward to the trip and, in the meantime, entered regional weekend rodeos (including two in east Texas) for the next month, to get in better shape.

At twenty-nine in 2005, Gabe felt fit and strong. He'd only suffered minor injuries from past wrecks with bulls, but he didn't suffer any delusions; he expected his turn would come— he just didn't quite know when that would be.

At that time, his life hinged on three things: writing, bull riding and teaching to pay the bills. He'd earned an MFA in Creative Writing at Tulane four years earlier and several of his short stories had been published and praised. His students respected him. Gabe taught with the same sensibilities he practiced with horses and bulls—returning respect, while expecting results. He spoke with his department head at the state college where he taught English to freshmen. The school granted him a version of family leave, and asked him to get in touch on his return.

He gathered his gear: spurs, long-wristed gloves, vest, bull rope, and several clean, pressed shirts. Not the best time of year to be traveling north, so he packed his warm corduroy jacket and wool vest. He could always buy long underwear if required.

Gabe hoped to return home with the prodigal sister in time for Christmas.

CHAPTER 19~RODEO

Her husband wasn't sure why he'd hired Gabe Belizaire (he'd once confided), but the reason he kept him on (if a purely unconscious one, thought Caroline) was this: Rufus had done a lot of horse trading in his day and this business of "windows to the soul" had merit. He knew the eyes of a horse could not betray, and so he'd always followed his father's dictum, "Look for *soft* eyes, Rufus, always," and this is what he'd tried to do, even with respect to folks.

So. It was in Gabe's eyes. That was it. *Now* she remembered. . .

It was January 2006. Caroline and Rufus seldom attended rodeos, but after selling off the cattle the previous fall, they had time on their hands, and a Stock Show and Rodeo would provide information regarding their next step. They were going into the sheep business.

Their daughter offered to come spend a few days at the ranch to feed, and to keep the water pipes from freezing—always a risk in winter. Caroline and Rufus seldom traveled farther than Cheyenne, Gillette or Rapid City, with the occasional trip up to Billings or to Sioux Falls—given the chores and responsibilities—but they wanted to look at sheep and confer with breeders, and this was what a stock show offered.

After wandering exhibits and gathering information for two days, Rufus finally settled on the Dorper breed. That evening, they attended the rodeo, choosing seats a third of the way down from the chutes, where Rufus like to be. Once seated (she on his right, as always), Caroline informed him she was hungry and thirsty, so he dutifully rose and negotiated the stands to buy hot dogs and Cokes. She was elated, but silently wished she'd brought a pillow for her backside. She seldom attended rodeos anymore. It seemed strange and noisy like a crazy circus. Clowns included. But she enjoyed the greasy pig contest and calf scramble.

Next came the women's barrel racing. (She'd competed when young.) Rufus looked forward to the bull riding, the last event, so they sat through saddle broncs and bareback riding until the very last rider was thrown, or qualified.

After his meal, Rufus wanted a smoke, so he left to find the designated area, to return just as the first bull rider bucked off.

"That bull spun him off . . ." Caroline reported, ". . . just like a top. I swear."

"That's all right . . . how he fell, I mean; he can get away that way. You just don't want to wind up in the well, inside the bull's spin, you see?" he reminded her. "You can get trampled. Not good. Nah, riding bulls is about timing and balance, Caro. Look. Watch the next one," Rufus provided a running commentary on the finer points of the sport.

"You draw the bull you're going to ride, you see, and riders tell each other how a bull is. It's just a thing they do—letting each other know the quirks. Right now, that rider—there in the chute? He's tying the rope around the bull—behind his front legs. You'll hear the cow bell. Those irritate the animal . . . make him madder—"

"Oh, well, that's intelligent," she interrupted.

"Now listen up, Caro. So the rider—who's just straddling the bull right now—his weight's on the side rails of the chute. Well, he slides the rope around so the bells hang under the belly, then his partner pulls the rope taut, while the rider— wearing those gloves, see? He puts powdered rosin on the tail end of the rope and the handhold. Makes it easier to hold on to, see? Then—"

The chute burst open and a whirling mass of testosterone (what Caroline saw) entered the arena and soon shirked its very own monkey (again, how Caro saw it) onto the ground. She hoped it was a softer spill than it appeared. The cowboy looked dazed for a moment, then swung his head around to locate the bull. The beast was at the other end of the arena, as it happened, between two mounted pickup men. The cowboy slowly stood, snatched his hat, brushed it off, strode to the side of the arena and climbed over the wall to safety.

Rufus resumed his discussion without missing a beat. ". . . Then his partner makes sure the rope is really tight, and the rider lays the rope tail across his open palm, then wraps it behind his hand, letting the tail come back across his palm." He demonstrated this, pretending to use a wrap. "Then he scoots up, almost on top of this hand, and when he's ready, he nods and the chute'll be opened. Okay, you see how that fella's holding his left arm in the air?"

"Can't help but see it—sorry . . ." Caroline couldn't help the sarcasm. Rufus had learned to ignore it.

"Well, they're disqualified if they touch the bull at all with the hand that isn't wrapped—it does help your balance, waving it like that. You want to find the "sweet spot," it's called, and they say the best bulls spin."

The rider made a spectacular short flight off the bull.

"Before, did you see him pointing his toes out?" he continued. "You don't want to get hung up; some riders split their boot tops down the back so they can kick 'em off fast if they need to."

"And why would they wanna do that?"

"Well, the spurs, Caro; they get tangled sometimes."

"How long do they have to stay on? Eight seconds, is it?"

"Yep. But even if they do, they're still judged. . . As it was once explained to me, you earn one to twenty-five points on how *well* you ride, and one to twenty-five on how your bull performs . . . and there are two judges, so if you get 100 points, that's a perfect score, do you see? Hardly ever happens, though," he concluded, drawing a toothpick from his pocket to worry his teeth.

They watched in silence as the next cowboy prepared for his ride, then Caroline spoke. "I just don't understand why anyone would want to get on one of those animals." She shook her head, but her eyes never left the arena. Rufus sat riveted as well. Senga's recent diatribe echoed in Caroline's ear. *We humans are compelled by our biology to be aware of danger. We will run toward an explosion, for instance, rather than away from it, to ascertain further possibility of peril. It's entertaining .We're suckers for chance encounters with our own mortality.*

"*Gladiators versus Lions followed spears against mammoths and saber-tooth tigers. Not to mention current battles among tribes. . . It all comes down to this—if you don't pay attention, you, or your family, might be killed. Simple as that.*"

Now it made a certain sense to her. *Always entertaining, having Senga to supper,* thought Caroline, taking a swig of her Coke.

Three more riders bucked off, one qualifying, two not, the clown and pickup men doing their jobs to distract the bull and lead it away. The announcer introduced the next contestant and named the bull, which drew reaction from the stands. Rufus raised an eyebrow at Caroline. "Must be a rank one."

They watched the chute. "A black cowboy," Rufus remarked, going for his shirt pocket under his down vest. Remembering he couldn't smoke, he huffed, leaned forward, forearms on thighs, spit out the old toothpick and replaced it. Caroline sat up straight—easier, she found, to watch from behind her husband's back. She placed her left hand there, patting his back in solidarity, letting it remain with affection. Concern too, she'd remember later.

The rider's partner finished his job and caught the nod, and the chute flew open. A brindle-colored bull exploded into the arena and Caroline held her breath. "Irritated," did not cover how this bull looked. The bell set up a horrendous racket, clanging louder somehow than previous entries.

The bull wasn't necessarily larger than the others, just livelier; maybe smarter too, Caroline figured. He wanted this rider off his back, and then he wanted to stomp him, with added insult, she decided. The bull was bucking hard and spinning, then he crossed the arena in a series of crow-hops. She was reminded of a locomotive engine working up a long hill, but one being chased by another.

This isn't going to end well. . .

"He's in trouble," Rufus said as they watched the rider lose his grasp on the wrap, until the hand was jerked completely out of it. The rider clamped his calves against the bull's flanks, using his spurs for purchase. In the next instant, the man sailed to the ground and hit hard. He looked stunned.

Then the worst happened.

The bull whipped around and charged.

The pickup men seemed preoccupied at the other end of the arena, the clown with them. Caroline nudged Rufus. "What are they *doing?*"

"What the hell?" Rufus called, looking in their direction, then toward the fallen rider. Other spectators were picking up on the looming disaster and the patent inattention of the staff. "*Depraved indifference,*" Senga would name it, when later told.

Caroline saw the rider try to scramble up, but the bull was already on him, having lowered his massive head to his groin, and, with his horns, he flung the man into the air, but did not gore him, she was relieved to see. The crowd was shouting. And then, with savage grace (*This bull's playing,* shuddered Caroline), the bull neatly lifted the man again, now from under his thigh. He fell back to the ground. The beast twisted around, his hindquarters squarely set, and he kicked—the right hoof finding the man's left shoulder. The crowd gasped as a halo of bright red seeped through the yellow fabric of the shirt.

All were standing now, some shouting for the help that should have arrived much sooner. An eerie hush descended on the arena as the bull, ever defiant, snorted once and turned, first to challenge one side of the stands, then the other. He snorted once more and trotted off toward an open gate at the other end, his bell clanging out of time, where the pickup men sat horseback. The clown held the gate open, as if this were his sole responsibility.

The injured man lay still a moment, before raising himself onto his right elbow. He twisted around and sat up on his heels. Reaching with his right hand for his hat, he pressed it down gingerly, then, with difficulty, he stood, and holding his bleeding shoulder and head askew, he limped away to applause delivered in timed claps—in acknowledgement, encouragement and admiration. His partner stood by waiting for him.

"Well, I never . . ." said Rufus. He looked at Caroline and, with a degree of self-control, told her to get her things. "It's time to go."

As it happened, the last contestant of the evening had just left the arena under his own power, after being mauled by a 1,700 pound animal, and Rufus had never seen anything like it in his life, he told Caroline, as they made their slow way through the crowds to the proper exit. They heard others discussing the incident, and Rufus wondered if there'd be an inquiry, "Or *something*, for chrissake," he muttered. And, in the manner of long-married couples, they felt the other's sense of shame.

They decided Rufus would ask about the man's condition.

The bull rider was all right, an official told them, but he'd need to sit out a season to mend. His shoulder and neck injuries were serious. He'd required eighty stitches and had pulled a groin muscle. The official added (with sadness, noted Caroline), "Doc says the boy will be in a bad way for quite some time . . . might have trouble with the shoulder and groin injuries."

Not a word about the appalling circumstances.

Rufus' face scrunched up in thought as he listened. Then, with no preamble, he wrote his name, address and phone number on the back of the rodeo program and, handing this to the official, asked him to give it to the rider, adding, "Please ask him to call that number. My wife and I would like to offer him a job."

And a place to heal up, she silently added.

They drove in silence most of the long way back to the ranch.

CHAPTER 20~NOR HIS SECOND

Deep barks startled him. "Comin', Gus," he muttered. Gabe snatched his work gloves off the neatly-made bed, patted his jean pocket for his knife then spotted his notepad beside the open laptop computer on the table. Morning sun sparkled through the window. The room came equipped with this new benefit, he'd written his parents, when he returned to Wyoming two years ago. The letter resided in a box on the table, to reread on occasion, dated June 2011, "a Tuesday," he had believed.

"Dear Mama and Daddy, here is your letter for this week, and I hope all is well. I am sitting here at my desk (really just an old table, but it does fine), and can see for miles down the valley. Ponderosa pine, bur oak, ash, box elder, chokecherry, juniper and cottonwood—just to mention a few—grow amid these park-like meadows and along creek beds, some dry, some flowing. I swear it's as if a landscape architect was hired. And I suppose you are both grinning now. I'll cry 'uncle.'

"Rufus (the rancher) kindly thought to install a wide, double-hung window a while back, and it faces due east—how this barn sits, square to the world. I mentioned my room was the tack room—still is, so I've included a diagram so you might see how it is now, compared to five years ago. No window in here at all back then. But I haven't thought to take photographs. My words will have to suffice for now. I am supposed to be 'good' at this, after all.

"The window allows good lighting during the day. I enjoy this unobstructed view of pristine Nature. Well, except for the sun shining in my face on summer mornings, when it rises more to the north. It says, Get on up, you silly bag of bones!

(Yes, Mama, I remember you calling me that.) I really don't
need an alarm at all, except during lambing, when Rufus and I
take turns in the shed. Besides, the missus still keeps guineas
and chickens, and between the two species, there's a heap of
carrying on at daybreak. She'd take care of them—she
informed me in no uncertain terms, when I signed on the first
time. To tell the truth, I think she—no, I *know* she thinks it's
hilarious the guineas sound as if they're calling 'Buckwheat!
Buckwheat!' when they carry on. Ha Ha.

"On some evenings I've seen the sun blaze out from under
a bank of dark, low rain clouds, and cast the remarkable light
that's called 'alpenglow.' Everything turns rosy, amber and
gold. And sometimes, if the light's just right, I can spot a
silvery, glinting thread of the Belle Fourche River way below.
And what wildlife! Every morning we see deer (mostly
whitetail; mulies range north, up on the flats). I see turkeys,
coyotes, bobcats; and Rufus says he's spotted mountain lions
and black bears. Elk roam higher elevations in the Bear Lodge,
near that guest ranch. Some have been spotted this way.

"Canada geese summer at a pond a little ways from here,
and the horses have learned not to shy at the ducks that fly up
when we ride past. Guess you'd call them 'bomb proof,' like
those horses the cops ride in New Orleans. Nothing fazes
them. Mine is a ten-year-old bay gelding named Hugh (don't
ask me why the name). He's quiet, sturdy and a joy to ride, but
I have to tell you, the romance sort of leaked out of the whole
deal after long hours of riding one day. Neighbors help each
other brand in the spring and my riding legs hadn't quite
gotten there yet. My butt was sore, too. I hear you laughing, so
quit.

"The Stricklands are wonderful people, I want you to know.
They treat me well, and I try to return the favor. When
Caroline learned I'm writing, she turned into Mother Superior,
directing Rufus to move a small table to the tack room and to
place it at the new window, which he did; I'm sitting here now.
She then brought out a lamp I expect has been in the family
for a century. A Tiffany-style. I'll ask her about it sometime.
I'm sure it has a story—like most everything around here. One
tale involves a car gate—or cattle-guard. Seems when Caroline

was around twelve, her father's horse spooked during a thunderstorm and ran into the grate. . .

"Well, I send my love to everyone, along with a hug. Please don't worry about me. I'm fine. But I wish you could see this country. You would truly love it. I know it's hard to get away.

"With love, Gabe," he'd signed the letter, one of many his mother had saved in a shoe box. Gabe had spared them a gruesome detail, that when the horse tried to wrench a leg from the grate, the sharp edge of the rung cut into his pastern, all but cutting off the hoof. Caroline witnessed this and the horse was destroyed before her eyes.

He'd revisited the letter when he flew home in August to attend his mother's funeral. Gabe asked his father if he could keep just the one. "Of course, son," came the choked reply. "She saved 'em all."

October already, he reminded himself. Hard to believe seven years had passed since first meeting the Stricklands. And how was his father getting on without Mama? he wondered. His sister worked as cook now and lived at home. It seemed her thirst for adventure had been slaked after New Orleans and Wyoming. . .

On the wall, to the right of the window, hung a print called *The Annunciation* by Henry Ossawa Tanner, an African-American artist who completed the work in 1898. The original hung in the Philadelphia Museum of Art. Gabe displayed it wherever he called "home." Home. The word bewildered him. Was it true of everyone?

One of his grade-school teachers, Sister Anne, used the artist's image in a lesson, combining theology and art. After Gabe received his Master's degree, he was surprised and touched to find a copy of the print waiting for him at home, sent by Sister Anne with congratulations, inscribed, "To Gabriel Belizaire—May you always strive to be a light."

In the painting, an attentive Mary is seated on her bed in Nazareth, beside a bright, incandescent wash of light representing the messenger-angel, Gabriel. His patron saint.

He closed the laptop and slipped the small notepad and stubby pencil, safe in their waterproof baggy, into a jacket pocket. He'd borrowed the idea from another writer who'd once spent her days working sheep and gambling the vagaries of Wyoming weather. In reading Gretel Ehrlich's essays, Gabe sensed a deep kinship, and he began to learn to love the life he lived.

He slipped into his jacket, pulled his hat back on and stepped through the door into the barn's capacious aisle. Then he halted, turned and stepped back into his room to the small fridge that served as an often too-noisy bedside table. He opened it and drew out the Mason jar of milk. Less than a pint left. He'd let Caroline know he needed more. After pouring a half-cup into a blue plastic dish, he carefully carried it out of the room, turned to pull the door closed and paused.

Funny, he thought, *I spend most evenings coming up with people and their stories, writing them down, while my real life just hangs around, waiting to be invited to the party . . . kind of like these cats.* He grunted, then stooped to place the bowl on the ground and strode to the other end of the barn. The sliding door allowed bright autumn sunshine. Several kittens paused their cavorting to watch him pass, then bounded toward the waiting treat.

That afternoon after chores, Gabe grabbed a duffle bag of dirty clothes, pulled the towel off the hook next to the sink, his Dopp kit from the back of the toilet and crossed the 150 feet to the house. Caroline was swinging a large container of ice cream destined for the freezer.

"Want some?" she asked, holding it up in question.

"Uh, no thank you, Miss Caroline, but it does sound good. What kind this month?" he asked, his resolve weakening.

The Schwann man delivered once a week. Ma's night out, Caroline called it.

"Rocky Road." She sparkled her eyes at him. "You can always run the north forty later." She liked to tease him, but, in an older, *much* older sisterly fashion, he understood. Humor went a long way with Caroline. When she wasn't peeved about something, she'd be laughing about it. She never let things get to her; she did not *stew.*

"Oh—why not, and thank you!" Grinning in anticipation, he added he had some wash and needed to take a shower; he planned to go out tonight, so wouldn't be eating supper with them after all.

"Well, haul it on in then. What . . . you have a *date?*" she asked, in a voice like a cat licking cream. In the kitchen, she set the bucket on the red Formica counter and reached into a drawer for the dipping spoon, then pulled a bowl from the shelf and began to scoop.

"I'll just go throw these things in and be right back—or, say . . . would you mind if I took a shower first? Put the bowl in the fridge for now? Please?" He raised his eyebrows in question, smiling.

"Oh, sure. Wasn't thinking. I can do that. . . So how is Francesca?" she called back, as he bounced down the basement steps, where washer, dryer and shower were found.

"Now, Miss Caroline—" was all he said, playing their game of, "What to Divulge Today."

Gabe knew she enjoyed gossip, the alternate currency for cash-strapped, curious folk in most parts. He had amended this to include the not-so-cash-strapped as well. And as Sister Anne once said, "There exist *degrees* of gossip; the class (she was Irish and used *class* for "kind"), the *class* that aims purely to poke fun and derision is sinful, but the *class* that aims to educate a person about the state of a neighbor's health, or his circumstances, in order to show where assistance or charity may be required, well, that is altogether different . . . and merely information, is it not?" Discussion had ensued. Some gossip was helpful—the consensus.

A sound like a wild African bird drifted down the stairs, Caroline cackling in the kitchen. Put him in mind of his grandmother, long gone, but ever present.

He gathered his toiletries. It felt good to be cleaned up. Wrestling with recalcitrant sheep made you sore all over and he wondered if Senga was feeling it herself yet. He sent silent thanks for her help, then, remembering the arnica oil she touted against aching muscles, he massaged some into his calves and shoulders. If nothing else, it soothed his dry skin, but he'd ample experience and faith in Senga's remedies.

They'd speeded his recovery back in 2006, though he still ached now and then. *But who doesn't?* Gabe didn't like to revisit that time, painful as it proved, but he guessed his healing had more to do with a caring regard for his spirit than simple attention to multiple physical injuries. Stationed around him, like The Seven Directions, he'd been nursed and brought back to wholeness of body and spirit by his sister, Caroline, Rufus, Senga, Father, Son and Holy Spirit. Senga and he seemed to read one another's minds. *The healer's gift?* he'd wondered.

Rufus returned home just as Gabe stepped through the front door onto the porch. Precariously balancing his bowl of Rocky Road ice cream, the duffle bag, towel and his Dopp kit, he eased down on the next-to-the-top step. Gear at his feet, he scooted over as Rufus made his difficult way up.

"Hey, boss," he greeted, ". . . now this reminds me of being a kid again, eating a bowl of ice cream out on the front steps," Gabe professorially waved his spoon in a slow circle near the bowl.

"I thought you all preferred watermelon. . ." Rufus paused then winked as he hobbled up the steps with the bag of mail tucked under his arm, the end of his cane tapping the wood.

"That too, that too. . ." Gabe chuckled.

He often found himself laughing outright at Rufus' occasional provocative remark, uttered in fun for Gabe's sake. From *The Virginian* (having taught the novel to his freshmen classes), he'd learned about expected behavior and attitudes in the West. But a quote from the book, "When you call me that, smile," rang a bell, one which clanged loudly. Gabe learned to listen for that bell when conversing with others. A sneer sounded hollow. Derision? Tinny. But villains also smiled, his Shakespeare warned.

"Good of Senga to stop by earlier," said Rufus, lowering himself slowly into one of the two new Adirondack-style chairs. He reached into his shirt pocket for his tobacco, papers and lighter.

"Senga? When . . . where?" Caroline demanded as she joined them on the porch. She searched the road as she sat down beside Rufus. Her face screwed up in displeasure,

"Humph, what do you think of these chairs, hon? I think they need cushions. Seem damn hard to me."

"Oh, she was heading for her root digging . . . saw Gabe here getting whomped by a sheep, so came over to res—uh, to help out. . . . She was here only a bit, but it sure greased the wheels, didn't it, Gabe? And yes, the plastic is hard, Caro. I wondered what possessed you. . ." Rufus placed his weathered, gnarled hand on his wife's forearm, which rested on the arm of the chair.

The large spoon heaped with Rocky Road sat poised at his lips. Gabe lowered it back into the bowl and turned to look at Rufus a long moment. His boss' expression looked indecipherable, as it often could. "Yes, Senga did his job for him, Miss Caroline," he said.

She chortled and he added, "I'm helping her Friday, as long as you don't have something else pressing?"

"Nah, but the weather's supposed to change; we're overdue. That's good—you helping her, Gabe. I'm sure she appreciates it."

He made a sound in reply, while swallowing another mouthful of ice cream, then he scraped up the rest.

"Well. That was wonderful. I'm going to hang out that wash now and then I'm off. Oh! And the cats need more milk, Miss Caroline." Gabe glanced skyward, "It's not supposed to rain or snow *tonight*, is it?" he asked, rising and turning toward the door to take his dish inside, and to get the basket of laundry.

"No, not that I've heard . . . have you, hon? By Friday, they're saying. Gabe's steppin' out tonight, mm-hmm," she informed Rufus, who grinned.

"I think you'll be all right . . . we're leaving around 9:00 . . . Well, you have fun and be home by midnight!" he said.

The screen door clicked behind Gabe.

He took pleasure in hanging out wash and it smelled good for the effort. The sun-dried fragrance recalled his mother. Lugging the heavy basket, he ambled toward the clothes lines, stretched between the electric pole and the trunk of an old bur oak behind the house. He noted which species turned first:

ash—bright yellow (something to look forward to, if working in the dark, piney woods); next, the tall, gangly cottonwoods along the creeks (yellow as well, but a darker, more serious color, he'd thought—*gold*, he'd supposed). The oaks had turned ocher-brown two weeks ago. The country had enjoyed a long fall. Last year an early, hard freeze had blasted the oak leaves to a dull, dusty brown overnight. They dropped shortly after.

Domesticity allowed for daydreaming, planning or letting it all just *be*.

Rhythmic repeated actions feed creativity, he'd once read. Walking; rowing; hanging wash—one piece at a time. Horseback, one's torso gently swayed in cadence with the animal's gait, in cooperation.

Gabe pinned the last sock to the line, mentally crossing his fingers that rain, or snow, would wait, then he lifted the basket and stopped by the front porch to retrieve his gear. He set the basket beside the door and strolled back to his barn room. Having returned the towel to its hook, and his Dopp kit to its place, he opened it again to remove a small green bottle of scent. Valencia oranges and cedar trees.

He tried to remember to wear it for Francesca, who'd given it to him. She'd brought it from Italy last May when she returned.

He crossed to the door, reached for his hat and jacket. His pick-up was parked behind the barn. He settled himself behind the wheel, turned on the ignition and pointed the truck toward what lay before him this evening. He hoped it was good.

CHAPTER 21~THE FRIAR

Joe Rafaela lived in the small rectory beside his church on the Northern Cheyenne reservation in Montana. His was a small parish situated on the eastern-most boundary. The site of General George Custer's epic last battle lay to the west on the Crow Reservation. A Franciscan friar when he arrived in 1988, he was ordained in 2003 after the necessary period of study. Now Joe responded to "Father," "Brother" or "Just-Joe"—the name given him by his adoptive Indian family, the Two Bears. A younger sister grew up calling him "Saint Joe," at times in earnest, at times skeptically.

He might have been content living out his life as a friar, but the little mission required a priest. The Cheyenne were his family now and he considered his calling in practical terms, that of helping where he could, regardless of bureaucratic procedural constraints.

A Franciscan sister aided in this considerable work. Sister Joan lived several miles away in a small mobile home. Raised and schooled in eastern cities, the fifty-year-old social worker brought street smarts with her: what she lacked in Indian cultural intelligence, she made up for in a mean shell game. The Cheyenne enjoyed games of chance. Theirs being one of the poorest reservations in the country, the basics—food, clothing and shelter—were uppermost on the parish agenda. Most of his neighbors were rich in spirit, *comparatively-speaking*, Joe maintained.

The Holy Spirit, depicted as an eagle on one of the church's windows instead of the usual dove, cooperated (in concept) with the Great Spirit or Great Mystery here. *Maheó* the Creator was all the same to his parishioners and Joe liked it that way.

On this bright mid-October morning, Joe reached into his mailbox and was delighted to find a letter from Senga Munro. Overhead, cranes made their trilling calls clear and he stepped off his porch to find them.

"There you are," he muttered and watched for several moments. The birds circled high above and his heart swelled.

He walked back into his home. Among the pieces of mail, he noticed another personal letter, two in one day, a small triumph against "tech meth," what Joe called the proliferation of devices and their insidious invasion into the lives of the people. He owned a computer but disciplined himself in its use. On and off quickly. No more than once a day, and no electronics on Wednesdays when he and Sister Joan fasted from all media. A hermit day. Phones could record messages, an irony not lost on them, and each would listen in case of emergency, of which there were too many.

Joe smiled and stuffed Senga's letter into his brown robe's deep pocket for later.

At the persistent sound of knocking at 3:30 a.m., eighteen Junes ago, Joe turned on a light, shrugged into his robe in a daze and opened his front door to a person sitting against it, face in hands; the picture of dejection. A woman, he saw when she turned. She reared back upon seeing him, stood up slowly and introduced herself as Senga Munro, and she'd just driven from Sara's Spring in Wyoming. Joe recognized the town, having often visited the Bears' Lodge nearby, a site sacred to the Cheyenne. It'd been ignominiously named "Devils Tower," in mistranslation.

"Come in, come in," Joe motioned, as he studied what God had put in his path so early that morning. She looked to be in her twenties or early thirties, he'd thought; her face on the wretched side. Mainly, she looked tired. Her hair needed washing, he observed, then chided himself for being uncharitable. A glance in the hall mirror explained her initial response: his usually neat hair and beard pointed in all directions. He'd alarmed her, he thought in dismay. *That's two of us*, he thought.

He had stopped wearing a tonsure and now wore his hair longer than his brothers might deem appropriate. Dark half-moons hung beneath his weary brown eyes; he'd been born that way, his mother had once told him. "My long-suffering saint," she'd quipped—partly in jest. And there was the matter of his considerable girth. The Cheyenne called him *ma'haeta* or, big. *E-ma'haeta-jo*, or, *Joe-He's-Big*.

"What can I do for you, ah—Senga?" he'd asked when they were seated and he'd tried to quickly smooth his hair and beard with his hands, finally excusing himself for a moment. He'd returned feeling more presentable and less the wild man.

"Yes, it's Senga—Senga Munro, Father."

"I'm *Brother* Joe, but if you need a priest, there is one down in Ashland—he comes here on Sundays. Ah, has something happened?"

She gave him a quick, weak smile, for his sake, he'd thought.

"About a year ago my daughter was killed, um, she fell . . . and I feel responsible. I—I'm a mess. I can't keep. . . I'm in trouble."

"Ahh," he said, his brown eyes holding hers. "I am so sorry for your loss." Then, "May I?" and covering one of her hands with his, he closed his eyes for a moment, then placed his right hand on the crown of Senga's head. "May the peace of God, which surpasses all understanding, preserve and guard the heart and mind of this woman, Senga, in Christ Jesus." He'd opened his eyes, smiled wearily and asked, "May I brew us some coffee? It will only take a moment."

He watched the woman think then say, "Amen—I mean— *yes*—that'd be good. Milk and sugar, please, if you have some," she'd called out as he entered the kitchen.

Senga passed the next ninety minutes recounting the tragic event and her present circumstances; her upbringing, her accidental settling in northeast Wyoming from the South, releasing Emily's father from her affections. To refuse love? Even such as it was? or wasn't, in her opinion, she'd admitted. She unleashed an angry but frightened wolf in telling her story, but he'd heard worse, *much* worse, and he was able to let Senga's confession—what this amounted to—pass through him like the pending pink sunrise through the window glass.

139

As a friar, he couldn't offer absolution, but this wasn't what the woman sought or needed, he suspected.

The telling was the thing, wasn't it? Telling a story, in his Cheyenne family's tradition, was medicine—healing the teller and the told.

My God, her child died, Joe reflected. *She is bereft and appears to have no people.* He remembered a time when he and Milo Two Bears had traveled down to Wyoming. They were driving the last thirty miles to their destination after dark—a waxing moon, he recalled—through cedar breaks, pine-ridges and sagebrush, when Milo sighed beside him and Joe asked him if he was all right.

"I feel sorry for these people, Joe—my heart hurts for them. Look! They have no people. Look how far apart everyone lives. . . It is no wonder they are so lonely. It is no wonder so many are lost . . . like wandering spirits. . ."

The occasional yard light shone upon a cluster of buildings, or a solitary lamp burned in a window far off the road. A stalwart mailbox next to a turn-out. Moonlit homes—as if no one lived there, he'd thought.

What Joe hadn't responded to his elder was his opinion—from experience—that isolation and loneliness can, and does, exist in large cities in the midst of thousands of souls. No, proximity of neighbors does not guarantee belonging.

The woman was telling him that her daughter's body had been taken to a funeral home, where it was examined by the coroner and cremated. A few friends and acquaintances from Sara's Spring attended a short service, but the father hadn't come. She'd added "callous" to the man's shortcomings.

"*Callow* too," she'd tacked on.

"I can't call her death an 'accident', Joe, and at the same time I can't call it anything else . . . so I'm kind of 'short-circuiting'—do you know what I mean?"

He had nodded, his heart aching for the woman.

She continued. "I've lost it—I'm drinking too much, smoking too much, reading too much—too much of *everything*. I'm starting to . . . *hell*, I don't even know. . ."

The woman turned herself inside out. And still he waited.

"If only she hadn't been wearing that backpack. . . I'd just helped her with it . . . I—I didn't think . . . she slipped—lost her balance, you see . . . and after it happened—when I held her—I kept thinking, *I can't imagine my life without you, I can't imagine my life without you,* over and over . . . and, so . . . it seems I can't. I cannot imagine my life anymore. I don't know how to do this. . ." She looked at him, entreating him for the answer.

"And, I've run out of tears. . ."

"It is not your fault, Senga," he'd said, gently. "And the other behaviors, well, they have run their course, yes? But your child's death was not your fault."

"What if I believe it is?"

He had groaned uncomfortably at this, knowing he was treading water. Belief raised the strongest barrier. A powerful adversary. Against both good and ill.

"Senga, I'm going to ask you to consider something differently . . . um—would you try?"

She had whispered yes.

He picked up his mug and drank, set it back on the table, closed his eyes a moment, then opened them and began.

"Belief and faith are not the same things, as you may know. Faith may seem the weaker of the two, but quite the opposite. As I see it, you stand at the edge of an abyss at this moment—not to put words into your mouth—it's just how I see it. You, however, see nothing. It's as black as the darkness was outside that window—you know, before the dawn?" he gestured. "Can't imagine anything before you; is this about right?"

She nodded.

"And I'm not talking about Faith, uppercase, as in, 'The Catholic Faith'—I mean simple faith, small 'f.' Ahhh, please forgive this simple analogy, but this is what's come to me. Close your eyes, Senga, and listen with your heart open, would you?"

He saw her tentatively nod, then close her eyes.

"A wonderful hot-air balloon with red, blue and yellow stripes hangs in the air over an abyss. Can you see the balloon? And the void all around and below?"

She nodded.

"The balloon's tethers—or ropes—hang over the edges of the basket. Senga, there is *always* the abyss. No one knows what is to come. But, we can simply and easily reach for one of the tethers . . . anytime. The distance between is an illusion. The balloon is faith, obviously, and it *will* support us, Senga. There are those remarkable few who manage to find themselves *in* the basket; they are the fortunate ones. I've known two Franciscan brothers and a sister who sailed most of their lives above the void, *in the basket,* so to speak. But most of us make do with a knot tied at the end of our rope. Proverbial or no. It's a useful device, no? I mean the analogy—but ropes are useful too. . . Do you still see the balloon, Senga?"

"Yes. And the ropes. There's a breeze from below . . . the ropes are waving back and forth—like grass in wind."

"Yes! Now, reach out. Can you see your hand before you, even in the darkness?"

"Um, yes—it's glowing—I-I can see it."

"Reach for the closest rope and step off the ledge. Go!" It had struck him just as he said this that he was asking the woman to repeat her daughter's fall. But it was what had come to him, and he trusted what came.

He watched as Senga groped in her darkness.

After opening her eyes, she told him she'd grasped the tether while stepping off into thin air. "I felt the breeze around me . . . then I felt light. I weighed nothing. . . Yes, I *see* it," she continued, "What you mean. . . Thank you. I get it. I just need the strength to hang on. And there's the rub, as they say. Besides, you're right; who sees what's ahead of them? Still, hope shines in darkness, huh? Or faith, in this case."

Joe regretted her glib remark. *A hard nut, then,* he decided.

"Fear is most powerful at a threshold or precipice, yet this is where we are often compelled to wait for some reason—um, like deer in headlights? Or maybe we simply feel more alive when experiencing abject terror. But thresholds are paradoxical too. It is where we numb ourselves." He raised his eyebrows for emphasis, "so we don't have to feel as much, for a respite. We have ingenious methods: the usual—drugs and alcohol; then there's food, exercise, television, reading, even travel, sadly, oh, and religion. The subtle one. It's even spawned a new spiritual disorder—'over-scrupling.' Do you see a pattern, Senga?"

"Anything to the extreme."

"Yes. I mention things one does, but doing nothing is included: despair—and what is called 'acedia' in our tradition—spiritual sloth or apathy—creates a vacuum of sorts, you see, for some of the, ah, 'usual suspects' to fill. Is this making some sense? I'm sorry for the contrivance, Senga, but—"

"No, it's all right, really; go on, please."

"We pray—or beg—for the strength to simply hang on, Senga. Our own weight grows lighter for it—and after a while we don't even notice the ropes—or the balloon floating away.

"Ah, there is a Catholic community in Sara's Spring," the friar in him lightly mentioned.

"Yes, I know. Em and I attended Mass sometimes, mostly on feast days. I guess it's how I was raised," she explained. "My grandparents. . . We lived a long way from town, in the mountains of North Carolina."

"Ahhh, I thought I detected a tar-heel accent," he said, smiling. They sat quietly a few moments.

"Tell me, child, if you can . . . why did you come here, I mean to this particular rectory? More coffee?"

She'd held out her mug. When he returned, Senga described the anxiety that was threatening to implode her inner structure, and near midnight she'd simply got into her car and began driving north. Winding up at the junction in Montana that ran east-west, she turned left with no plan. She'd practiced slow, deep breathing most of the way, she told him, to allay panic.

Hearing this, Joe stood and left the room, to return shortly with a plate that held a fat cinnamon roll.

"Eat, please," he instructed. She did and resumed.

"When I read I was entering the Cheyenne Reservation, I just followed my nose, as my Grannie used to say. . . I turned north and drove a ways, then I saw the church from a distance and turned in that direction. You can see the bell tower a long way—having a light in it that way."

"But there's no—" and he'd stopped, wondering if moonlight glinted off the surface of the bell, ". . . Ah, yes, I see. . ."

Joe had liked Senga, her transparency and, while *fervor* couldn't describe the quality, she conveyed quiet determination in her demeanor, even in the throes of despair and grief. He had witnessed this in the Cheyenne too. A notion surfaced,

"Do you have Native Americans in your ancestry?" he'd asked with no preamble, causing her to blink.

"On my mother's side, back a few generations," she replied, "Cherokee."

"Mm, yes, I don't mean to pry; it's just . . . I've become used to certain responses," he added cryptically, "So—would you like to rest for a while? You must be worn out. I can offer a clean pillowcase and blanket for this couch."

He watched her consider the horizontal surface wistfully, and pointed out the bathroom; he'd bring the pillow and blanket.

They corresponded by United States Postal Service, Senga's discussions and questions reflecting a fertile—if fanciful—mind, but Joe was struck by her disinterest in theological conundrums. ("Isn't it all just too obvious?" she once quipped.) She accepted and cultivated Mystery. He'd found some of his course work tedious in that regard—exegesis "taught," versus a kind of grace, and having to hold paradox in one's head. But then, it was a Benedictine college he'd attended and Benedictines tend to inhabit their heads more than—He stopped, ending this observation with a quick prayer for his fellow religious and clerics, and an equally quick, "Lord, have mercy."

They met in 1995, Joe figured in his head (what heads were good for), and he smiled. She'd visited on occasion since, and he'd stopped to see her when traveling to the national monument to attend a summer ceremony with members of his family and parish.

A month after their initial meeting, she wrote her first monthly letter to tell him she was "better," and thanked him for his kindness, his coffee and his couch.

He finished his lunch before pulling the envelope from his pocket. The postmark was dated recently, but he knew the letter may have been written over the course of several days, as Senga often required time to grapple with a notion, or life simply intervened. One page revealed a colored-pencil drawing—a portrait. He glanced at it before setting it down, to take up October's letter.

"Dear Joe," it began. "Peace be with you. A good crop of apples this year. Several bushels in the garage, the rest still on the trees. You could come down for a box—a contribution! The fall colors are beautiful, no? But we're due for some weather, I hear.

"Pleasantries nearly aside—how go your old bones? And Sister Joan's? Last missive I received, you'd both caught some bug. Do you need more Echinacea? I have some to spare, you know, for mendicant friars and the like. Remember, it's ten days on, ten days off with the doses, unless you have symptoms, then it's every few hours; for you—three droppers! Half for Sweet Sister. Let me know. Or, ask Moona'e. She makes it, but possibly without alcohol. Not sure.

"We were discussing time last time. Here's one for you— it's a goody, so listen up: I was waxing my table after an early supper, just before twilight, so light enough to see. Out the south-facing window, I spotted a nice buck, a whitetail with a drop tine on the left side, drinking from that small pond below the cabin. I admired his rack, a five-by-six, then started to turn back to my task, but was distracted by quick movement out the east window, and this was no fantasy or hallucination—well, God knows; I don't. An Indian, can't say which tribe, wearing buckskins; a tall man—judging by the distance—was standing beside a ponderosa—behind it, from the deer's perspective. I watched him slowly bend (genuflect?) to one knee, nock his bow and draw down on the buck.

"It was over in maybe five seconds. I looked back to the buck quickly, in time to see him turn his head in the man's direction and bound away. I looked back and—nothing—there was no one there. With my eyes, I searched high and low, and then I hiked over to the spot and saw no sign whatsoever. You'd think there might've been an impression in the pine needles or something. Nada. It gave me chills, Joe; then I felt a tingling sense of wonder. I sat down to catch my breath and spotted the buck way below, antlers up, alert and moving along quietly. I had a bandana with me and tore a strip off to mark the spot where I thought the man's head could have reached. He was about six feet tall—or more.

145

"Hunting season's not until November 1. Bow season—last month.

"As I say, it was nearing dusk, so the light was waning, but I saw this, Joe. I've included a rough sketch. From the cabin window, where I sit now, I am maybe seventy-five feet away; it's directly across the ravine—you've been there. Near that old-growth stump.

"I believe this is where our notions come from, seemingly impossible theories, which lead to broader perspectives—at least this one stretches my puny brain. Miracles? Your conclusion of reflected moonlight on the bell the night I found you. Remember the moon was waning that night. Two days to new. But back to the hunter. . .

"I'm considering dimensions, Joe. (I know—so much for accepting mystery.) But what circumstance could account for my being there at a particular time, at a particular place, to overlap with a scene from, oh, the 1850s or earlier? My hunter may have carried a rifle later. But the buck knew it—that's the thing. . . That's the part I can't wrap my head around. If the buck had also "been" in the earlier time period, would that arrow have found it's mark? Is it something about (other) animals? Also, my cabin was invisible to this person; else he wouldn't have remained in plain sight.

"Enough. Another bone to chew from your favorite fancier of old-timey letters. Tell me how your latest project is going; steering your young away from numbing themselves, toward a more hope-filled future sounds Herculean. Hope is indeed the thing with feathers—of eagle, turkey, flicker and crow."

She had signed it, "Faithfully yours (still small f), Senga."

He reached for the drawing and, like a suspicious dog, felt his hackles rise. From a shelf, he brought down a large volume of George Catlin's works and found the page: a painting, dated 1832, showing *Né-hee-ó-éé-wóo-tis*—Wolf on the Hill or, "High Wolf," a chief of the Cheyenne Nation. Catlin described him as tall, and as, "a man of integrity." Senga's subject looked a younger version of the man; the hair less adorned, if just as luxuriant, the features less chiseled, softer; but the *eyes*—there was no mistaking the eyes. *Hooded and far-seeing*, Joe thought and, catching his choice of phrase, he grunted. *A paradox.* Even the buckskin shirts looked similar, but no decorative scalp locks on Senga's man; the quill work patterns—the same. Cheyenne work. She might have seen the image once and imagined the likeness, he supposed, but no, he didn't think so. He'd show the drawing to Milo for his impression. *And do I really want to do this?*

CHAPTER 22~A DAY'S WORK

On Thursday morning, while gathering wood from the nearby rick, Senga smelled snow in the air and heard bright honking of geese. Their V-shaped slice headed due south. Earlier, Sand Hill cranes had passed, a loud spiral of rolling R's on a thermal, meeting the current of moving air.

Depending on the season, the drive to Sara's Spring could be made in as little as twenty-five minutes, or take as long as an hour. The town had grown from a small logging settlement in the late nineteenth century into a community. At town center stood Sara's Spring's Community Building. Decades past, it was called "The Hall," and hosted Saturday night dances. As it was, the place accommodated funerals, auctions, blood draws and anything else a larger gathering required. There the Senior Citizens met. Senga preferred to call such "elders," and said so at every opportunity, but this fell on deaf ears. Perhaps literally.

As she rolled into town, she noticed Rufus' outfit parked on Main Street, the four-horse trailer hitched behind, repurposed for sheep. *Probably having breakfast*, she guessed. Her habit was to take her wash to the laundromat once a week before work. On her lunch break—in rain, shine or snow— she'd return, fold the pieces into her basket, and return to the library.

But today, she pulled first into the store parking lot, stepped out, grocery list and canvas bag in hand, and entered. At eight o'clock, several customers were already lining up at the counter. She found the items she wanted and took her place.

Senga usually recognized folks, even if she wasn't acquainted with them. Not the individual who waited in front of her. Of similar height, he was scruffy and unshaven, with short-short hair. His clothing smelled like wood smoke and gasoline. A tattoo shouted from his neck behind his left ear. Some sort of symbol, she thought: two jagged, parallel lines.

Just then, the door opened and in walked Gabe, dressed for town, wearing his hat, brown corduroy coat, clean jeans and requisite silk scarf (*burgundy*—*no*—*plum*, she decided), the large square tied around his neck like a stock. Fellow bull riders often wore them while competing, but "I never," he'd once admitted to her.

Gabe held something in his right hand. *An index card?* He turned to the bulletin board, located a push pin and tacked the card to the wall. *What's he selling?* When he turned, he spotted her and beamed, tapped his hat brim and walked out.

Senga heard the man in front of her make a derisive grunt and mutter, "Wash that grin off your face, nigger," in a tone she recognized with sickening dismay.

Oh, dear Lord . . . she thought and, amending this under her breath, said, "No. *No* way."

Senga carefully lowered the hand basket onto the counter, having to reach behind the man to do it, then, after a deep breath, she whipped him around by pulling his right shoulder toward her, pulling him off-balance. Then she grabbed the front of his shirt-jacket in both fists, causing him to drop his few items, including a dozen eggs (of which several broke). She shoved him backwards into the nearby soft drinks cooler, rattling the contents inside, his eyes widening in surprise.

"Are you crazy? Or just plain stupid?" she demanded in an even, controlled tone.

The two cashiers and three other customers stood stunned.

"What are *you* doing, *bitch*?" the man countered. "You a nigger-lover or what?"

Senga's anger reached flash point and she barely registered the motion of unsnapping her scabbard and drawing out the Hori Hori. She had it raised half-way to the man's face when someone grabbed her arms from behind and dragged her backwards, her heels scraping the linoleum.

Instinctively, the man had raised and crossed his forearms.

149

A voice at her ear said, "Whoa there, woman—settle down. . . This trash ain't worth hard time."

Grinning in her face, the individual slowly lowered his arms. His were yellow-stained teeth, and breath, like the song said—hard as kerosene. She knew she needed to leave, and right now, but her arms were still pinned behind her. She wanted to spit, but refrained. The object of her considerable ire glanced at the door, then to his groceries, seemingly debating what to do.

Her restrainer spoke. "Here, let's put this, uh, what *is* this anyway?"—about the digging knife he carefully took from her to inspect. He then replaced it in the scabbard and snapped the strap. "Hunh."

"It's her digging knife, Tom," piped up the cashier, also a client of Senga's, adding, "She digs roots, you know—makes medicines."

At this information, her foe jerked his head in her direction, mouth shut now. His eyes registered interest or, perhaps simple curiosity, but he remained cool.

"I'm okay . . . I'm *okay*," she insisted, without taking her eyes from "Yellowtooth," what she dubbed the racist. "Put that stuff on my account, please, Ellie . . . and, I-I'll pay for the broken eggs. I'm sorry—" Senga cut her eyes to the cashier in speaking her apology, then returned her gaze.

"You got nothing to be sorry about, Senga," said the cashier, adding, "Who's next? I mean—next to check out?"

The customers (except Tom Robinson) stood near paralyzed. Finally, one tittered and moved forward, all eyes on Yellowtooth, who vibrated like a coiled serpent before it strikes.

The cashier handed her the bag containing her items and she stepped to the door, pushing it open with her right shoulder while keeping her eyes on the man. He glared at her with the dead-eyed expression she'd only witnessed on the faces of rattle snakes.

Outside, Senga inhaled deeply and the sharp October air filled her lungs with a needed dose of nitrogen. She spotted the Army-green, flatbed dually pick-up, with a large Confederate flag decal adhered to the window. Beside it another decal read,

"Wood." You didn't grow up in the South without learning the flag's other, implicit significance.

The truck belonged to Yellowtooth.

After stowing the groceries in her car, she drove to the Laundromat and, finding she was alone, she broke into tears. "God . . . what just happened?" She shook for a moment then pounded a fist on the washing machine, in frustration or anger, she couldn't tell. The resounding kettle drum-like sound dispelled the emotional jag, and she reached into her basket for a towel, wet a corner in the wash basin, wiped her face and rearranged her demeanor. Then, she proceeded to attentively shake out and place each item into the washer, measure soap, close the top, add the necessary coins, adjust the dial and push the "Start" button.

Will the idiot press charges? she wondered, but only for the time it took to think it. The rhythmic drone of the washing machine was calming, and her mind settled. When the cycle finished, she moved the wash to the dryer. Then, she gathered up the sack containing detergent, et cetera, put it in the car and plucked her lunch bag off the car seat. A short walk around the corner and she arrived at the library, where she expected the news had already been delivered.

It had.

CHAPTER 23~THE FOOL

Chief Charlie Mays was waiting for her. All three-hundred pounds of him. He was approaching retirement age and sorely needed to lose weight if he wanted to live to enjoy it. He was chatting with the librarian, Senga's supervisor (also an herbal client *and* the chief's girlfriend). Senga corrected her posture and made for her corner, where a not-quite-filled, rolling cart of books awaited her organizing skills. She sighed, then turned to a small refrigerator to store her sack lunch. After draping her jacket over her chair back, she arranged her sweater hem to cover the scabbard, for form's sake. Sensing the scrutiny of the chief of police upon her entry, she endeavored to reflect grace, sanity and care.

"Good morning, Muriel. Charlie," she greeted. "And I expect I know why you're here," she said, betraying no emotion and easing down into her chair.

"Muriel, would you mind if I spoke with Senga in private? I mean is there somewhere you could go for a minute?"

"Mornin', Senga," Muriel offered quietly, with a smile. In her mid-forties, she carried a little extra weight herself and wore her usual, navy blue cardigan. "I've got to visit the 'ladies.'" She stood and walked around the counter, toward the hallway, to leave them alone. It was still early for patrons.

Charlie pulled a chair over and sat down.

"Shit, Senga," was all he said. Then, he waited. She didn't look at him, but sat impassively staring at the desk blotter. Her hands neatly folded.

She finally raised her eyes. "I lost it, I know. But the guy had it coming, Charlie."

"Christ, woman, if Tom Robinson hadn't intervened, what the hell would have happened? Can you tell me that?"

"Tom was good luck, I'd say," she said, grinning into Charlie's face and quickly wiping it off with the back of her own hand.

"Aggravated assault. That's what you could be charged with, you know that?" His frustration rose with the volume. "That—that *knife* you carry, Senga, is what we call a 'deadly weapon' in Wyoming, or has this never occurred to you? And whatever he is—"

"He's a racist, Charlie," she interrupted, ". . . and I could string other colorful adjectives to that, but won't. . ." She searched his eyes now, with concern, to reach a part of him she knew understood. "Charlie, that guy doesn't even *know* Gabe, but that's beside the point, isn't it? How can anyone be allowed to talk like that, and . . . use such tripe?"

"What—tripe?" Charlie asked, "Thought it was intestines or something. . ."

"Trash, then," Senga amended. "And yes, I know what you're going to say, freedom of speech and all that, but this was in our *grocery* store, with everyone minding their own business, and this guy just decides he can call someone—never mind a friend of mine—one of the ugliest words. . ."

"O Senga—" Exhaling loudly, Charlie leaned back in the chair, causing it to groan, and his shirt stretched too tightly against his abdomen. Then, he rolled his head down and around in a circle, to loosen neck muscles.

"You sore?"

"Yeah—and this business doesn't help, Senga. What, you've got a potion or something?"

She pulled open the drawer on her left, lifted out a small jar and handed it to him. "It's just a salve—arnica. Good for what ails ya. Use it a few times a day; take a warm shower, let the water run on the area for a while, Charlie, then rub more on." She inhaled and released it all at once.

"Uh, thanks, but I'm good," he said.

"Go on, take it. It's not a bribe or anything." She winked at him.

"Senga, knock it off, but . . . okay, thanks, I'll try it. . . Look, you took it personally, what the guy said . . . I mean, you don't even know him, do you?"

"Damn right I took it personally, and who cares if *I don't know him personally*. . ." she lowered her voice to a forceful whisper. "So what happens now?" she asked, seeing Muriel return, glance in their direction and discreetly move to the far stacks.

"We wait and see if there are charges filed, Senga. Ordinarily, the state would file against an assault, and we wouldn't wait for the uh, *aggrieved* party to do it . . . I talked with Tom and Ellie, and they both thought the twerp deserved it, but now I'm going to have to go out to his place and get a statement. You made work for me, Senga, and I don't much like it. . ."

Charlie stood up, arranged his hat back on his head, called over to Muriel with "Later." Senga's hands once again rested on the blotter, a blank expression clouding her face.

"Cheer up, gal; could've been worse. It'll be all right, I expect." Then, as an afterthought, he added, pointing with his chin at her Hori Hori, "I'd leave off wearing that thing for a while, though—just for the sake of appearances."

Senga slowly raised a finger, at which he chuckled. "Ha. Didn't think that'd fly . . . but it's a damn good thing for you I've got a sense of humor." Then he left.

Senga tucked the incident in the drawer labeled Ponder Time, and passed the remainder of the morning mindlessly sorting and returning books to shelves, while Muriel said nothing.

At noon, she pulled on her jacket to go collect her laundry, asking Muriel if she needed anything from the store, quickly amending the thought to, "Oh, never mind."

Muriel shook her head and returned to her monitor.

Charlie started out for the old Berry place, a county sheriff's deputy en route to meet him at the junction, following protocol between city and county law enforcement offices. Charlie didn't think he needed another body with him, but the sheriff insisted. Its remoteness—his reasoning. Besides, his rookie deputy needed experience. *Wonderful*, thought Charlie. The place was located some five-to-seven miles off an isolated logging road, deep in the wooded area of the Black Hills National Forest.

It was late afternoon when he arrived at the old homestead, and growing darker with heavy cloud cover. He wondered if he had the correct location. The place looked deserted, despite two vehicles and a thin column of smoke rising vertically from the chimney.

He pulled into a sort of yard, devoid of vegetation, and stopped, leaving the SUV running but shifted into "park." The deputy pulled in alongside, and both were just stepping out of their vehicles when the *zing!* and *pop!* of a bullet forced both down, behind their open doors. Charlie drew his gun and looked quickly up and over in Carter's direction, then toward the house.

"What the *hell?*" Charlie said under his breath.

An elderly man in a long gray beard and unkempt hair stepped through the door wearing crusty blue overalls and a red plaid flannel shirt. Two large, muscular dogs that resembled a cross between a Pit Bull and a Rottweiler rushed out past him.

"Duke! Daisy! Stay!" the man rasped, and Charlie blew out as the dogs stopped in their tracks and sat down on their bulging haunches.

The chief didn't like to shoot dogs. *Where's the banjo music?* he wondered.

The man peered at him and the deputy, then, turning his head to the right, he yelled to someone, "Joey! Quit! We got company." Then the old man slowly took a few steps toward them and stopped, apparently waiting for someone to speak. Charlie watched the man slide a large folding knife from his pocket, and proceed to clean a thumbnail with it.

Oh, for crying out loud. . .

"Tell, uh—Joey?—to come out where we can see him," Charlie directed the man and Joey appeared from the side of the house, a .223 in his hand, the other hand raised palm up.

Now there's a mixed message.

"Target practice . . ." the kid explained, ". . . turkey and deer season coming up." Then he grinned, and Charlie noticed the kid's teeth. But he also recognized the pretext of target practice as intimidation, and felt his blood pressure rise. Not a good thing in his case. He suspected the SUV and cruiser had been spotted on the winding lane and their presence reported, *but by whom?* he wondered.

"I need you to put the rifle down, now, son," Charlie told the boy. To his surprise, the kid complied immediately and stood back up. The deputy looked at his colleague, in question, but Charlie remained cool and holstered his SIG Sauer. The deputy lowered his, and they both rose from behind the relative safety of the car doors.

"I need to speak with the fella who was in Sara's Spring this morning. I understand he lives out here?"

"You have a lot of needs, dontcha, big guy, but yeah, that would be Dale. This is his little brother, Joey," the old man tipped his head in the kid's direction, speaking in a voice that sounded as though he needed to cough up something—*like a hairball*, Charlie thought.

"I'm Chief Charlie Mays from Sara's Spring, and this is Deputy Carter from the Sheriff's Office in Sundance—and who might you be, sir?" Charlie asked.

"Oh, well, *nice* to meet you too, Chief, Deputy. I'm George, George Canton," the man replied, still digging the dirt—*and God knows what else*—from under his nails.

"Well, is he here?" Charlie inquired, "This Dale?"

"Could be . . ."

This was becoming tedious, Charlie thought, as he glanced at Carter, who looked as though he'd rather be anywhere than here just now. Charlie recognized his colleague's sentiment, that of one's skin crawling with a bad feeling, such as realizing you had a tick creeping up your back and you couldn't reach to remove it.

Charlie took the opportunity to further survey the buildings and surroundings. An old travel trailer had been brought in and set up several yards from the old house, which, for all the world, did not look fit for human habitation. *What some folks will do.* Structures from the former mill lay in a heap. A flat-bed pick-up was parked haphazardly next to an old Bronco. He memorized the Bronco's plate numbers. The flat-bed's weren't visible. Then the door to the dilapidated house squeaked opened and who must be "Dale" appeared.

"Ya wanna speak to me, Occifer?" he asked, and Charlie instantly understood Senga's revulsion. The man wore a sleeveless t-shirt, his bare arms tattooed with varying degrees of "supreme white pride" invectives, and Charlie recognized the prison organization's *Peckerwood* image, a pissed-off woodpecker, with the word "WOOD" on his forearm. The symbol on the man's neck Senga had described appeared to be two white lightning bolts, and another clue. *Jesus*, thought Charlie, when he spotted the "88" in a beautifully rendered design. He knew it stood for HH or, *Heil Hitler*.

After Charlie marshaled his sensibilities, he looked Dale in the eye and said simply, "I need a statement about this morning."

The man must have felt the cold, given the quickly dropping temperature. *But he wants me to see who, or what, I'm dealing with, the fool.* "So, do you want to sit in my outfit, or do we go inside?" Charlie asked as he casually jotted down the Bronco's plate number in his notebook from memory. Dale gave him a look that said, *I am no fool* as he headed for the SUV, without a word.

Carter holstered his gun and waited beside his cruiser, while Joey strolled back to his target. The deputy spotted it with a sigh: a rough outline of a man's torso, this stapled several times onto two lengths of lathing. A bull's eye had been rendered in white chalk or paint, on the chest area. Black poster board was used. Several visible holes marked direct hits near the heart, Carter noticed, and he slowly moved his hand down to rest on the butt of his weapon, the safety strap unsnapped.

The target was placed in front of a berm of sorts. The high pile of dirt appeared seemingly tamped, with its nearby source left casually untended—a large hole employed, apparently, for garbage. Then his gaze moved to the two dogs, still quietly sitting at attention. Carter felt relief, and a kind of amazement, all at once.

The old man sauntered back over, possibly in hopes of eavesdropping, and Carter warned, "That's close enough, sir." The old man shot him a belligerent look, then pointedly folded his knife. Returning it to his pocket, he turned and shuffled back into the house, barking something to the dogs, which followed on their master's heels. The squeaking door slammed shut behind him.

Where are the women? Carter wondered. He saw no evidence of children either. *An old man, another man and his brother; is that it? Can't be,* he thought. And it didn't sound as if this Dale was the old man's son; *he would have mentioned it, but maybe not.*

Just then, the door to the trailer opened and a young woman dressed in jeans, boots, hat and a heavy coat carefully descended the two metal steps. She glanced warily in his direction. Carter felt his stomach lurch, and the woman turned back to a five-or six-year-old girl. The woman beckoned and reached for a small mittened hand. Finally, reaching up, she lifted the child and set her on the ground.

Chief Mays wouldn't see the woman, or the girl, from his position. From where Carter waited, the woman stood maybe a hundred feet away, but even from this distance, he spotted her badly bruised cheek and bloodied black eye. He had also watched her distinctly shake her head at him in urgent, silent appeal.

Aw, shit, he thought, *now what? Looks like we've got racists, wife beaters and God knows what else.* He watched the woman quickly pull a woolen hat down over the child's bright red, curly hair. The girl caught sight of Carter and tentatively lifted her wooly hand to wave to him, but the woman touched the child's arm to stop her. She whispered something. Then she stood up and took the child's hand. They turned in the opposite direction, away from Carter's line of sight, and into the forest.

On the drive back, Charlie wanted to confer with Carter. Before they reached the junction, he radioed for Carter to stop at the roadside café.

Charlie chose a booth and each ordered coffee. After the waitress brought their cups, filled them and left, Charlie began.

"We've got problems."

"Uh, I'd say so . . . there's a woman and kid out there— about five, I'd say. The woman's been beaten—her, ah, face. . . She made it plain she didn't want help. They walked into those woods behind the house while you were getting the guy's statement. I'm wondering if she was trying to leave or something. . . Come to think of it—*damn*, why didn't I think of that before?" Carter sounded distressed.

"It's getting ready to snow, Carter. Were they dressed for it? Oh, hell. I don't like any of this," Charlie said, adding, "That Dale is bad news. Spent seven years in the pen in Texas and is decidedly *not* rehabilitated. The opposite, I'd say. You know what the Peckerwoods are?"

"We studied prison gangs at the academy, but I've forgotten some of it; you'll have to remind me. So what're they all doing up here?"

Charlie had his suspicions, but kept them to himself.

"I need to look into something and get back to you. I'll give the sheriff a call. And he'll want to talk with you, too. . ."

"Did you see that target the kid was using?" Carter asked.

"Yep, when we drove out, and that's only the tip of this iceberg," Charlie added without explanation as he stood. He reached into his jacket pocket for his wallet and pulled out a five-dollar bill for the check and tip. Carter pulled his hat back on and stood. They'd left their jackets on. The waitress thanked them for coming in and told them to come again. Charlie smiled at the woman. Outside, Carter thanked him for the coffee and started to walk around to his car door, when he stopped and turned to Charlie.

"Someone told them we were coming. You know that, don't you? And where *was* he—or she?"

"Yep. Thought of that too. Best get on home before the snow's bad, Carter. We'll be talking, and say, I appreciate your being there today. . . Well, goodnight," and Charlie opened the SUV door and slid in (with some difficulty), as the first snowflakes fell. He started the engine, shifted into gear and drove onto the highway.

He saw Carter in his rear-view mirror gaze skyward, as growing swirls of falling snow sparkled in the café's receding light, and he thought of the woman and child, hoping they weren't out in this, but equally hoping they weren't back in that mean trailer, either.

CHAPTER 24~SEA CHANGE

Earlier, on her way home from work, Senga wondered if she were losing her mind. At Strickland's turn-off, she abruptly veered onto the county road and found herself bouncing east, toward Caroline. Rufus and Gabe would still be away and not expected home until after suppertime. They'd probably stop at Earl's in Alzada.

An old-fashioned hen party was called for. Caroline would offer wisdom, if not quite a shoulder. Senga rolled over the car gate into Strickland's yard and pulled up.

"Yeah, I heard," said Caroline, as Senga exited the car. Her neighbor was busily rolling up a garden hose against the probability of frost or freeze overnight. The cold front's icy fingers were already making inroads, the afternoon's temperature dropping twenty-five degrees in three hours. The apples could wait until morning, snow or no snow. *Chances are, it won't be a hard freeze,* Senga hoped. So much prayer hung on hope and faith.

"I suppose it's all over town," she said.

"Well, ha! What do *you* think? But folks around here get a kick out of any kind of tussle. Don't matter what the politics are. . . You know that, Senga."

"Charlie went to talk with the guy—to see if he's going to let it go."

"Grab those two pots there, would you, hon, and bring them on up to the porch."

Senga did as instructed, then surveyed the yard for other weather-dependent tasks.

"Want some coffee? Or maybe something stronger? We're getting snow tonight," Caroline added, in passing, just as she spotted Gabe's wash still hanging on the line. "Here, come help me with this too, then we'll go in. Thought he was going to get this down this morning—may not have been dry yet. . ." she said as they both began to pull the clothespins off and drop the clothing into the basket. "Ha! He'll owe me one," she snickered. "Woulda been frozen by tomorrow, that's for sure."

When they finished, Senga picked up the full basket and carried it to the porch.

"Just set it inside the door, hon; he can get it later. Come on in and take a load off." Caroline motioned her inside then closed the door behind her.

"Let's have a drink! What do you say?" Caroline proposed as she bustled over to the hutch. "The sun is over the yard-arm, as Rufus says . . . whatever that means . . . do you know? Of course you do. . ."

Senga removed her jacket and laid it on the back of an easy chair. "Sounds good, Caroline. . . Um, it's a nautical term. The yard-arm is part of a ship's mast—a horizontal beam the square sail hangs from, and after 11:00 a.m., I guess, the sun was usually 'over it' you see, so a crew could have their elevenses . . . and thanks—what have we got?" she asked.

"Hunh," Caroline digested the information, snorted at her neighbor, then looked back at the cabinet. "Well, Jim Beam, or beer in the fridge, or the makings for Slippery Nipples—but that don't sound good right now."

"I'll have whiskey in a little water with ice; thanks," Senga said. Caroline agreed with her choice and she set about making them.

They sat in the kitchen, its bright wallpaper and red counter tops more cheerful than the large front room, still furnished in 1950s décor (save the television, a gift from their children for Christmas last year).

The kitchen was the room to visit in, and always had been.

Basil, rosemary and onions filled the air. Senga detected a single note of wet-dog as well. "Gus in here?" she asked, looking around.

"He was earlier . . . why? He'd been down in the creek, so I kicked him out."

"Just wondered. . . I should have greeted the guy," she said, a non-sequitur.

"What? What guy? You mean *the* guy?"

"Grannie taught me to always greet someone, that it could actually change their behavior, in so many words. I didn't recognize him . . . it wouldn't have taken much to say hello. He might not have said that thing—and I wouldn't be here talking to you about it."

"Well, cheers," Caroline toasted, her eyes wide with amazement or disbelief, and they each took a sip. Then Caroline stood up, crossed to the pantry and brought a sack of chips back to the table. Now all contingencies were covered; now they could begin. . .

"What's the matter with me, Caroline? I could have *killed* the guy," Senga admitted.

Caroline made a sound. "But you didn't, and I probably would've done the same thing, you know? I mean, Gabe's like a son. But listen . . . ahh, are you—*could* you be going through your change?" she asked, not knowing if she should be affecting embarrassment at the question or not.

"What?" Senga asked, eyes round, then realizing what Caroline meant. "Oh, my—*aw jeez,* you know? Boy, do I feel like an idiot now." It occurred to her she hadn't missed her courses—as in *unaware* she wasn't bleeding anymore—but when had been the last one? *Over a year now.* Last July, when she joined Gabe and Francesca for an overnight ride in the peaks. *I wondered if it was the last time, as I'd only spotted . . . and I wondered about mountain lions—if they'd pick up my scent.*

"You don't have to feel like that, hon; you are no idiot, Senga, but I remember becoming, uh, feistier than I already am. . . It was hell on wheels for poor ole Rufus. Ir-ri-ta-ble, *whoo-ee!* That was me . . . but you really haven't thought about this? I mean you and your herbs and all. . . Ah, never mind; healers are lousy at taking care of themselves, they say."

"I have felt in a fog of sorts, but then, I have for years." Senga paused for a long moment. "Caroline, I'm going to tell you something, and I need you to just listen, please, until I'm through . . . and don't worry, it's not a 'True Confession,' or anything like that. . ."

"I'm here, Senga. Go on," her neighbor stated simply. Then she said, "Wait a second," and rose to turn off the heating soup. She poured two glasses of water and brought these to the table, setting them beside their whiskies. Once seated, she turned her full attention to her friend. "All right—" she prompted.

"I know we didn't get to know each other until after I moved to the cabin. It's been that long," Senga added, almost to herself. She spoke while gazing into her drink, "And here's the thing: I'm not sure *where* I've been all this time, Caroline, and this is going to sound crazy—" She glanced up at her friend, then into the amber liquid, "but sometimes I feel like Rip Van Winkle, as if I've fallen asleep in the woods, and woke up to learn years have passed—or remember what used to be called Fairy Land?" *Maybe it still is,* she wondered.

Senga peered into Caroline's face to gauge how she was receiving this, and was gratified to see Caroline's demeanor as impassive, rather than shocked or showing concern.

"Oh, *aye,* the *wee* fairies. . ." Caroline said with no emotion. "Tell me more."

"I mean, I have lived here, I'm conscious of this. . . I've even been somewhat involved with the community, but on so many levels, I've felt apart and utterly alone, as if there were a membrane of sorts between me and everything else. Does this make sense, Caroline?"

"Well, you *have* been alone, haven't you? At least I don't think you've got a man locked up in the garage, do you?" and not waiting for a response, she added, "You lost me, Senga. Membrane? You mean like what's between muscles?" Caroline meant the *fascia* between muscles, having butchered her share of meat.

"Well, yes, something like that. Or, a see-through veil. Does that work better?"

"Mother read us fairy tales when we were little," Caroline began, "She told us fairies ain't all sweetness and light, Senga. That's how she said it; that they have trickster-like spirits, you know? Like the Indian Coyote figure."

"Yes . . . and?"

"Well, mysteries abound, I do know this, and if you got it in mind that you've been away with the fairies, one way or another, for the past twenty years or so, then this is you making sense of something difficult—even impossible—to explain. Ha! I knew Walt Disney wasn't doing kiddos any favor when he made his movies with cuddly pixies," she cackled. "But I'm wondering if it ain't all just one, big, tangled-up ball of yarn. . ."

Here, Caroline picked up her water glass and drank, all the while holding Senga's gaze, then continued, ". . . Your change, this foggy feeling, the last twenty years. . . Mourning? Feeling lonesome? Not being able to see through a veil, membrane—whatever. . . You know, not seeing how to get on with just plain ole living . . . and you working at that library, year in and year out, hon—now *that* would numb the dick off a devil. . ."

Senga choked into her just-raised glass. Caroline always laid down her more shrewd observations couched in humor, to ease tension, and Senga was grateful for it. Nervines and calmatives came in myriad forms, this she knew, but a good belly laugh trumped all.

Part of living behind a veil of any sort, Senga also knew, was ignoring instances when people guarded their speech, for fear of raising an unpleasant, even horrendous, memory. *Like walking on shards of glass or, at the very least, egg shells*—how Joe in Montana had put it, in relating how people might react to her when she returned to society.

So she hadn't, at least fully.

Emily's presence permeated the Sara's Spring house, not as ghostly; more as an imprint, so Senga searched for another home and discovered the small hunting cabin. "Retiring to the Enchanted Forest?" Rob had suggested, furthering fantasy's foothold on her wounded soul.

But was it . . . is it harmful? Came the reply—*No.*

"When I went through my change—oh, twenty-five years ago or so . . ." Caroline began, "there were books about it, so I read 'em. My body was telling me something, but in a different language. Back then, doctors said hormones, so I did, until other doctors said no, so I stopped, but I think they helped. I guess the main thing was, I just wasn't 'juicy' anymore, and that bothered me. Sleeping with Rufus just plain *hurt*—I was so dry—sorry to be blunt, Senga, but it's the plain truth. Trouble was, I'd always liked sex."

Senga felt supremely uncomfortable hearing about Caroline and Rufus' love life. "What else did you do, um, about the other symptoms? You said you were irritable?"

"Oh, hell yeah, still am—like you haven't noticed—but maybe not as much. Okay, let's see. . . I found that making time for me helped; you know, just slowing down to smell the roses, it used to be called. I think our bodies tell us it's time to start winding down. We can still do stuff, we just do it smarter, more *slowly*, and pay more attention . . . know what I mean? Like cleats."

"Like what?"

"You know those things you strap on your boots or shoes when it's icy out. . . Cheaper and *way* less painful than a busted hip."

"Oh, those . . . and I know what you mean, at least I think so, Caroline, but working at the library, well . . . I have to make a living, too," she injected, ". . . besides, I must *like* working there or I wouldn't be doing it still, right?" In her mind's eye appeared a college course registration slip, similar to the one her high school English teacher showed them in class one day. This one read, "Trance 101."

"Hmmm . . . but frankly," she continued, ". . . it's been a handy way to learn, without costing a lot." Senga squirmed, then shifted in her chair. She took a few chips; her appetite had returned. "You may not believe it, but I was a pretty good student . . . I wanted to go on to college, but, well—life sort of squeezed in there first."

She paused to eat another handful of chips and realized she felt no regret, not an inkling regarding college. She'd simply made do with what was at hand: the library's stacks of books, arranged in useful order, to check out for as long as necessary (as long as they weren't the latest best-seller—rarely her choice anyway). She devoured atlases, herbals, textbook-like tomes on biology, chemistry, physics; histories of all kinds, and Shakespeare, for his language—and moral conundrums.

Francesca once described an Italian phrase: *l'arte di arrangiarsi*. Translated literally, it meant, "the art of arranging oneself" or, "to come to an agreement with oneself." But philosophically, she'd explained, it signified the concept of making do, or getting by with what you have at any given moment, and, given the Italian sensibility, to exquisite effect; the "art" part, Senga noted. Library work claimed a certain appeal when viewed in this light. She'd noted a pattern: time spent in study passed more quickly when she was absorbed in a subject. . .

As Senga sat in Stricklands' darkening kitchen, an image of a vast tidal rhythm rose in her mind, as viewed from forty-thousand feet. *So, is the tide coming in or going out?*

Listening, Caroline waited, ear cocked, as though hearing Senga think. And in the fading light, the older woman quietly stood, stepped to the switch by the door and flipped it on. The lamp hanging over the table cast a soft yellow glow, like a diminutive sun, illuminating their world, the corners of the kitchen consigned to outer darkness. Shivering once, Caroline crossed to the thermostat on the wall to adjust it and the heater clicked on.

Senga was given that she'd been "out to sea," in a sense, mixing her metaphors. *We are allowed more than one,* she insisted, recalling the line by the Persian poet Rumi. *There are [indeed] a hundred ways to kneel and kiss the ground.*

"When I was young, oh, around twelve," she said, "my grandparents took me to the seashore, and Papa showed me how tides come in and go out, but I remember him saying it so, oh, you know, in that way that says you need to listen hard?"

Caroline nodded.

"Well . . . between these *rhythms*, my word, Papa said there's a gap of sorts, a *mighty stillness,* he called it."

Caroline mumbled, "Mm-hmm."

Like spaces between musical notes, perfectly necessary, if laws of time are observed; which they are in this dimension. Senga stared out the dark window.

"Do you know I've never been to the ocean?" Caroline declared. "Well, unless you count the one that used to be here . . . but that was a while back, wasn't it?" she asked rhetorically.

"Eighty-million years ago. . . You must go, Caroline; I hope you will. Has Rufus ever?"

"Nope."

Senga took another sip of her drink. The liquid shone in the overhead light, reflecting off the ice cubes. It smelled sweet, and tasted warm and comforting. Doing its magic of sedation. Restoration. *Dosage and frequency, dearie,* Senga heard. The warmth from the furnace made her drowsy.

Caroline said something, then. "Hey, gal, you in there?"

"Huh?" Senga looked up and smiled. "Sorry . . . but *this* is *good,*" she said, lifting her glass. Whiskey now as veil, as membrane, as brick wall perhaps. . . "Thanks for being here and letting me go on, Caroline."

"Well, as I was saying—I heard those people up at the Berry place are looking for trouble."

"Who?" Senga looked up, confusion on her face. "Oh, you mean the guy. Ugh," she grunted, "Yellowtooth. Disgusting dental hygiene. There are *more* of them?"

"Charlie and a county deputy went up there this afternoon, but I haven't heard anything else. A couple of weeks ago, Rufus overheard the old man ranting while he was getting gas . . . going on about this state needing to secede and everybody better be getting ready for a revolution and collect guns, food and water—all this horseshit—and every other word was the "n" word. Rufus told me his guts 'bout twisted listening to it. He couldn't wait to be out of there—Rufus, I mean . . ."

"Did he say anything to him? Y'all know the man's name?"

"Nope, and yep—George Canton—he's the one ordered these two lambs a few months back. He called us so didn't recognize Rufus . . . Rufus, he just went on pumping his gas, paid for it, asked the cashier who it was, came out, got into his truck, he said, and drove away. A few folks were still standing around, hanging on to the man's every damn word. I suppose in the old days the guy would've been good at selling snake oil or Nebraska beachfront property, you reckon?" Caroline added. Then she raised her glass and, finishing it, announced, "I'm ready for the other half; how 'bout you?"

Senga drained hers and, setting the glass down, said, "Sure, for medicinal purposes, you bet," and she smiled warmly at the friend who'd elucidated at least two mysteries Senga hadn't considered—her *change,* as Caroline called it, and what the man in the store was about.

"You might as well stay for supper, hon. It's ready."

"Thanks. I'd love to, Caroline. It smells great. What is it?"

"Black beans, onions, carrots, celery . . . uh . . . salt pork, tomatoes and some seasoning. Oh! And them fancy herbs—rosemary, basil and bay leaf. I made it yesterday, but I like my soups better the next day," and she stood up to get bowls, spoons and napkins. The red oil cloth made plates and place mats unnecessary. "I'll just put these out and we can dish it up when we're ready. But I want to finish this first," she said, referring to the whiskey. "It's good to have you here, Senga. You could come around more, you know," Caroline chided.

They sat quietly for a long moment, listening. The two women permitted the wordless interlude. The gap between notes—measured ticking of a clock, hum of refrigerator and creaks an old house makes in its deep, wooden recesses. Then, a rushing gust of wind rattled the window and Caroline rose to investigate. Another gust and a splattering of sleet pelted the metal roof and the north facing window near them.

"Here it comes," Caroline announced, and, returning to her seat, she fixed Senga with a gimlet brown eye, and said, "You know what I think?"

"No, Caroline . . . what do you think?"

"I think you're like those purple daisy flowers that bloom in September. Don't recall their names, do you?"

"They have several common names, depending where you find them. They grow all over the world."

"Well, what are they called *here*?"

"Asters, Caroline. . . A species of aster. Myself, I like the name Michaelmas Daisy, because they're usually in bloom around the feast of St. Michael in September. September 29."

"He has his own day? Well, I suppose," she added. Then, "No, I mean it, Senga, you're just what we used to call 'a late bloomer.' You know, I hear you talkin' about all these fancy things, like time and dimensions, and when it all comes down to it, it's *only* about time, and I don't mean it like, 'It's about time!' Ha! I guess I could, but what I'm saying is . . ."

And here, Senga swung her head over to Caroline, eyes wide and mouth open, and Caroline drew back, swallowing her next words.

"What?" Caroline finally demanded, then, "Shut your mouth, hon, we got us some flies."

Senga's mouth clamped shut, then her eyes and, after a moment, she raised the glass to her lips, eyes still closed, took a sip and set it down. She squinted and watched the red of the oil cloth shining through the amber drink.

"Grannie used to say that a lot, to shut my mouth, hmm, but also this thing about timing. She called it the 'right phase of the moon;' I haven't thought of it in a long, uh, time." Senga twisted to look behind her, to the window and the sleet, then continued. "Not literally, the right phase of the moon, as in astrology. Grannie always said things are more easily done when circumstances are more favorable. Something like that. Makes sense, doesn't it?" This to Caroline's smile. "But I remember her saying we don't always have that luxury. . ."

"Hunh. I wish I could've met your granny. Sounds like a smart lady."

"Yes, she was, and I miss her. She raised me, you know, she and Papa, from the time I was eight, almost nine, when my daddy got killed . . . then there was my mother's—no; I really don't want to go there right now. . ." Senga finished her whiskey, followed by a long drink of water. "All right, maybe I *am* an aster; my birthday's in late August, so that fits. I'm a Virgo. Supposedly good with detail . . . and thanks for reminding me that all things have their seasons, ah, even me."

Another pause as they listened to snow splattering the window.

"Hope Rufus and Gabe get on home soon. . ." Caroline said after a moment, "just to get it out of the way."

Caroline employed the latter phrase to mean a prayer sent into the "ether," as she called it. Then Senga stood, carried one of the bowls to the pot, removed the lid and ladled some soup. She handed the bowl to Caroline and repeated the action for herself.

Humming approval, they agreed the soup tasted wonderful. Caroline returned to the pantry for saltines and they ate in silence, save moans of pleasure, having exhausted all pertinent topics of the day. The sleet changed to snowflakes, the snow changed the landscape, and the landscape changed for Senga.

CHAPTER 25~A COLD BED

Friday morning found Francesca Albinoni between sleep and wakefulness in the warmth of her bedding and memories of lovemaking two nights ago; Gabe holding her close—*spooning*, he'd described it. She'd replied in Italian, "*Ahhh, spooning a letto, sì, sì! Ah, caro mio*," then, she'd laughed and told him the expression was the same in Italy.

Francesca spoke English well. Gabe haltingly used an Italian word now and then: *prego; grazie*. He delighted in her language. It paired with her fiery appearance, he told her once—*and with your temper,*—he thought.

They met in August of 2012, three months after his return to the area, at The Cottonwood in Sara's Spring, where Gabe now and then looked over his writing. Having printed his latest pages, he'd sit at a table, order a beer and do his "red pen" work, as he called it. First drafts required the silence of his room in the barn but, for editing and polishing, he found he could ignore customary bar sounds; however, not a band like the one setting up for the evening across from him.

He had raised a bottle to his lips, when an unfamiliar woman entered the premises with a band of revelers—some dressed a mite too obvious, he thought. The woman was discussing something with a younger man who didn't appear to be part of the group, judging by his appearance. He looked to be just about drinking age, but was apparently on the job that night, and Gabe was impressed by both the woman's and the boy's consideration for their troupe. The boy's parents owned The Blue Wood Guest Ranch, Gabe later learned.

The three-piece band soon had the place rocking, and loudly, so he tucked his work in a folder and returned the red pen to his shirt pocket.

Gabe liked Francesca right away. From the moment she walked through the door, her bearing exuded distinction. Exotic wasn't *le mot juste,* he thought; too showy a word. No, this woman held herself with respect. With dignity.

She was short, maybe five feet, two-inches, with a full body—hips, wide, and buxom—her breasts shown to advantage by a light jacket worn over a blue V-neck. Gabe noted her cleavage. He admired expressive black brows and large doe eyes, voluminous dark hair, cut mid-length and layered, clearly by someone who knew what they were doing. She probably spent some money on that, Gabe decided.

He caught the woman's eye, and her response.

He had once read a paper on the more esoteric codes of aristocratic women's fan gestures, how they communicated solely with their eyes above an open fan, which covered the rest of their faces and décolletage. The eyes of Francesca communicated *something.* He recognized a wry expression when he saw one and chuckled to himself.

She returned her attention to her company.

Well, they sure aren't from around here, he decided. The cafés and bar catered to three guest ranches in the county, and the tourist promotion board encouraged seasonal events to attract visitors to the area. This particular evening's entertainment included a horse and rider plodding through the bar during a break in the music, in one door and out the other, to cheers and raised drafts of beer.

Gabe sat at his usual table to the rear of the room and watched in amusement. In bars, he always sat with his back to the wall and identified the nearest exits, something his father had taught him. From his corner, he watched the woman settle her charges and assist in ordering their meals; bar grub mostly, but elk and buffalo burgers featured on the menu. Simple and evocative.

He ordered another Stella Artois, but needed to visit the men's room. When he returned, the woman was seated at his table, nursing a glass of red wine.

From his vantage point, the lovely breasts drew him and he quickly sought the woman's eyes. The waitress had brought his beer and a large serving of sweet potato fries and a hamburger; the woman's supper, apparently.

"Hello," said Gabe, as he tipped his hat. He'd learned you needn't remove your hat in a bar in this state, so he didn't, but he enjoyed the old etiquette.

"Hello . . . my name is Francesca Albinoni, and what is yours?" she asked, smiling, while holding out a dimpled hand—to be kissed or shaken, Gabe didn't know. Her Italian accent sounded *mellifluous,* he decided. He reached out, took her hand and held it a moment, then sat down. Slowly.

Oh. My. Lord. . .

"My name's Gabe, ma'am—I mean, um, miss?"

She nodded.

"Gabe Belizaire," he said, swallowing.

And their mysteries let out gracefully, like fly-fishing line into a sparkling, laughing brook, where shiny, slick-sided trout dart headlong onto baited hooks, one after the other, the difference in this case being a desire to be caught and then lifted out reverently, from snow-fed, icy waters onto a sun-warmed, grassy bank. To be admired, fussed over and then lovingly devoured.

The fishing expedition took eight days.

Francesca invited Gabe to the ranch the following Saturday afternoon. Owners Lee and Mary Rogers welcomed him warmly. The prospect of meeting them had him fretting (as his mother would have called it) on the drive into the peaks where the ranch was located, but Francesca assured him her employers were *molto brava gente,* very good people, as if this simple declaration might ensure his acceptance.

The guest ranch had sold since his sister's employment during the fall of 2005 and early 2006. When Gabe arrived, he found her and her girlfriend relatively stable after their ordeal in New Orleans post Hurricane Katrina. Crediting the environment and personnel, he had thanked the owners and staff profusely.

Gabe found it easy to tell Francesca his circumstances: how he first came to be in Wyoming; about finding his sister at The Blue Wood; how he'd entered a couple of area rodeos in Montana and North Dakota. That he wrote, and rode bulls. Francesca had him back up. "You are . . . a *writer?*" she asked, a bit too incredulously, he thought, for comfort.

"Yes, why—yes, I am . . . um, is this too hard to believe?"

"No! Not at all. . . You will permit me to read your work sometime, yes?" she asked, "And what do you write?"

He told her, "stories," leaving it at that, wishing to return to a prior thread. He wasn't ready to enter that place with her yet. He held it tender.

"When I caught up with Allie, the owners invited me to stay at the ranch, and I helped out where I could. She and her friend begged to work another month or so. As you know by now, there's always work to be done on a ranch, even a guest ranch."

Francesca and Gabe were in her suite at The Blue Wood one evening, leaning against the headboard, sheet drawn up to cover their nakedness. His scar piqued her curiosity, so he told her about it, relating the events of that bull ride without rancor, by simply stating what had happened. Her eyes rounded. She was appalled—he could see by her expression. He'd accepted the Strickland's hospitality, he told her, what it truly was, for he could not work. Francesca studied the mark that ran above his collarbone, almost a keloid, moving her finger along the crescent-shaped raised line, then she leaned over and kissed it. Gabe told her it tickled.

Francesca had listened to Gabe's story with equanimity, and a growing sense of connection—love by any other name— prompting her to share her circumstances. *Quid pro quo*, as she understood it, greased the wheels of social momentum.

Born and raised in Lucca, Italy, she had three brothers; one older, two younger. Her parents, grandfather and one of the younger brothers lived in the same house they'd occupied since the war. In Italy, it wasn't unusual for sons to continue living at home, she'd explained, to Gabe's quizzical glance. Rent was high, ". . . and boys like their mama's cooking," adding, "*I* like my Mama's cooking, as you can see," and she laughed.

"The cities are—" and she gestured to suggest overcrowding. "This is why we *so* love your West and her—ah, *wide-open* places?"

Places, spaces. He understood all this. *And Louisiana isn't even that crowded.* Gabe noticed her feminine reference to the West. *Is my writing a feminine thing?* He wondered if the attraction for the

West wasn't merely a matter of leaving somewhere behind, but rather, a heading toward elsewhere, without the over-thinking and tedious analysis.

Fascinated, he watched and listened as Francesca carefully chose her words in English to describe her past and present: she had enjoyed school and had attended university in *Firenze*. Tourism drove Italy's economy—Florence's especially—tempting her to consider the hotel trade. In the end, she'd chosen art history and languages, and followed her heart's dictates. English and French she spoke well, and she was studying Spanish and Russian. Her favorite period was the Renaissance. *No surprise*, thought Gabe.

Her facility with languages, and a background in art history, all but assured an opportunity to earn the all-important license to guide professionally, without which—at least in the larger cities—she could've been fined. Gabe mentioned the same arrangement regarding hunting guides in the state, at which she raised her glorious eyebrows and made a moue with her mouth in acknowledgement. She told him she particularly enjoyed driving carloads of "women of a certain age" around hill-top towns, their enthusiasm and joy obvious. This was her favorite job, and they usually tipped well.

"I remember one such day. I was hired by three such ladies. Their inn was located in the countryside. Near Ulignano. The owner told them next time, they must rent a car. They were exited as *bambinas* on Christmas morning. We met in the breakfast room to discuss the tour. They wished to visit a winery, so I explained where we would go—Piombaia is a beautiful, small estate vineyard and winery near Montalcino. I also drove them to Pienza, where Zeffirelli filmed scenes for his *Romeo and Juliet*. I think of these ladies as *Le Tre Grazie* or, The Three Graces."

Gabe interjected a groan. "I *loved* that film—*Romeo and Juliet*—watched it, oh, probably two dozen times . . . used it for a Shakespeare class . . . I could watch it again right now." *So now she knows you're a romantic.*

"Yes, we love it too," Francesca added, "It marked a reawakening of the rest of the world to the wonders of Italy; it was *so* well-produced. And for the principle actors to have been so young, though it was, ah, evident in some scenes. . . It gave a, *ah, come si dice? Ah, sì!*—a vul-ner-*ability* and preciousness to their plight," she concluded.

His American students couldn't express themselves in their own language as eloquently. And now, Gabe was completely reeled in and hanging above water, figuratively speaking, and Francesca?—the ample net beneath him.

One day, while searching the Internet for a suitable guest ranch for clients, she had discovered The Blue Wood and, after her second trip, she was invited to join the ranch staff, as liaison for European guests. She had agreed.

"*Hmmm*, this is why they name this place, 'The Blue Wood?' Look. See the lines of blue in the wood, *Gehh?*' Two nights ago, Gabe was lost in nuzzling her endlessly inviting neck, luxuriating in the weight of her thick, black hair as it fell over his face and neck. A scent of jasmine mingled with her own scent. And her breasts . . . He'd never seen anything so *damn* beautiful—round as baby watermelons (his writer described); they were firm and had heft, and he became a child, laying his head against one, to lose himself in the other. He began to call her *chère* and *sweet Francesca* on account of her body, not necessarily her temperament.

"Um, yes—" he said, returning to her query, "because of the blue in the wood. Bark beetles—an insect—causes it, and it eventually kills the trees . . . a sad problem."

"Ah—*bella* wood, though," and she ceased examining the wall near the bed to face him. Grinning, she reached down for him. "It is like a Spring Roll, *sì?*" she suggested, and he made a sound. He knew what she meant. A Chinese appetizer, made with translucent rice flour wrapping.

"Delectable *teed-beets*," she added, enjoying this word, as she pronounced it, repeating it as she edged beneath the goose-down comforter.

He moaned. After pulling her up to him, he judged her delight and the trust in her eyes the closest he'd come to that which he called God, and he loved her fiercely for it. His strong arms and his chest became the entire world for her spirit to play on, and he loathed having to leave her, but Rufus expected him in the morning to help take the sheep to town, and Gabe did not let people down. "I need to go."

"*Ohhh, cuore mio*, my heart . . . then I say goodnight to you."

She lay still in her bed, the comforter pulled up just below her breasts. Gabe recorded the image in his mind.

"I'll see you soon, *chère*," he said, as he leaned over and kissed her forehead, then he reached for his clothing. She watched him with unabashed curiosity, and told him that hers was an educated admiration, that his body was worthy of being sculpted. He feigned discomfort but was secretly pleased, feeling a blush rise.

"And you *ain't* so bad yourself. . ." he responded, followed by regret, then, looking at her, he felt the age-old male response.

"O my sweet Francesca—"

She smiled, and with one motion, pulled away the cover as he stripped again and fell on her.

After, Gabe quietly opened the door to leave, gingerly stepping down the hallway to the front door of the lodge and, walking out into that good night, he inhaled in recollection and let it out slowly with pleasure. He climbed into his pick-up, started the engine and drove away, imagining Francesca listening for every step of his bitter-sweet passage away from her.

Into the near recesses of her mind, Francesca released her reminiscence. On this new morning, she gradually made out the cold sound of gusting wind blowing through trees, and with such force as to cause boughs to snap and slap against the side of the lodge. It summoned her to full consciousness.

Looking out the window, she realized it wasn't so much the wind breaking limbs, as the sheer weight of heavy, wet snow. Through the white-out, she barely perceived jagged, broken branches hanging from stubborn strips of peeled-away inner bark, clinging tenaciously to trunks. The sight repeated itself through the snowy curtain.

A white tornado doing its worst.

Francesca shivered, climbed out of bed and grabbed a thick robe from the closet. She stepped into sheepskin slippers Gabe had given her, especially welcome this morning. She gave a thought to him, knowing he'd be working in this weather, feeding, or any number of chores that may be required during, or after, a blizzard.

After making her toilette, and dressing warmly in a dark gray cashmere sweater, she walked into the commons where the staff met for breakfast. This usually included young Pete Rogers (the owners' son); Jim Wilson, the weathered wrangler; a middle-aged housekeeper named Carey; a young, pretty cook named Lupita and herself.

The owners' log home stood a hundred yards from the lodge. Mary Rogers normally enjoyed playing Lady of the Lodge, but not this morning.

"Where is *Jeem*?" Francesca asked, looking around. He was usually finished with morning chores by now.

"Two of the yearlings got out. . . He's looking for them. . . Took the four-wheeler," Pete said as he buttered his toast.

"In this? How can he *possibly* find them?"

"He thinks he knows where they went. They've done it before. For some reason, they like the shed in the south pasture. . ." He took a bite of his toast and swallowed before responding. "Don't ask me to figure out a horse's psychology," he said. "Anyway, that's where he was going to look, and if they aren't there he'll return and wait for this to blow over."

They ate in relative silence, save howling gusts. Francesca only ever ate a slice of toast and a boiled egg, with coffee, for breakfast, while Pete enjoyed a plate full of sausage, hash browns, eggs and toast. A fire blazed in the hearth—not best for heating, given most of the heat rose straight up the chimney, Francesca once observed. Pete had agreed and suggested his parents install a large woodstove with glass door and fan. Lee Rogers could see it, but Mary preferred the more "romantic" ambience of an open fire. More "lodge-y," she'd said. "And she'd know," Pete had quipped to Francesca.

Her eyes paused on the large painting above the mantel: a rendering of Devils Tower, with covered wagons trailing in the foreground, done by regional impressionist Tom Waugh. "Self-taught," Lee had once described the painter, with esteem.

How did immigrants and settlers survive blizzards in those wagons? she wondered with a chill.

"Sounds like Jim's back," the boy said, as he cut into his sausage.

Upon meeting him, Francesca thought Pete looked quintessentially American, with his blond, good looks and his straight, white teeth. Wearing an expression of baffled wonderment most of the time, she thought he looked as though he had just awakened to a room full of treasure. He'd graduated from high school in May, and was taking a year off before college.

Jim Wilson had wrangled for guest ranches most of his life. He was nearing forty-five, and had told Francesca he could see doing this work for only a few more years, and then, he wanted to go live in southern New Mexico—where it did not snow. He was getting *plum tired* of it, he told her. Francesca kept a list of his expressions.

He looked every bit the part of wrangler, she decided, even while eschewing the trappings some guests expected, such as: chaps (though worn when necessary), the ten-gallon hat, the fancy, television cowboy shirts and boots, the buckskin jackets with fringe, an old-fashioned kerchief tied as a large triangle around the neck and shoulders. In marked contrast, Jim always wore a black, silk scarf in winter, and none in summer, though he carried a bandana in his back pocket. No, Jim dressed plainly for the job.

When he burst through the door, he was wearing only his boiled-wool vest over a wool shirt, his red plaid Scotch hat, snow-encrusted jeans and overshoes—pulled over his boots.

The oversized and magnificently carved lodge door opened to Jim saying in his usual laconic fashion, "I need some help," and he whipped back out. Pete and Francesca exchanged glances, pushed back their chairs, got up and followed him out, Pete pulling the huge door closed behind them. They weren't dressed for the weather, but Jim's tone sounded urgent.

The four-wheeler was pulled up to the steps, under the portico. The snow wasn't plowed, and wouldn't be until the storm passed. She thought she saw two figures, one astride the seat, and another curled up on the rack behind the seat, wrapped in what looked like Jim's buff coveralls, now mostly white.

"Help me get them inside, and call the hospital; we may have to get them there," he added quickly, moving to the slumping person on the seat.

Between Jim and Pete, they brought the woman into the lodge and laid her on one of the overstuffed sofas before the fireplace, and Francesca carried the young girl, still wrapped in Jim's coveralls. She laid the child in the chair near the fire. She knew too much heat could be harmful, and gauged the distance.

"Pete, you call the hospital; I don't want them to misunderstand because of my accent," she told him. He nodded and left.

The woman and child were alive, but dangerously cold. Jim asked the cook to bring something warm for them to drink—not too hot, he cautioned. Did she have any broth she could warm up?

Francesca told him he looked frozen himself. She began removing the little girl's coat, shoes and other wet clothing, with Jim doing the same for the woman.

"You must get warm, *Jeem*."

"I'm all right."

"What—*where* did you find them?" she asked. The woman moaned.

"God damn, Francesca, they were lying in a goddamn snow bank, half-covered with it. I was returning from that shed . . . found the yearlings . . . left them to wait out the storm. There's hay enough," he added then shivered violently. Francesca's brows knit with concern.

"*Jeem*, look at me. . . look!"

"I *am* looking—*what*, woman?"

"Go remove those clothes. We can take care of them. Go, *now*." Francesca spoke in a tone that meant business, so he turned and was back in a matter of minutes, dressed in a heavy wool sweater, a pair of wool trousers and slippers. Carey fed the fire, while Francesca pulled the woman's soaked sweater over her head. Carey then handed her one of the fluffy towels she'd laid beside the sofa.

Jim continued. "I happened—just happened—to see the little one's hair out of the corner of my eye. I thought it was a buried cow, but the shade of red was off. I would've missed them completely, hadn't been for that. *Goddamn it.* And look at the woman's face . . . it's—" Jim was upset, Francesca knew; he never swore.

Francesca and Carey had noted it, with alarm. By turns dark red, purple and yellow, it was horribly bruised. The woman's one good eye was opened half-way; the other split above the eye-lid, and black with dried blood. She moaned, then slurred, "Where my baby?"

"She is here; she is all right—you will both be all right," Francesca told her, not certain it was true. She detected an accent in the woman's speech.

Carey brought duvets and two heating pads, which she plugged into the floor jacks next to the table. "Lupita's bringing some broth. . . Pete's gone to tell his folks," she said.

"Did he reach the hospital yet?" asked Jim.

"He couldn't get through. Downed lines, he thinks."

The wrangler swore under his breath. He lifted the woman's wrist and checked her pulse.

"It's weak, but steady. . ." Then he checked the girl's, had trouble finding it and reported that it was slower still.

He peeled off the woman's socks and carefully patted her feet with a towel. They were too pale, Francesca thought. The woman groaned this time in pain and again asked, "Where my baby?"

"She's right here, darlin'," Jim assured her as he gently moved her head so she could see the girl out of her good eye. "We'll need warm clothes, and a cloth with a bowl of warm-to-hot water to clean her eye . . . she doesn't need an infection on top of it all," he said, but Carey had already thought of this and produced a bowl of steaming water with a soft cloth. He set about dabbing the woman's eye and cheek.

Years of minding horses and their scrapes earned him more than a few useful skills in the doctoring department. The water turned a reddish-pink.

"*Ai! Like needles . . .*" the woman cried, ". . . *Feet . . . ooh. . .*"

"I know, I know, darlin', it hurts, but it'll get better—it will."

"My baby, why she no move?" she whimpered, as Jim pressed the warm, damp cloth to the woman's eye, purple and swollen nearly shut, with a blood-shot slit peeking out; one of the worst he'd ever seen—he'd later say.

The woman was young, in her mid-twenties, *maybe*, Francesca guessed, as she finished removing the child's wet clothing. Then, she spied the ugly, yellowing bruises on the torso, and the same on the small upper arms. She turned to Jim, who'd just noticed them. He shot back a glance and returned to his task, grimacing.

Wrapped snugly in the duvet now, the child whimpered as Francesca gently massaged her as Jim demonstrated, to slowly encourage blood circulation. After several moments, the girl showed signs of coming 'round, and Francesca held a cup of broth to her lips. The steam, or maybe the fragrance, roused her. She opened an eye. "Mama . . . *Mama?*" she groaned.

"What is your little girl's name, *cara?*" Francesca asked.

"Tanya."

"Tanya. A pretty name." Francesca looked back at the girl, ". . . And what pretty hair you have—" she added. Tanya tried to smile, Francesca noticed. *Bene*, she thought. Good.

The child sipped the broth and, when Jim had cleaned her mother's face as well as he could, she swallowed some of the broth—with appetite, they noted. Both took a deep breath at the same time.

Tanya whimpered again.

"I think you can put someone in a not-too-warm bath and this helps with pain," Francesca said.

"We put newborn lambs in warm water sometimes, if they're caught in the cold, but we've got something better. . . Carey, let's put them both in one bed in the closest room with an electric blanket . . . turned to low. You don't want 'em to warm up too fast." Jim stood up. "I'll carry her in and come back for the girl. What's your name, darlin'?" he asked the woman tenderly.

"Larissa," she said.

Ai, mamma mia. Francesca recognized a Slavic accent.

CHAPTER 26~APPLES

"Oh, God. . ." The wind had howled all night, keeping her whiskey-induced dreams bad company, and Senga predicted a blizzard. Her bedside clock read 7:00 a.m., and her head felt as though it had been repeatedly struck with a ball-peen hammer. An oatmeal morning for certain. Senga sighed as she got up her nerve to throw off the covers.

Should've drunk more water. . .

She performed her stretches slowly but mindlessly and half-staggered to her bathroom. A fire in the woodstove next. Then coffee. She put the water to boil, unconsciously. After, she squeezed two droppers of St. John's Wort tincture into a glass, added milk thistle and water, and swallowed the concoction.

She hoped Gabe would stay home. Judging from the drifts out the window, she thought the road would be impossible. The plows may have passed, but she doubted it, and with a flick of a switch she turned on her radio to a local station. No school, the announcer reported almost immediately, then he gave the details of the storm. Overnight temperatures had reached thirty-two degrees, but the wind chill brought that number down. Higher elevations had received over three feet of snow in the last twelve hours. Deadwood and Lead had recorded thirty inches and expected another foot and a lion's share of moisture.

"*Damn,*" she swore under her breath, recalling yesterday's run-in at the grocery store. She picked up her telephone and dialed Strickland's number.

"Hey, Caroline . . . yes, I'm warm—have a good fire. Y'all all right?"

She asked after Rufus and how the sale trip went, then thanked her friend for supper and last night's visit. "Gabe isn't coming, is he?" she inquired, stooping to rearrange kindling in the woodstove and adding a chunk of oak.

"I'm going to knock snow off branches and pick those last couple trees. Tell him he really doesn't need to come, Caroline . . . and thanks for last night . . . all right. . . Later."

After water, oatmeal and two cups of strong coffee, she layered on clothing, banked the fire and pulled out her coveralls. She gathered three quilts from a high shelf above her bed, and with stocking hat pulled down and warm cashmere scarf tied around her neck and face, Senga walked out into the storm.

The trudge to the garage wasn't as difficult as she'd feared. Using her boots, she scraped away enough snow to be able to yank open a door. The snow hadn't settled enough to make it too heavy, yet. Her hatchback was buried under a deep, white blanket, conjuring *Baked Alaska*. Snow swirled and drifted around its south side. *No sense in shoveling yet.*

Inside the garage, Senga pulled shut the door and inspected the bushels of apples that lay in ordered rows on pallets. Rufus had suggested it might help in storing them. Even in the cold, their fragrance lingered, sweet, and somehow warm. She quickly laid the quilts over the array, overlapping where she could until all were covered. Then, she checked the thermometer—thirty-five degrees. *Good.* But the forecast predicted colder temperatures tonight; she hoped this measure, the quilts, might prove adequate. Soon, she'd load as many bushels as possible and deliver them to the farmer's market in Spearfish where they sold well. Her local customers stopped by, or they met in Sara's Spring.

Surveying the space, it appeared just enough room remained for the rest of the crop. She grabbed three stacked boxes, the broom, her courage, and left the temporary shelter.

Through all the years Senga had tended the orchard, knocking snow from limbs tested her resolve and perseverance, along with setting the bow saw to broken branches. The chores illustrated Papa's *rocks in the garden* metaphor. The proverbial hard parts of life. But these particular demands visited infrequently, *so there art thou happy!* she heard. However, she hadn't prepared herself for the sight of the orchard.

Branches bowed and sagged under the weight, and from the eldest tree in the orchard, the most venerable, the one she never failed to address, she thought she could hear heavy breathing; a near-gasping, *Where have you been?*

Senga quickly dropped the boxes, turning them over, against their being filled with falling snow. She thought to go systematically, from one tree to the next, shaking the limbs, save those still bearing apples, for fear of losing them in the deep powder. This tree required more time and care, as she high-stepped through deep powder. The broom reached high branches.

"Oh, my *dearies*, I'm so sorry, but you'll be all right." And thus she continued. On two occasions a branch bounced back up, dislodging its icy burden into her face. Her fingers stung with cold, but her toes stayed warm. Two branches required the saw, having cracked under the weight. Good producers too, she lamented.

After an hour, she waded back to the cabin to feed the fire, mourning too the oaks and pines whose crowns had snapped, and guessing more damage lay beyond her myopic field of vision. *It'll look like a bomb was dropped,* and she shuddered. She had unburdened half the trees so far. This wasn't a too-hard freeze, she decided, and the crop would survive. Frost gave the fruit its crispy, sweet taste, after all.

Having brushed off several more trees, she retreated to the cabin to warm her fingers and stoke the fire. A stomping on her porch steps startled her. She rose from her chair before the fire to open the door. Gabe, covered in snow, was busily brushing it off, mahogany eyes glaring from beneath the bill of the gray *Stormy Kromer*. A scarf hid most of his face.

"Hey, girl."

"Hey there," Senga greeted, "You walked in from the road?"

"Yep . . . wasn't sure of your roadsides. You might think about planting some of those markers. . ."

"I'd just knock them over with the car. . . Come in . . . and get warmed up, uh, before we go back out . . . but there are only a couple more trees to brush off, then the picking. Won't take too long."

"This is supposed to hang in all day," Gabe reported, unwinding the scarf and removing his gloves to warm his hands.

"I asked Caroline to tell you not to come. Had you already left?"

"Well, I suppose I had," he said, with sarcasm, Senga noted. *Been living with Caroline a while.* . . "I got your message," he added, "Chose to ignore it."

"How about some coffee?" she asked.

"Sounds good, thanks."

She poured him a cup, having placed the French press into a pan of water on the stove to keep it warm, added the rest of the scalded milk and two teaspoons of sugar, and handed it to him. "Wait," she said, stepping to a cabinet for a fifth of brandy, raising it and her eyebrows to him in question.

"Now we're talking . . ." and he flashed his laughing Buddha smile as she added a splash to his raised mug. "Aren't you having some?"

She frowned at the sight of his right hand but let it go. *A fight?*

"Uh, no. Caroline and I got into the Jim Beam last night and my liver needs a rest—for a month at least, I figure," she joked, but realized it was possible. The liver *can* regenerate itself, but needs a period of clean living to do it.

"Yeah, I heard you were by. . . But let's help out your trees," he said, giving her a look that brooked no argument. He downed the brandy-laced coffee, rubbed his hands together a few times, fished a gumball from his pocket, then pulled on gloves, hat and scarf. Senga did the same and zipped up her coveralls.

They worked quietly. Wind in the tree tops whisked snow down around them—*like frantic ghosts, lost, trying to find their graves.* Senga conjured them out of the corner of her eyes as she made her way to the next tree. Gabe picked quickly but carefully twisted the stem from the limb. Gloves proved unwieldy and he stuffed them into his pockets.

The cold chore completed, they settled onto low stools in the garage to cull blemished fruit from perfect, but only after they'd warmed up. She pulled a pot of soup from the refrigerator and set it on the stove, turned to low to warm slowly.

"You'll stay for soup." A statement, not an invitation.

"Yes . . . I expect I will. Okay, let's go."

Senga loved to inspect the different varieties: Honeycrisp, Cortland, McIntosh, among others. Some grew large as grapefruit; others stayed smallish, like the Liberties; ripening to a dark red, they summoned tears when polished. *Like holding an enormous ruby globe in your hand; shining, enticing. No wonder Snow White succumbed.* She held it up to Gabe (who grinned), took a bite and handed it to him.

After drying the fruit with towels against spoilage, they carefully laid each into a waiting box. "We'll have about four bushels to press, I think," she said.

"Might be simpler to take them to the ranch, rather than bring the press here like last year."

"You're right. . . Well, I think that's it. We're done," she observed.

"We are, ah, *finished* . . ." he corrected, "Sorry. English teacher in me," and he winked.

"And you from the South—where we're taught not to correct our elders." She stood up, winced and stretched, then said, "This is *so* much more pleasant work in sunshine."

They covered the fruit with a quilt, then Senga gathered the towels and hung them over a line stretched between walls, usually reserved for herbs. Several apples went into a box and they walked outdoors. Gabe pushed the door closed and latched it and they made their way back to the cabin, earlier footprints snow-filled once more. Wood smoke drifted by, caught in a downdraft; a comforting smell, Senga thought. From a quarter-mile away, came the heavy scraping and trundling of the state snow plow.

"Hope my truck's all right," Gabe muttered.

"And my mailbox," Senga added.

Snow plows were lumbering beasts that paid no mind to what lay in their path, except snow, which they cleared in spectacular fashion; but woe betide roadside objects. Senga's closest neighbor cleared her drive, and had for all these years, but he waited until the storm passed. It was a good idea to have a store of water, food and firewood—Rufus' words to the wise, after Senga moved to the country and met him and Caroline at a branding.

"I didn't hear anything get run into . . ." Senga spoke over her shoulder at Gabe, as they trudged on, ". . . Or should that be: 'I heard nothing into which got run?'"

He chortled, saying nothing.

Indoors, she invited him to remove his coveralls and hang them behind the woodstove. She stepped out of hers and hung them beside her hat, gloves and scarf. The windows would soon steam opaque with humidity. *Better keep the fire hot.* Squatting at the woodstove door, she added more kindling and, with a fluid motion, rose to stir the soup. Then she transferred the pot to the woodstove to save electricity.

She brought out bowls and bread and cut three thick slices, putting these on a plate. The butter and jam were in place. Utensils next.

"More coffee or—something else?"

"Ah . . . how about some water now and coffee after?" Gabe asked.

"You got it," she said, and took down two glasses, filling them at the tap.

Her water happened to be good, which couldn't be said for every household in the county. It depended on the aquifer or source. Hers was an artesian well, her landlord once explained, and the water escaped having to be softened—unlike some in the area. Gabe guzzled one glass and held it out for another, which she filled.

"The soup's warm. You ready? Or want a minute?"

"Senga." He looked at her squarely. "Sit down, girl—and I know you are my elder, but not by much—no, not by enough to count; *sit,*" he instructed.

She sat and shifted in his direction, where he still faced the fire.

"What *the* hell, girl? Caroline told us what happened at the store yesterday. . ."

"Well, I'd like to know whose version she heard . . ." she replied. "I never asked last night."

"Tom Robinson's," said Gabe, and Senga believed it would've been accurate; Tom was acquainted with Caroline and Rufus, but not with Senga—having only heard them mention her; it was the cashier who suggested he call Caroline to make sure she was all right. He had.

"Oh." Senga said. "Gabe, I—"

"No—I want *you* to listen, Senga, and listen well—I am *so* pissed, it was all I could do to keep from ripping those apples off the trees. I thought I held it together pretty well, considering, but that's over now—the trees . . . and I am fixin' to give you a piece of my mind, so you just sit there and do *not* say a word."

Senga's eyes welled up. No one had scolded her since Grannie had, more than thirty-four years ago. She felt mortified and, strangely, she also sensed his affection. Gabe cared enough to light into her, as she'd cared enough to light into Yellowtooth—though, there was a difference, she knew. She slowly nodded and held his gaze.

"These people are dangerous, Senga . . . People who spew slurs in public places, well . . . they're dangerous because they're also ignorant and, together, it's lethal. What's the matter with you, pulling a knife on one of them like that?"

"Gabe, Charlie's already—"

"*Hush*, I said," and he stood to pace a moment before sitting back down.

"Look, I appreciate your sticking up for me, Senga, really, I do, but I don't think you have a clue about what you're dealing with. I do. . . I've lived around it all my life, do you hear me? My folks, my grandparents—Lordy, Senga . . . Louisiana was no cake walk, you know, and I'm not going to review Black History with you, but *damn*, girl." He paused and looked out at the blowing snow. Senga noticed his eyes were moist.

"When Caroline told us last night, after we got in, I walked outside," here he lifted his right hand, knuckles up, to her eyes, ". . . headed to the nearest post and fuckin' punched it—'scuse my French." The knuckles were bruised and abraded, she saw.

188

She'd noticed he was handling the picking more gingerly than strictly necessary. She went to touch the knuckle, but he drew it back and covered it with his other hand.

"Oh, no you don't—you don't get to play nursemaid—I'm not through," he said to her, his volume rising. "I *choose* to live here, Senga, and I'll take care of my own . . ."

Here Gabe paused and Senga, finding purchase, jumped in:

"Horseshit! Now that's a *load* of it, as Caroline says. If people wouldn't sit by and let stuff like that go by. . . Gabe, I couldn't *help* myself, I swear, I had no choice."

By now tears had sprung and she wiped them on her sleeve. Gabe frowned and Senga knew he regretted raising his voice at her, but she knew it was fear, and he told her.

"Senga. *Chère.* I was afraid for you, is all. Pissed, yeah, but that's how it shows, huh? The guy could have tried to defend himself and gutted you right there with your own knife! He's been in prison, did you know that? No; I see you didn't. The shit . . . *stuff* they learn there . . . well look, *please,* girl, *please* don't do anything like that again—swear it, come on, you've got to promise me," and his entreaty warmed her like the brandy she wanted right now.

"I-I promise, Gabe, but—"

"No 'buts,' Senga; leave it alone. I'll deal with it—or not," he said, searching the fire for a moment; then, "You know the story about the little girl who picks up a snake on her way home from school, and puts it inside her coat to keep it warm?"

She shook her head.

"Well, this snake tells her he's a snake, and she says, "I know," and she keeps walking; by and by she's bitten and falls to the ground and, as it slithers away, it looks back and says, 'You knew what I was when you picked me up.'"

"Point taken . . ." She sighed. ". . . So, do you want to eat now? I could eat . . . I guess."

Gabe did, with appetite; Senga—no. After one serving, she offered him another and he accepted. It was the chicken stew, and medicinal. She added *astragalus* root powder to her soups in the fall and winter to strengthen the immune system. And, it thickened the broth.

"There's something else—" Gabe began. After eating the soup, bread with butter and chokecherry jam, she guessed he wasn't quite sated yet, so she rose and stepped to the silverware drawer, pulled it open and, reaching her hand to the back, drew out a large bar of dark chocolate.

"Sounds like I'll need fortifying first," she said as she laid the bar down. "I keep it out of sight," she added sheepishly. "Have some."

"Why, Senga, you have vices!" He feigned surprise.

"Like everybody," she said, unsmiling, as she unfolded the end of the wrapper and broke off several pieces. "Dark chocolate, taken in moderation, is good for the heart, you know." She picked up a piece. "And savoring is the secret of life." He took a square and she smiled, but only for an instant.

They sat quietly savoring and gazing out the window. A *whoosh* from the woodstove turned Senga's head, as a pitchy log caught, followed by a roar of hot flames. The pause provided Gabe breathing room; at least Senga thought he seemed less preoccupied.

"So what else?" she ventured.

"On the way over this morning, I got a call from Francesca, and don't ask me how in this storm. . . Pete had tried to reach the hospital on the landline . . ."

"What's happened?"

"They're fine, Senga. Just listen. Some phone lines are down, but Jim took her on the four-wheeler to where they can get cell service . . . you know, we've been there—west of the lodge, where you come over the crest of that hill?"

"Yes, go on—"

"Earlier this morning when he was out, Jim discovered a woman and her daughter lying in a snow bank. Francesca thinks they could be Russian. Anyway, she thinks they're all right and both are in bed under an electric blanket—oh, and they drank some broth." Gabe stood up and stretched his back. He crossed to the south window, gazed out and continued. "She reached the clinic before calling me, and they told her they were doing the right things, but to check toes and fingers for frostbite, and to bring them in when they can."

"Do they know how they wound up in a snow bank?" Senga asked, appalled. "They need a lot of liquids too," she added. "Oh, Gabe. . ."

"Francesca tried the sheriff's office too—but didn't get through. Both the woman and the child had been beaten." He turned to face Senga. "And now you'll understand why I was so angry with you—your guy? Sorry to call him that . . . well, he lives with some other folk about six miles from The Blue Wood. As the crow flies." He paused but nodded his head once.

"How do you know?"

"Charlie Mays talking on the radio last night. . . Rufus and Caroline have a scanner—a lot of folk around here do, you know. But he—Mays—must've switched something off, because right after his mention of the Berry place, it went dark—or however that's described." Gabe liked to read spy thrillers—far and away from his own genre.

In the mind of Senga, a drop of smoky ink dripped into a glass of water. A wraith-like miasma of ink, suspended, slowly sunk in slow whirls among the clear molecules of water, to eventually cloud it completely. Her head shot up and their eyes met.

"Gabe," was all she said for a moment, then, "Who *are* these people? What do they want?" She didn't know why she'd asked the latter, but it occurred to her, *What does anyone want, and what happens when they don't get it? Is it a question of desire—or more of a need? A mere requirement for living?*

"Senga? Where are you, hon?"

She heard Caroline. *Hon?* Still, it touched her. *Tenderness, ah yes,* she'd forgotten. . .

"It's okay—I'm all right, Gabe, but does Charlie know? I mean, about the woman and little girl?"

"Oh, I don't know—but let it be. Let them do their job, Senga."

Her telephone rang and she lifted the receiver from its cradle.

"It's Francesca," Senga said, reading the caller I.D., "You want to?" she asked, holding it out.

"No, go ahead—she knows I'm here—I'll talk to her after you."

"Hey, Francesca . . . Yes, Gabe told me. . . How are they? Good. Hey, may I put you on speaker? Gabe's right here—we just ate lunch—and the trees will be fine; thanks for asking." Senga switched the phone to speaker.

"*Ciao, Gehb,*" came Francesca's voice. *Adorable,* thought Senga. She loved her friends' relationship. It nearly qualified as vicarious, but no; she enjoyed their romance with a step removed from envy and longing. It was akin to savoring her chocolate, a simple joy—this delighting in her friends' happiness.

"Sweet Francesca," said Gabe, and Senga watched his eyes gleam. "How are your foundlings?"

"My what?" she asked, "Oh, *found*-lings, I see . . . they sleep now; I *jess* saw them, and before, I looked at the toes and fingers like the clinic said, and they are *all* pink, so I think there is no freeze, ah—no. *Frost-bite,*" she reported slowly, as she knew her accent could be confusing.

"Francesca," Senga spoke, "Gabe said they'd been beaten—"

"*Ai, mamma mia,* yes, Senga, but *Jeem,* he is good with that, cleaned the—ah, places—but we don't know if they could be, ah, bleeding *inside,* you know?" she said, and Senga groaned.

"This is Jim—" he broke in, having apparently commandeered Francesca's cell phone, "We need to get back to the lodge. Francesca wanted to check in, but we gotta go—look, call the Sheriff, will you? Tell them what's happened, and about the woman being Russian—I don't know if they know—it may be important, and Francesca says *ciao.*" The phone clicked off.

"Well." Gabe sat staring at the phone, then out the window once more to the heavy snowfall, swirling around the eaves of the cabin, visibility as poor as when he arrived three hours ago.

CHAPTER 27~MEANWHILE. . .

B lue Wood owners Lee and Mary Rogers had lived in Florida all their lives and, at retirement, Lee dreamed of something other than traffic and old folk communities. Florida offered more rustic alternatives, but when Lee spotted an ad in a magazine showing a Wyoming guest ranch for sale, the machinations of his mind eventually wound around an as yet-unidentified wish. Oddly enough (to Lee), Mary had agreed—she confided to Francesca one evening at dinner when they were becoming better acquainted.

Mary had experience with entertaining and hospitality, two requirements for their new venture. Of course (she told Francesca) they would retain the present staff, and this was a fairly simple, if not easy, solution. They made only one change, that of hiring Francesca. The rest of The Crew, as Mary termed it, had stayed on. *Simple-but-not-easy* entailed the staff learning new employers and their expectations. Tricky. But all had finally arrived at a working rhythm and, as Jim had once told Francesca, the Rogers were also willing to learn, something he'd worried about when informed of the turnover.

Florida chic translated well to the Western variety, give or take a few changes in wardrobe. During the months with guests, Mary embodied and played her role well, wearing high-end western styles and handsome boots to match. Laden with silver and turquoise, she didn't mind that Wyoming was not the Southwest.

"The West is the West," she once quipped to Francesca, after Lee had made a comment about her "dripping" Southwest style—spoken with love, Francesca noticed.

During the off-season, Francesca noted that Mary dressed more casually, in jeans or warm-ups. She might even skip her carefully applied make-up altogether and simply use mousse in her short hair, combing it off her face. Mary was *bellissima* and of indeterminate age; she had taken care of herself, Francesca thought, like her own mother in Italy.

Lee Rogers was sixty-six years old. Pete, his son from a previous marriage, had always spent his summers with his father and stepmother, with whom he got on. When Lee was young, he'd spent several summers at a dude ranch in Colorado, and the romance seeped under his skin. He sent his son to the same ranch for three weeks each summer when Pete was between nine and twelve—to relive the experience, Lee fervently hoped.

"There's something about being around horses and all that fresh air and—God forbid—*chores,*" Lee had impressed upon Jim this last point. At his childhood dude ranch, the guests were expected to muck out "their" horse's stall each day and feed them. When he arrived to first inspect The Blue Wood, Lee was disappointed to see the horses were kept in a paddock, near a long shed built against the north wind, and not stabled in individual box stalls. Furthermore, guests did not participate in their care and feeding, save for grooming before and after a ride.

In the end, he decided times were indeed different, and parents' expectations too, especially regarding their children's experiences. What Lee hadn't counted on was the interest from Europeans and their more mature age group. It was a different animal altogether, he realized, with a little sadness. He still wished to provide a Wyoming ranch vacation for youngsters, but he'd have to confer with the right people. And, he'd prefer to invite kids who weren't already jaded. In other words, not spoiled.

Hell, what's the opposite of spoiled? he'd wondered.

He and Mary were ill-prepared for the cold. Lee would trim his beard before returning to Florida, January through the middle of April, in order to escape Wyoming's winter. Not having understood the season could begin in early October and last through the middle of May, Lee had told Jim and Francesca recently that he "missed the sea." Francesca had nodded and said she understood perfectly. She was preparing to return to Italy in three weeks herself, to the utter dismay of Gabe Belizaire.

After reaching Gabe, Francesca and Jim returned to the lodge, the four-wheeler just managing the deep snow. Jim pulled under the portico. This gave onto a wide veranda to either side, snow-covered now with high drifts. They brushed one another off before walking onto the large Persian carpet that anchored the sofa and chairs near the fireplace.

Lee and Mary sat at one of the tables, drinking coffee. Anticipating Jim and Francesca's return, Lupita had brought a carafe of coffee, a small pitcher of half and half, spoons and assorted sugar substitutes and sugar in a bowl.

"Mary. Lee," Jim greeted, nodding as he brushed snow off his hat onto the hearth to a sizzling *pshhhh*. Francesca and he stood, warming their backsides.

"Good morning," said Lee. He and his wife were bundled in what appeared to be their entire winter wardrobe: down jackets over vests over turtlenecks; mukluk-like boots on both. A wool hat for Lee and one of fur for Mary. The high ceiling of the commons, even with the fan to push the warm air down, made for a chilly atmosphere during a blizzard. "Carey and Pete tell us we've had a morning of it," said Lee. "Mary looked in on our guests and they're sleeping. That's all right, isn't it, that they're sleeping?"

"Well, they don't have concussions, as far as I know, Lee— if that's what you mean—so yes, sleeping is probably good. They likely didn't get much during the night," Jim added. "Gabe Belizaire is calling the clinic and the sheriff . . . I couldn't get through, except to leave messages." He joined the Rogers at their table, as Francesca brought mugs from the kitchen.

The rest of the windblown, snowy afternoon passed quietly, after a hot soup lunch—Lupita's creamy chicken and noodles. An on-going picture puzzle awaited interest, and much of the time found a taker in Carey. The woman's usual chores followed a routine, and these she worked through until Mary told her to take the rest of the day off, "like everyone else." Francesca took up her knitting before the fireplace. Lupita, however, continued to cook, a task she found calming. Lasagna for dinner. Mary called it dinner, instead of supper, and that was that.

Late afternoon, Francesca noticed the woman in the hallway glance in their direction and then to the left. She appeared to be dazed. Francesca laid down her needles and rose to go to her.

"Larissa, would you like to come by the fire and have some soup now? And how is your little Tanya?"

"She sleeps, thank you, and thank you for helping us," and at this, the woman began to crumple. Francesca, just in time, put an arm around her to hold her up.

"*Jeem?*" she called, and he was there, scooping Larissa up and carrying her to the sofa, where Mary covered her with a throw from the back of the couch, now put to good use.

"Larissa, *cara,* how do you feel?" Francesca asked.

"I am sorry . . . I make trouble for you," she spoke in her thick accent, and Jim shot a glance in Francesca's direction. Russian characters had occupied the American cultural milieu for decades, but this was Wyoming.

Lee and Mary were visibly shaken by her appearance, Francesca thought, Lee more so than his wife. The couple hadn't yet met nor properly seen their guests. Larissa's back was turned earlier when Mary quietly opened the door to their room. It was Mary who spoke to Larissa now.

"We are so very sorry this happened to you, but you're going to be all right. Do you understand?"

Larissa nodded slowly, her eyes darting to Francesca.

"Could you eat a little soup, do you think? Beef and vegetable barley, or chicken and noodle?" Mary asked the woman, hoping to entice her. Lupita often kept two soups on hand.

"I think Larissa needs something for pain," Francesca said while looking at her. The woman nodded again. She looked miserable.

"Carey, would you please go get a bag of those peas from the freezer?" Mary asked in her soft Florida accent, "and Tylenol from the medicine cabinet—a glass of water, too?"

"She had a bag with her in her room, ma'am," Carey replied, ". . . it's probably thawed by now," she said and everyone saw Mary's eyes grow wide in frustration. Carey abandoned the puzzle for the freezer.

"And Carey, do change out the peas regularly," Mary added.

"Yes, ma'am," Carey called back.

A cry from the hallway pulled their attention away and Larissa tried to rise, but Francesca said, "I will go to her, *cara.*"

CHAPTER 28~POST STORM

Saturday morning found Senga once again in the orchard wielding her broom. The sun shone brilliantly, however, making the chore less baleful. At a glance, she guessed eighteen inches had fallen, but much had sunk into the ground. Later, as she ate her soup, she watched long cornices of snow slide off her roof, to create high berms on either side of the cabin. She expected her neighbor and his tractor in the afternoon, and reserved a bushel of apples for him and his family. He always objected, but Senga felt obliged, and she knew Papa would have done so.

The apple crop had been good and Senga blushed with gratitude, satisfaction and accomplishment—Gabe's help notwithstanding.

She sat back, blankly chewing on a torn cuticle. Nerves. *The purposes of work are myriad,* she heard. "Indeed," she spoke aloud and stood to go clear her dishes. After washing the morning's oatmeal-to-soup bowl and pan, she started on the cup, but changed her mind. She'd enjoy another cup of coffee later.

Not exactly at loose ends, Senga sensed a fragmenting—as if nerve ends were unraveling a bit. *Io sono frammentati,* Francesca had once told her: I am fragmented. They'd been discussing *l'arte di arrangiarsi,* and Senga now wondered if the concept, executed, held a charm against being *frammentati . . .* doing one's best with what's at hand . . . against disintegration.

You're thinking too much again, dearie. Senga shook her head to dislodge the interruption, its message unheeded. She hadn't digested all that Gabe had told her the day before, and his reason for having to, having fallen asleep early. Now, fresh coffee in hand and a blaze in the woodstove, Senga relaxed in her chair before two views: a burning fire and diamond-like, sun-encrusted snow out the window.

Thinking and contemplation weren't the same at all, she knew. Fire as thought, but a snow scene as contemplation—an allowing, a *steeping* in a thing, an infusion. She permitted the energy of Gabe's speech to soak in, like one of her salves, only this ointment might be better described as a counter-irritant—a distraction.

Yesterday, after she and Gabe had eaten lunch, she'd brought out her calendula-St. John's Wort salve, smeared some on his knuckles and massaged the hand against his protestations. He finally relaxed and accepted the attention, but told her the salve would just get wiped off by the glove after she applied it.

"Not if you let me rub it in," she said, looking up in annoyance.

"How's it going to soak in . . . through the skin?"

"Yes, through it . . ." she replied, "the skin is—come on! You know this—the skin is an organ as much as anything inside, and it absorbs matter, some say spirit too. You know—the emotions? Through the cells. . . You aren't *that* thick-skinned, black man." Senga raised her eyes to his. Gabe made a noise. She resumed her discussion: "How do you think lotion makes your skin soft? And medicinals, such as tinctures, are absorbed quickly, as much from being taken under the tongue as what actually slides down your gullet . . . that's why you're always to take my tinctures in a little water, because the alcohol they're made with could cause mouth cancer; those tissues are sensitive."

"I guess I did know that . . . about the skin, I mean.

"Do you have any of this at home?"

"Uh, I think I only have the arnica oil, so—no," he said, as he opened and closed his hand after Senga's ministrations. "And thanks—count this as an apology—on account of losing my temper on *your* account, and that's too many *counts* in one sentence," he said and smiled. "Speaking of sentences . . . how goes the writing?" She brought a small jar to the tableto transfer some from the larger jar, using a spoon and a butter knife.

199

"Well, I'm waiting for word on a submission, and I'm almost finished with another story. Been busier than usual, it seems . . . not writing as much as I like, but it's a seasonal thing, too. It'll come."

"You could have been writing instead of helping me today," she observed, "but I appreciate it, more than you know."

Senga pulled open the drawer in the walnut table to reveal several pens and masking tape among her correspondence supplies and journal. She tore off an inch of tape and marked it "St. J's Salve, with the date. Apply as needed. RUB IN." Then she handed it to him with a smirk.

"I thank you, and no worries. Besides, you helped with the sheep—it all works out—somehow . . ." he added, then, "Let's try the sheriff again." The line had been busy earlier. "And how about that! My hand feels better."

She smiled and returned the jar of salve to the shelf. "I'd put some ice on it later. Why don't you call them. Somehow, I don't think it should be me."

"All right, but I want to call Charlie first, since he went out there."

Gabe dialed the number and Charlie answered the phone. After pleasantries and weather talk—the two being interchangeable—Gabe told him what Francesca and Jim had related, remembering his journalism to report only facts. Gabe told Senga Charlie cursed after hearing the account. He asked Gabe if they were going to take the woman and kid to the hospital. Gabe thought so, but when the road was clear, which would have to wait until the next day. Gabe mentioned the woman and her daughter were Russian. Charlie cursed again. He told Gabe he'd get in touch with the sheriff, thanked him for calling and told him to say hi to Senga.

Bundled up again, Gabe left shortly after. Into the storm. Senga offered her antique snowshoes but he declined.

"Fool," she called, as he stepped off her porch.

"And who's calling the—ah, proverbial kettle *black?*" She laughed and thanked him again.

Lulled by the warmth of the fire, and sunshine streaming through the window onto her face, Senga dozed in the wing chair. Between dream and unconscious memory, an image of Black Baldy steers and heifers rose behind her sleeping eyes. They were traveling away from her, not at a run, but in haste, the yips and yells of riders goading them on.

Astride Sadie, Caroline's chestnut mare, Senga rode flank. Drawing up to wait for other riders to move ahead of her, she was left behind and alone. But not quite. . . She spied movement in the trampled grass and reined over to look. On the ground lay a newborn antelope, trampled, yet somehow alive. It lifted its head and squealed when she approached. Senga dismounted—dropping Sadie's reins. She opened her pocket knife and kneeled down to *take care* of it. This is what she recalled later, the phrase—*take care*.

With the sound of hooves still rumbling in her ears—a vibration underfoot—a night hawk swooped, whirring above her.

Placing her left hand over the fawn's head and eyes, she murmured, "I'm sorry," and put her knife to its throat. The blade was dull. The squeals pierced—stabbing her own heart. *Take care!* she heard again. And by dint of force, she at last broke through the windpipe and the antelope died. Cutting the artery, to allow the kid to bleed out, had been her intent.

The incident left her shaken. She resolved to mind her tools better as she took up the reins and mounted.

First, do no harm. She'd done harm. In her zeal to be helpful. *Sometimes it's better to let things be. . .* Sometimes it's better.

A chugging sound pulled Senga's awareness from the small animal to which she'd given death. The fawn lay far behind in her sleep, along a dusty trail. She glanced at the clock, surprised to see she'd slept for over an hour. No flames licked behind the woodstove window. She rose to add a split log, and bent to blow orange coals to life. When the new wood caught, she closed the stove door, rose and stepped to the sink window facing her road.

Her neighbor had arrived, announced too by a glint off the tractor's side mirror, an instant blinding flash.

Plowing took time. No simple matter of setting the plow and moving forward, at least not for this tractor. Employing the front-end loader, her neighbor had to continually dump the burden off the side of the road, making the chore tedious. It would take at least an hour. It was now 1:00 p.m. Senga contemplated a trip to Spearfish to deliver apples and to pick up a few items. The highways would be cleared by now, surely, but she'd call for a road report, in case.

Cabin fever. And only the end of October, she thought. The aftermath of the first blizzard. But she'd pull herself together and get on with it; if not a blizzard, it'd be something else. . .

She had time to *make time* for herself, as Caroline advised. So, she peeled off her clothes, dropped them in the laundry pile, turned on the shower, waited for the water to run warm and stepped in. Several years ago, she'd bought a small, teak stool in a second-hand store, perfect for the narrow shower stall. On this she sat and indulged in the luxury of hot water pouring down upon her. Water as sacrament. *In all its manifestations*, she believed. Baptism was as much about the sanctity of water as anything else.

When ease replaced strain, she took up her hair cleanser and soap. Before stepping out, she rubbed oil onto her body and face, then gently patted herself dry to allow the oil to penetrate.

She dressed carefully, feeling a renewed sense of herself. After towel-drying her hair as well as she could, she braided it and pulled a stocking hat over it against the cold. She cleaned her teeth and added another thin layer of oil on her face and lips. Long underwear, fresh jeans, a navy-blue turtleneck, wool socks and boots and she was ready.

The highways were snow-packed, she learned, but open, and the car's tires good. She would go.

Senga made sure she had her thin wallet—all she ever carried, besides a pocket knife. The Hori Hori rested in its scabbard on her shelf for now. She wouldn't require it to dig roots for the present, nor to threaten errant bigots, she thought with a wry grunt.

She lifted her scarf off the hook and tied it jauntily around her neck, like Francesca had shown her when presenting it to her. Senga checked for her gloves in her jacket pockets. She turned to survey the room for anything out of place or left on. Grown accustomed to a certain order, the attitude included her surroundings, close as they were. Too, it was a question of safety, when one was solely responsible for oneself.

Satisfied, she pulled the door to, locked it and replaced the key on its nail. Taking a deep breath, she lifted the snow shovel from its hook under the eaves of the porch. Gathering her wits, she assessed the aftermath of the storm. The two purposes melded in her consciousness now.

"O God . . ."

As far as she could see, tree branches dangled from their pale sinews. Tall cottonwoods along the creek bed stood bravely, like wounded warriors returned from battle, their limbs hacked away. Damage from wind and heavy snow had been great. As most of the trees still wore their foliage, this compounded the devastation. The picture was disturbing, and she shook her head quickly from right to left to rid her of its impact. *Gather wits?*—she asked. *And how, precisely, do I go about this, please?* The memory of the fawn crossed her vision, and her eyes burned with it.

I am so tired of death and destruction—weary unto death—but I'll listen for how you're going to rationalize this. Am I to reconcile it, somehow, for myself? Or must I continue to accept it as Mystery?

Senga wasn't only thinking of recent events; therefore she listened with concentration: the motor of the tractor as it continued its task, the cracking of more limbs and their soft *whomp* as they fell onto pristine, deep snow. But no caw of crows, no wildlife at all in evidence; the assault of the blizzard too fresh, she suspected. Nature remained hidden, burrowed or buried. She sighed.

The snow weighed much now, having settled, and Senga lifted smaller scoops and eventually shoveled the porch, steps and path to the garage. Now, the car. From the garage she retrieved the large broom and used this to push away the car's snow crust. Her road had been cleared to within a few feet behind and she'd shovel the remainder. The neighbor wouldn't risk a mishap. Senga paused every few minutes to stand and breathe; it was hard work and she broke a sweat. *So much for taking pains . . .*

When finished, she placed the shovel inside the garage and stepped into the car, started it and pulled around so she could load the boxes more easily.

All that remained in the garage were bushels for locals, and seconds to press. She placed her good neighbor's box on the passenger seat to give him on her way out.

She had just turned onto the highway when it came: *All three. You will accept this as a rationalization and reconcile yourself to it, and—the mystery it represents.*

"That makes *no* sense," she said aloud. Then, she was sitting among the underbrush with Papa, on a long-ago fall day, waiting for a deer to wander by, below on the trail.

"*Shhh*, girlie, we must be quiet—no *talking*." She'd been busily peppering him with questions about this, about that, knowing to whisper—the woods somehow demanded it—but on their way home (with no carcass), Papa had told her that *needing* to know things all the time was akin to always having to peek at yourself in the mirror every time you passed one.

"What do you *mean*, Papa?" she'd asked. Senga was thirteen at the time and her changing appearance significant to her.

"Hmm, well, there's *a lot* to know, for one, and curiosity's important for certain things, but when we don't let certain things just *be* what they are—you know, sort of like the Good Lord's saying it's so, then we're sort of being all puffed up about our own self. *Vain* is what it is."

"But how is that like 'taking the Lord's name in vain'?"

"Well, I think that means, 'for no good or worthy reason,' and that's akin to looking at yourself in a mirror every time, for no reason. Always needing to know things, 'just because,' is vain, in other words, girlie; 'specially if you don't mean to use the knowin' somehow. I guess it's . . . prideful, do you know?"

"Grannie's told me some of the same, but in different words . . . but how do I tell the difference?"

"I expect she's mentioned it, and learning the difference, well, *I'm* still learning the difference, girlie, and I'm an old man. *Law*, enough. We'd better get on home or your Grannie will be feeding us cold food." He spit off to the side.

Three days later, Papa collapsed and died. His heart quit, Grannie said.

The image of her neighbor plowing her road rose before her as she drove through the white landscape. There had been, naturally, a "proper" time for the plowing, *a time for every purpose*, after the snowfall ended; he was doing good toward her, being a good neighbor, expecting nothing in return. He'd appreciated the apples but told her it wasn't necessary.

Our way is cleared sometimes if we but look. The ultimate *arte di arrangiarsi;* "God making do . . . ha!" she quipped and grinned and drove on with care, avoiding icy spots and watching her speed.

The farmer's market looked to be closed, but Senga spied a light and pulled in. The parking lot had been plowed. The owner told her to haul the boxes in and he paid her for them— a good sum—then Senga browsed the produce and chose three onions, two beets and two large buttercup squash. She added a baking pumpkin to the collection and settled up. The owner told her one of the greenhouses had collapsed. Snow caved in a large section of the roof. "It wasn't insured."

She expressed sadness and asked if he'd prefer to take her apples on consignment, but he shook his head and assured her that no, the apples would sell—no worries—and thanked her for the thought.

Destruction was evident everywhere. Crews busily gathered limbs and filled pickups with debris. After buying vodka for tinctures, she stopped by a coffee shop to buy a cup for the road and noticed *gallery* on her list. Yes, she'd wander the exhibits—to antidote recent images.

A bell tinkled as she entered, and Senga greeted the docent. The petite woman with white-hair, who sported rimless spectacles and a shocking shade of pink lipstick, volunteered her time for "the noble sake of art," she once suggested. Senga was acquainted with her from a past herbal workshop on making one's own face cream. *Appears she's using it,* Senga observed.

"You're the brave one, out in this," the woman said. "No one's been in."

"Hi, Betty, how are you?"

"Excellent! And you? What are you doing out today?"

"I—um, needed to get out, so drove over to sell apples . . . and I need to sit and stare at something pretty. I haven't been in for a while. Don't mind me," Senga told her and Betty smiled, returning to her book.

The gallery's dimensions ran long and narrow, and an exhibit of sculptures and wood carvings on pedestals split the room in half, with space to admire one one half of the room and return the other way. Two long benches, covered in dark red leather, invited patrons to sit and contemplate. Senga perused the oils on one side, then paused to study a wood carving—the intricate waves of a child's hair. Delicate. Perfect. Crying to be touched. She resisted.

The last exhibit included large photographs, several two-by-five feet, printed in black and white, in an eerie resolution that drew the eye, forcing admirers to wonder if the images were somehow real, and only waiting on the other side of very clean glass. The first was made of a roiling creek, in horizontal format, sunlight filtering through trees and sparkling on the water.

Senga found herself having to step back to consider the next photograph. She reeled as recognition dawned, nearly careening backward over the bench. Groping for its edge, she lowered herself down.

"Senga? Everything all right, dear?"

She heard the docent and slowly nodded, her eyes riveted to the print.

The photograph had been taken at the very place where she'd held Emily for the last time.

The stone slab anchored the bottom of the image. In the background, and pulling the eye up, the falls shed their long, white tears. At the very top, Senga saw where they had stood. And for the next twenty-five minutes, she sat engrossed, her eyes never wavering. Betty walked over once, but sensing Senga's concentration she crossed to the back of the gallery, where the office and restroom were located. After several moments she returned to her desk.

A high tinkling indicated another visitor, but Senga remained transfixed. Betty greeted the person quietly.

"Ah, Mr. Hansen, so good to see you. I was sorry to hear about your aunt. I liked her very much . . . she was frequently in, you know. Are you in town for long then?"

"Yes, actually. I have moved into my aunt's home, you see, and I am working from there," the man said.

"How nice. . . Oh!" Betty interjected, "You have an aficionada of your work, Sebastian; Senga has been admiring that photo for the longest time." And by these words, Senga slowly turned to the two persons standing near the door and groaned before slumping over.

CHAPTER 29~SADIE'S TANGO

R ufus could just manage to climb up into the cab of the tractor, if painfully. But pressing the clutch proved impossible, so he gingerly inched back down and informed Gabe he'd have to do it. The day had dawned cloudless and the road needed to be cleared of snow.

His hired man gave him a jaundiced look.

"*Patron*, I'm not familiar with this . . ." Gabe added a sheepish grin, ". . . no snow in Louisiana to plow."

"Oh, now, you'll be all right . . . and I'll explain. Go on—get on up there," which Gabe did, then Rufus hitched himself back up the steps to show Gabe the ropes.

"I keep the key down here." He showed Gabe the spot, under the seat. "This is a diesel; you know they have to be warmed up first?"

Gabe raised his eyebrows in negation.

"Well, yeah, they do," said Rufus. "So, put it in neutral here . . . here are the gears," he indicated, ". . . clutch here, brakes there on the right. And you don't really have to use the accelerator on the floor—use the fuel lever—pull back on it to rev it if you need more power." He explained the hydraulics for the front-end loader, and how to read the tilt and angle of the bucket.

"Don't lug it, for chrissake . . . see the tachometer? Keep it between 1,000 and 1,500 r.p.m."

"Boss, I don't know. . ."

"You'll be fine. Every self-respectin' rancher drives a tractor, Gabe—you'll do."

Rufus had him clear an area near the house first and, after a couple of fits and starts, Gabe indicated he might have it. Rufus waved him off and returned to the warmth of the house,

Caroline's cinnamon rolls and another cup of coffee. There were sweet consolations to being laid up. . .

This tractor's a tank, Gabe observed. He was feeling righteous, and now had something to write home about, Senga's use of "Fool" notwithstanding. *No good deed goes unpunished, they say.* . .

The day before, he barely made it back to the ranch during the blizzard, and his pick-up's four-wheel drive earned its name. He missed the roadside twice due to poor visibility, but managed to lurch back into the tracks.

Upon his return from plowing to the highway and back, Gabe noticed the horses following in the wake of the tractor, with Sadie leading. They'd holed up during the storm in an old sheep shed (as Caroline had hoped), and had made their way to the road, tractor noise often signifying hay. He crossed the snow-covered car gate into the barnyard and set the front-end loader down to finish, feeling smug satisfaction. For a too-short moment. A glance in the cab's side mirror froze his blood. Sadie had stepped into the car gate and was "all-fours" standing therein, weaving her head back and forth on her outstretched neck.

He lowered the bucket, put the gear in neutral, set the emergency brake and calmly climbed out, knowing any alarm might frighten the horse. Attempts to extricate herself would land her in trouble. She was quiet, save the neck swinging. At least the hole beneath the grate wasn't deep. Gabe walked quickly to the house, knocked, and when Caroline came to the door, he said, "We've got a problem," and pointed. She shuddered, said, "Shit," and pulled her coveralls and hat from the hook.

"Rufus!"

"What is it?" he yelled from the bathroom.

"Sadie's in the car gate—we're heading out," and they stepped into one of the worst circumstances Caroline had ever dreaded, Gabe knew.

He had heard the story about her father's horse having to be put down. Rufus had related it to him when he first hired on, to impress care around car gates—unnecessarily, he'd thought at the time, as Gabe had grown up around them. He put all that in the back of his mind now and thought what to do. *Stay calm.*

They approached calmly, Caroline speaking in hushed tones. The other horses had wandered back down the road and stood in a kind of vigil, being still. Caroline believed Sadie would be all right; the horse was a quiet one, and they'd be able to get her out; she just wasn't sure how. Gabe was speaking to the mare—thus to Caroline—saying what they needed to do, both knowing it wasn't so much what you said to an animal, as how you said it.

"We need to bring up your legs somehow, and get you to lie down on the grate, then pull you off—so what do you think, Sadie . . . and Caroline?"

He omitted the "Miss," she noticed in a detached way.

"Uh, yeah, but . . . oh hell, Gabe. . ." she said now, in a strangled voice, and she feared going to pieces, but she took a breath and slowly stepped to where she could rub Sadie's neck. She spoke to her horse.

"It's all right, girl. . . You'll be fine . . . we're here . . . we're going to get you out of this mess."

Rufus had brought the mare home to her as a gift some fifteen years ago, and she was now twenty and getting on, which might work to their advantage, Caroline hoped.

"We'll need rope, chain and the tractor," said Gabe, and Caroline wondered if he wasn't at all sure of this strategy. *But it's what's come to him*, so she stood back up.

"I'll go. You keep talking to her and rubbing her neck, Gabe," and she stepped back over the rungs and turned toward the house. Rufus appeared on the porch, meeting her.

"Rope—nylon—we need a good length, and after she's hog-tied we need the tractor brought 'round with chain to drag her off."

"There's rope here, Caro," and he pointed behind the door where a length hung in a coil. This he lifted off and handed to her. His tone betrayed his fears, but she ignored it. Stepping up to him, she looked him in the eye, then leaned in and kissed his cheek. *For luck*, she figured.

"When we get her tied, Gabe will get the tractor . . . unless . . . you think you can?" she asked, her expression between despair and dismay.

He stood a moment, considered, then said, "I'll do it," and turned for his coat and hat.

Gabe stroked Sadie's neck, back and flank, murmuring continually in low, soothing tones. Only once did she offer to lift a back leg between the steel rungs, but these were *rounded* poles, he had noticed—no sharp edges. It would take all their strength and resolve, he thought, even a miracle. "Lord—give us a hand, please?" he asked.

Caroline returned with the rope. He told her to cut it in lengths of about six feet, handing her his pocket knife. They began by lifting the front legs carefully, one at a time, and binding them together quickly to prevent their dropping back down. Sadie's considerable weight now rested on the rungs. Then they worked at freeing the hind legs. The horse objected, and Gabe's wrist was wrenched as he wrestled to control her movement. She settled again and Caroline was able to tie the back pasterns together. Sadie lay on her side and Caroline stooped, poised to lie across her if necessary, to keep her quiet. Gabe produced his scarf to cover the mare's eyes.

It required sheer perseverance and undaunted will among them, but Sadie cooperated. Gabe's neck scarf reduced her tension, and she allowed Caroline and Gabe to manipulate her limbs, as though she were sedated. Such is the power of calming presence. When Sadie lay tied with Caroline seated near her flank, they recognized the horse needed to roll over, so her legs faced the tractor side.

"Okay, Caroline, Sadie—this will take the three of us," and Gabe stood on one side raising the back tied pasterns, and Caroline the front, with Sadie on her back. They kept her thus steady even as Gabe circled to Caroline's side. No small feat given the footing, or lack thereof. They each pulled on the ties, and Sadie rolled like a hinged lever. Then they tied the ends of the two ropes to either side of the car gate, around the posts, to immobilize her while they considered their next step.

"Good girl . . ." crooned Caroline, *". . .* that's my *good* girl," and Gabe gestured to Rufus, who put the tractor in gear and pulled up, squarely facing the scene. He gestured for Gabe.

"She won't drag on that grate, Gabe; I don't want to do that. . . We'll need to lift her a bit while we're pulling her off."

"Um—how's that, boss?"

"Tie a length of the rope, oh, a little wider than the loader, between her front and back hooves, and stretch this across *under* the loader, after I've raised it. I'll lift her slowly, then pull her off."

Gabe did as instructed. The loader rose until the rope pulled taut, and most of the horse's weight just off the grate; then, incrementally, Rufus laid just enough pressure to gently pull Sadie away, her legs stiffened out before her, but she didn't complain.

Caroline's defenses fell at this time and she exhaled, "Oh, thank God . . ." Gabe's face broke into a wide smile.

They unhooked the rope from the back of the loader. Rufus opened the door to the cab, gingerly stepped down and hobbled over, clearly hurting, Gabe thought, as he worked to untie the ropes from Sadie's pasterns. He removed his scarf from her eyes and stuffed it into his pocket. The mare lay breathing hard, her flanks heaving, but her eyes were mostly calm. He knew she was in pain from the pulling—that her ligaments and muscles had suffered damage.

"What do you think, boss? We need to let her lie still a few moments before getting her up?"

"I expect so. Damn, Gabe, I don't believe this . . ." And he turned to his wife, to hold her as she whimpered; Gabe wondered if she might be in shock. He knew she was cold; so was he.

"Look y'all, I'll wait here a while and give Sadie time to figure out she's all right—she'll be sore. I'll give her some bute. Probably wrap her. Not sure yet until we see how she goes. . .

"Y'all could go on in and get warmed up. Rufus, I think Caroline needs to sit down a while—better yet, lie under a blanket with her feet raised," and he shot Rufus one of his Mama's looks.

"Come on, Caro," Rufus said, acknowledging Gabe, ". . . let's get you inside. Enough excitement for a day—hell, a whole year. . ." and Gabe watched them huddle back to the house, each holding up the other.

He turned back to Sadie. "Damn, girl," and tears sprang to his eyes. "I'm *sorry*, I'm *so sorry* . . ." He believed the near tragedy had been his fault, that he should have shooed the three horses away when he spotted them in the mirror. The mare raised her head and nickered in answer, then laid it back down on the snow.

She's chilling down. He needed to lead her to a stall soon and cover her with the woolen blanket. She raised her head and nickered again, and Gabe thought she might be ready to rise.

"Okay, old girl . . . let's do this." He fashioned a make-shift halter from a length of rope and fastened it over her head, then he sat back on his heels and waited. After a moment, the mare gathered herself up, tucking her legs beneath her great mass, and with a mighty grunt, Sadie pushed herself up onto front and then back legs, and stood. She shook, a full-body tremble, like a wet dog shaking off water. She seemed to be mentally assessing her situation.

Gabe grinned and rubbed her neck, then moved his hands all over her, down her back and her hind legs to check for anything amiss. Sensing nothing but incipient swelling and soreness, he held her by the short length of rope left hanging on the hasty halter and asked her to step forward. She complied, and slowly, he turned her in a circle, in both directions, and watched her movement.

In the stall, he spread the heavy blanket on her. Her far hindquarter proved stiff, but *all things considered*—as they say—she seemed otherwise sound. He gave her bute for the pain, fresh water and some oats (which she ate—a good sign) and filled the hay rack. He'd have company for the next several days.

After leading the other horses back to the paddock, and giving them extra rations, he fed the sheep, Gus, cats and fowl, and passed the rest of the afternoon in his room. He'd administer pain reliever for the next few days and rub down the mare's legs with snow or cold water, to relieve swelling.

At suppertime, he walked to the house, to the comforting smell of fried bacon. Caroline was cooking a "breakfast supper," one of their favorites: eggs, bacon, and pancakes, with plenty of maple syrup. Rufus brought out the bottle of Jim Beam and they each downed a couple of shots—*medicinally*, Gabe figured.

"Truth is," said Rufus, after Gabe expressed guilt, "the thing was nobody's fault, least of all yours. And a lead mare will always do some dumb-ass thing." Rufus had stated this in all sincerity, and, to lighten the mood. "Hell, we should be celebrating!" he added, and Gabe felt a little less horrible. Absolved, in a way. *What's my penance, then?* he wondered. But his appetite had returned and he finally felt warm inside.

Caroline beamed as he prepared to return to the barn after supper. She reached up to embrace him, saying, "Thank you— I mean it, Gabe. *Thank you.*"

Rufus still couldn't believe it, adding that, "Stock and car gates, if they tangle, rarely, *if ever*, come to a good end. . . Good night, son."

Later, Gabe stepped into his coveralls and wandered up the passable road with his cell phone. He left a message for Francesca. It would have been handy if Stricklands had Internet service, but the rural monthly rate for bandwidth was exorbitant. Still, it'd be nice to email in relative comfort.

He trudged back to his patient, Sadie, to his warm room and, finally, to his story. At 1:00 in the morning, worn out physically and mentally, he fell asleep in his clothes.

CHAPTER 30
~THE BLUE WOOD

Pete Rogers preferred the lodge to his father and stepmothers' home, a question of privacy for all concerned. He woke on Saturday in his rustic surroundings, sunshine glaring through the window into his eyes. He'd slept in. His clock read 9:35. It was one of the things he loved about Wyoming—sunshine on average 300 days a year, give or take. In Florida, they called rain "liquid sunshine," but cloudy days spoiled the effect.

After gaining his bearings, Pete recalled yesterday's events and wondered how the woman and girl were doing. He'd never seen anything like it, and supposed he'd been rather protected in his childhood, even cherished. How could someone beat a woman and child? Pete felt debased by what he'd seen and the knowledge that the woman was trying to escape. But he wanted to know how they were. *The shower can wait.*

As he wandered into the large commons area, he heard conversation. Larissa was seated before a plate, with Tanya next to her, eating a bowl of something. Francesca and Lee were beside them, *drinking coffee*, Pete suspected. The place ran on coffee. He didn't care for it. Mountain Dew, however. . .

"Good morning—how's it going?" he asked, as he drew a chair over to their table. Lupita noticed him, nodded and returned with a glass of his favorite eye-opener. "Thanks, Lupita," he said as he smiled at her. She smiled back.

"Mornin', son," said his father. "Seems the storm has passed. Forecast looks good, at least for the next week. Jim's still plowing."

"*Buon giorno*, Pete," Francesca greeted. "Larissa, this is Pete, Lee's son."

Larissa offered her hand to Pete and nodded. The skin around her eye had ripened to a muted purple-ocher color, with a yellow tinge. The swelling was down, but she lifted the sack of frozen peas to it, as much to conceal it as anything. "Cold good," she said.

"Larissa, *cara*, how are your teeth? We did not look," Francesca asked.

"Teeth good, but—here hurts where hit," and she touched her jaw. Would she relate what happened? Pete wondered. Francesca murmured for the child to be taken to the kitchen, to Lupita. Larissa understood and nodded. Francesca stood, took up Tanya's bowl and glass of orange juice and understood Larissa telling her daughter to go with the nice lady, in Russian. *They haven't been here that long, then,* Pete thought. He wondered if the girl spoke any English.

"How're you doing this morning?" he asked her.

"Good."

Well, it's something, and he smiled at her. Tanya returned it, a beautiful, heart-breaking grin, and it only served to raise his blood pressure against the persons responsible.

"I'll take her," Pete offered as he reached for the bowl and glass from Francesca, tilting his head toward the kitchen to Tanya. Larissa again told her daughter to go, and Pete led her into the kitchen.

Lupita lifted the child onto a stool at the island, to watch as she mixed chocolate chip cookie dough. She handed Tanya a heaped tablespoon, followed by "*Shhh.*" The girl reached for it greedily. Pete was satisfied with the arrangement and walked back to the table near the fire. He'd just sat down when the lodge door opened. Jim, Charlie and Deputy Carter walked in.

Lee crossed over to them. He extended his hand to one, then to the other. "Lee Rogers. Wish it were under better circumstances, as they say," he said in his soft Floridian voice.

"Chief Charlie Mays from Sara's Spring and this is Deputy Carter from the Sheriff's Office in Sundance. And, yes. . . May we see the woman and child?"

Jim stood by a moment, then entered the kitchen hallway, where he removed his coveralls and winter gear. The plowing had taken nearly three hours. He'd been at it since 7:00, but a new tractor was one of the improvements the Rogers had made when they arrived and Jim had no complaints; its heater worked well. He noticed Tanya in the kitchen and ducked in.

She held up the spoon of cookie dough, offering him a lick, to which he grinned but said, "I like my cookies cooked!" The child's giggle sounded like a high mountain brook.

"Jim, come look at this drain, will you? It's too slow," and when he bent to look, she whispered the woman was going to say what happened.

"It's all right, Lupita . . ." he played along, "Just pour boiling water through it." He winked at Tanya and told her to help Lupita cook those cookies, that he wanted the first one out of the oven. The girl gave one curt nod.

Carter was astounded by Francesca's acumen in English. *Authorities?* He supposed it was a word you'd learn if you were in the tourist business. The bruising on the girl's back and arms had subsided somewhat, but was visible enough to warrant attention, "medical, and from the authorities," Francesca was explaining when the wrangler returned from the kitchen. Chief Mays and Carter had only to look at Larissa to agree, and Carter felt a punch in his own gut for not following-up the other evening.

"Larissa what? Your last name, please," Mays asked, as he reached for his notebook and pen.

"Larissa Ivanovna; my daughter—Tanya. . . I tell you what happened—my daughter and I be safe, do you hear? We *no* return to that place, please."

"No, of course not. How did you come to be here, Ms. Ivanovna?" Mays asked.

"Please to call me *Larissa*; I tell you. It is long tale. Can I have this *Ty-le-nol* again, please, Francesca?" she asked, and was immediately brought a glass of water and two tablets.

Long story long, Charlie thought, as he struggled with details: Larissa had arrived in the United States five years ago as a mail-order *fiancée* or, "Internet" bride-to-be. She'd met her suitor

217

online. He lived in Idaho and had picked her up at the airport in Boise, having sent her the means. It was all a pretext. Once in country, she'd been taken into the Idaho wilderness, where several girls and women, most foreign nationals, were treated *"like animals,"* hissed Larissa; under unspeakable conditions, Charlie gathered. Francesca used her halting Russian to fill in some blanks, as Larissa struggled to find words. They resorted twice to a translation application on the lodge's computer. Charlie wanted an accurate account.

"Um, but how did you come to be *here?* I mean at the trailer," he asked, not to cut to a chase, but he needed to know; there would be time to review Idaho.

"I don't know this word *trailer*. . . ahh, where we sleep?"

"Caravan," Francesca suggested.

"Ah, da; this man buy me for—ah—sex, and he bring me here, where there is *nothing*—like *taiga* in *Rasiya!"*

Francesca explained the taiga in Russia as largely wilderness. She told Charlie later she thought the woman might have spit, had she not remembered herself.

Charlie and Carter exchanged glances, and Charlie wrote in his notebook. Carter spoke up:

"You saw us the other day . . . why didn't you say something then?"

Larissa's one good eye grew large. Against juxtaposition with the other, she communicated wordlessly, then said simply, directly, "I afraid of these men. They *like* to hurt me and my little Tanya. So, I say nothing and we go. Better sleep in snow than that bed . . . and, I *know* what this is, this . . . *this*—ah, this *droog* now in *Rasiya* too . . . make people look dead. Teeth fall out; they *crazy.* Men want me to help 'cook'—they say—in *caravan.* And there I sleep with my little Tanya—*chérti! D'yávoli!"*

Charlie looked at Francesca.

"Devils," she translated.

"Cook, you said? Are they cooking meth, Larissa?" Charlie asked evenly.

"Yes, that is word, *met,"* as she pronounced it. Then she pronounced "methamphetamine" in Russian.

"Do you know the names of these persons?" Charlie asked. By now, Carter had taken out his notebook. Carter leaned over to Charlie and said under his breath, "Is this the iceberg you mentioned?"

"Yep. Foil on the trailer windows . . . didn't count on the rest, though."

"I write names for you," Larissa said, and Charlie was encouraged, but kept it to himself. He slid the notebook and pen toward her.

"You help me and Tanya, yes?"

Charlie knew better than to promise anyone anything anymore. "We'll take you first to a clinic where doctors will treat you and your daughter—and they may keep you overnight—then we'll take you to what we call a 'safe house.' Do you know what that is, Larissa?"

"I know *safe*. If true, then, yes," and she proceeded to scrawl the names of the men residing at the old Berry place, using the Latin alphabet. Charlie recognized the names of the old man, George Canton, and Dale and Joey Scobey; she listed another—Jacob Brady. Probably the one who'd alerted the others of their arrival. The look out.

"Which one, um, bought you, Larissa?" Carter asked this time, "and when did you come here? Can you remember?"

"*Iakov*," she pronounced the name, with a sneer, "I come to America in 2008."

Francesca supplied, "Jacob."

"I need lie down, now," Larissa said, and Francesca quickly stood and helped her to the sofa. "I *here* sixteen months," she said, gesturing out the window. "Come in July with *Iakov*. He father of Tanya. . . She born in *A'i-da-ho*," she said as she closed her eyes. "In *caravan* I write on paper when moon, *ah* . . . *kak skazat*—when moon *big?*" Larissa wrote *16* in the air. Sixteen full moons.

Francesca brought a hand to her mouth and looked at Jim, whose eyes were closed and whose jaw was clamped tight; then over to Lee, Mary and Pete. Charlie viewed the exchange and guessed they were contemplating the proximity of such—

"*Mama!*" Tanya came running into the room, holding up cookies in both hands, and seeing Larissa on the sofa, asked, "*Mama—kak tih? Mama?*"

"*Ya hahrasho, dyevachka*. Speak English, Tanya—we in America," she said, accepting the cookie, then Tanya turned and, spotting Jim, trotted over to him with the second. He made a show of eating it with delight, and told her she was a good cook, with a nod toward Lupita, who stood in the doorway.

"May I bring anyone something to drink? More coffee—cookies?" she asked.

"Chief? Deputy?" asked Lee.

"Yes, thanks, coffee . . . and we wouldn't turn down a cookie or two," Charlie added. They took a much-needed break. Carter copied the names into his notebook. After, Jim gestured Charlie and Carter toward the door, where they might speak out of earshot.

"The woman's been repeatedly beaten—her body's covered with bruising," and noting Charlie's expression, "Ah, well, we needed to change her out of the wet clothes. Francesca was with me," he added. ". . . and anyone who would do that isn't going to sit back and wait to see what happens next.

"And look, when I was out this morning a guy rode up on a snowmobile. I thought it was strange, his being alone. People usually go out in pairs. Anyway, he stopped and wanted my attention, so I geared down and opened the cab door. He kept his helmet on, so I can't really describe him. He asked if I'd seen anyone wandering around, and I said, 'In *this* snow?' you know, like he was crazy, and he just moved his mouth funny, I remember thinking at the time. . . I could see his mouth."

Jim held back a card in the telling. He didn't exactly know why, he just did. The man had asked him if he wouldn't mind plowing him out—that there was a problem with his rig. Jim asked where and he recognized the old Berry place. He agreed and said he'd get to it around lunchtime.

"Well," Jim continued, "the guy thanked me and was off—headed south toward the logging road out there. . . You know, I've lived here for years and we used to take trail rides in that direction. We'd show guests a sawmill from the twenties, but a year ago last May we noticed a string of electric wire'd been strung—two strands—along their boundary with the national forest, so we just avoided the area. Didn't think much of it at the time, except it was weird . . . but folks come stranger and stranger these days. . ."

Charlie took a deep breath and asked, "Is that it?" and Jim nodded, thinking, *I'm going to have to tell him, but later.*

A long speech for Jim, Pete thought as he overheard; it couldn't be helped. Jim was worked up and didn't realize he was speaking louder than necessary. Pete also noticed, when Jim glanced toward the sofa, Francesca, Lee and Lupita turned their heads away quickly.

Francesca busied herself with Larissa, asking her if she'd like to take a shower; that they could place a stool in the stall for her. Yes, Larissa answered, and could her little Tanya join her? *"Kanyeshna, cara, of course,"* Francesca answered—in a medley of Russian, Italian and English.

Pete saw Francesca look to Lee, who then asked Lupita to ask Carey to find a stool for the shower. Such was the chain of command at the Blue Wood this morning. Evidently, Mary was sleeping in.

The deputy drove Larissa and Tanya to the clinic when they were ready. Carey had thought to wash and dry their clothing. After they left, Jim wished he could've told them, "You clean up real good," but the shower only served to highlight the peculiar shades Larissa's skin had turned.

Tanya's injuries were hidden beneath her clothing, but with their wet hair, smelling of coconut, Larissa and Tanya resembled nascent beings. Otherworldly. Almost—*larval.* Jim didn't know where the image came from, but they both looked far too frail to be exposed to the bright light of day.

After devouring a large brunch of scrambled eggs, sausage, toast, stewed prunes and more coffee, Jim once again pulled on his gear and headed out the door to the waiting tractor. He made sure his rifle and ammo were secured behind his seat where he kept them when plowing. Varmints were everywhere now. . .

PART THREE

Before she lost consciousness, the image of the falls seared into Senga's mind; the memory of the day, nineteen years ago, reduced to a mere shutter-click. Yet—as entranced as she was—the memory of Emily's fall evolved into a time-delayed photograph . . . in reverse. The photo had been made, and the long interval passed in aftermath; *life-delaying*. In black and white, the frozen scene impressed itself upon her soul as a poignant still-life. The gap between notes. Epiphany-like (even as she succumbed), she sensed the long spell, or curse, lifting. The Indian through the window, she recognized as harbinger, a sign of something coming.

This? The sound of the bell announced a presence, then a voice, and it had all proved too much.

CHAPTER 31~STILL; *LIFE*

Senga! Oh, my, Mr. Hansen, *go* to her, will you? Why—I can't imagine . . . I have some lavender oil here *somewhere*," In a dither, the woman reached for her handbag. "It was Senga told me to carry it always, and I *do*; it's here somewhere. . ."

Sebastian heard Betty's distress as she rummaged through her bag.

Moving quickly, he was behind Senga in an instant. She lay slumped over on the bench. He knelt behind it and held her up before him. Betty arrived with an ounce bottle of lavender oil and held it under Senga's nose, at which she reared back into his chest, shaking her head, "Wh—*what?*"

"You fainted, my dear," Sebastian said to her.

"I-I do *not* faint. . . My God, you smell the same . . . sun-dried . . . Is it you? Is it really you?" she asked. Sebastian watched her try to focus, her head turning up toward him. She sat up then bent over again, lowering her head between her knees. He placed his hand on her back with a light pressure.

"Senga," Betty asked, "are you all right, dear? What happened? Shall I call the EMTs?" Betty stood before them (blocking the photograph) clutching the bottle of lavender oil. "I'll turn the sign to 'closed,' shall I?" and before waiting for answers, she scurried away.

"I am sorry, Senga," he said, ". . . this was so—foolish of me. I had not thought of your ever viewing my. . . I didn't think. Stupid of me."

"No. No, Sebastian, they're beautiful, truly," she replied and sat up. "Please . . . don't think that, and . . . and I'll be . . . all right," she added with some difficulty. He sensed this and moved around the bench to sit beside her, draping his right arm around her shoulders. (Yet again.) He pulled her against him and Senga relaxed at once. *Like a marionette puppet being laid down*, he thought.

Betty returned with a cup of water for Senga, which she drank.

"Thank you, Betty . . . I'm sorry I scared you," she said to the woman. Betty asked again if she was all right. Senga nodded, and the woman returned to her desk.

"You have not aged. How is this possible?" Sebastian asked.

"Hunh. And you need glasses . . ." she said wryly. It was true that her braid, roping down her back, appeared the same shade as nearly two decades ago, bar strands of white. But, when she reached to remove the wool hat to show him, he noted the white at her temples and the strange streak growing from her widow's peak. His own hair had turned a sandy-white and was thinning.

"And I do have some lines; so do you, I see," she said as she examined his face. Then Senga's eyes filled with tears and, smiling through them, she said, "God, it's *good* to see you, Sebastian."

After thanking Betty for her concern, and quickly discussing the issue that had brought him into the gallery that day, he turned to Senga and asked if she'd like to go have a bite to eat.

"I don't want to go to a restaurant, Sebastian . . . Um, could we go to your home instead? I could scramble eggs or something—"

"That will do, but *you* will do no such thing. I have something I think you'd like."

As she pulled her hat back on, Senga thanked Betty once more as the couple left the gallery. When Senga heard the tinkling in their wake, she said, "Well, someone just got their wings," and Sebastian looked at her in question.

"Clarence in *It's a Wonderful Life?*"

"Ah, yes, I know it; wonderful film. About second chances, I believe."

As Sebastian led her toward his car, Senga glanced over her shoulder and saw Betty behind the glass door, arms crossed and staring after them with a bemused expression—*or is it a "knowing" expression,* Senga wondered. The air felt and smelled crisp, cold and sweet, she thought. *Like my apples taste.*

Sebastian suggested she leave her car where parked, in the town lot, and he opened the passenger door to his Volvo for her. He noticed (in her wide-eyed reaction) the simple courtesy came as surprise.

She is nervous, he thought, and decided it was the chance meeting—extraordinary, to be sure—but with an added ingredient; mystery. He turned onto a snow-packed road that led them toward the National Forest. They came to a narrow, snowy, graveled road.

"Something 'gulch,'" she read as they turned onto it.

"Jasper's Gulch. The National Forest borders my aunt's property . . . fortunate," he explained, while keeping his eyes on the road, then, "The storm devastated so much . . . near you as well?" They had driven by more snapped-off crowns of trees and debris in the road—larger limbs having been cleared earlier.

"Yes, it's bad. . ."

He watched the woman move her head to the left and back again, but said nothing.

"I've never been up this way. . ." she continued, ". . . um, how long ago did your aunt pass? I—ah—overheard Betty earlier; I'm sorry for your loss."

"Thank you. It happened three months ago, approximately. I flew over as soon as I could—from Copenhagen. But I was obliged to arrange several things from there. It was difficult."

"Did your aunt have anyone here to help her?"

"No, sadly, she did not. Well, there is a friend, but she is *very* elderly herself, you see, and while Aunt was remarkably capable on her own, she had not quite prepared for the inevitable, shall we say."

"Ah."

The car slowed, and he steered onto a hidden driveway, to arrive at a timber-frame home, peeking out behind a tall, wooden fence, fashioned of pointed staves.

"Oh, my . . . look at this . . . it's Baba Yaga's yard!" cried his surprised passenger.

"It is rather—picturesque—yes? And you know Baba Yaga?" he asked. The Russian fairy-tale was less popular than some. But he enjoyed being in the company of those introduced to his aunt and uncle's creation for the first time, so clearly whimsy and folly. And now it belonged to him.

He parked, opened his door and hurried around to open his passenger's. His guest swung her legs out and stood, wonder written on her face as she took in the surroundings.

Beyond the parking area, a shoveled walkway led to a gate, then several more feet of cleared path to steps. The elevation in the foothills accounted for the deeper snow—at least two and a half feet.

"You were busy this morning," she said, inspecting piles of snow and broken limbs.

"I am used to the work of winter . . . I don't mind. And you? Did you receive much snow where you live?"

"Yes, but not quite *this* much . . . Oh, Sebastian, this is wonderful!" she cried as they made their way toward the house.

His name spoken in her voice felt as warm as this place in his memory. The home was built in the Scandinavian style, with five steps leading to a porch and a fanciful wooden door, arched at the top, whose planed boards had been white-washed then wiped off, giving it an antique appearance. She passed her fingers over the unusual hinges; he would tell her about them.

The outside walls of the house were constructed of squared timber and field stone. A high and wide, prow-shaped bank of windows ranged nearly to the apex of the pointed roof, facing south; reds, corals and mauves giving the time of day in the glass. Snow reached the edge of the narrow porch, surrounded by one-of-a-kind, crooked, peeled log railings. To the right, a lean-to shed stood directly off the path, filled with split wood.

"How long ago did your aunt and uncle build this?" Senga asked.

Sebastian heard enchantment in her voice, and a deep calm. They would remain outdoors for this conversation, he thought. Warming rays of the sun caused loud dripping from the high eaves; by the end of next week, much of the snow would be melted, if forecasts were accurate.

"Uncle Harold was a geologist. American. He met Aunt Karen while in Copenhagen for a conference. She was a lover of rocks, you might say—absolutely adored stones—and she enjoyed attending these lectures now and then. That was . . . oh, fifty years ago now—I think. They built *Fred* about forty years ago.

"The place is called *Fred*. It means "peace" in our language. Do you see the sign there?" She looked where Sebastian pointed and smiled. A brightly painted, oval-shaped wooden plaque, with the single word painted in the middle, as a greeting (Sebastian had always thought), hung beside the door.

"Most of the stones and rocks for house and chimney, they gathered themselves. The Hills are studded with them—as you undoubtedly know—but they also brought back boxes and boxes from their travels around the country . . . you cannot see them now for the snow, but there are several, ah, *mountains* of rocks around the house," he added, chuckling, and holding out his hand for Senga to grasp as he stepped ahead toward the unique front door.

This he opened, then stepped back to let her pass.

"You don't lock it?"

"No."

The high-ceilinged entrance foyer was painted white; the interior walls built of horizontally-laid, rough-cut timber, mellowed now to gray shades. A wrought-iron spiral staircase rose to the loft. Dashes of color in the form of textiles, art, braided rugs and lamp shades greeted her. Gorgeous cloth prints in rose, orange and yellows and gilt-framed paintings decorated the walls.

"None of your photographs," Senga idly remarked.

Other wrought-iron fixtures, including a simple chandelier, gave the room a weighty dimension. The fireplace—a ceramic, tile-covered woodstove, glassed doors on two sides—stood in the center of the room, its large stove pipe rising to the vaulted ceiling. Beyond, lay the kitchen area, beneath the loft—with an island commanding the area.

"Let me take your coat, and no, none of my work here; oh, maybe a snapshot or two. . ."

She pulled off her stocking cap, stuffed it into her jacket pocket and he helped her out of her jacket. He stepped to a hall tree and hung it on one of the pegs.

"I'll take my boots off."

"Not necessary, but there are slippers if you like. Aunt always keeps—ah, kept—several sizes for guests . . . Hallowed ground and all, you know. . ."

He watched her look for a suitable place to sit, cross to a bench in the foyer, and begin to unlace her boots. Sebastian reached her, knelt down and sat back on his heels. He lifted her hand away from the ties and finished unlacing the boots himself. They said nothing. He felt her gaze as he worked. When he'd at last loosened the long laces, he gently pulled one boot off and then the other. His aunt's collection of slippers lay neatly in a row according to size, beside the bench near the hall tree.

"Um . . ."

"The green ones look about right."

She gestured with her chin, and so the green ones he reached for and brought back to her feet. Yes, they fit well enough. Then he removed his own boots and slipped on moccasins—his uncle's. Happily, they wore a similar size.

"I'll light the fire. Please make yourself at home, my dear," Sebastian told her; then, "The bath is down the hall to the left, if you would like to 'freshen up.' I believe this is the phrase, yes?"

"Mm-hmm . . . You speak English well, Sebastian. When did you learn it?"

"Thank you. We begin our English instruction very young in Denmark. In fact, *most* countries begin English early. It is rather necessary anymore, as the language of commerce, flight and, with apologies, politics and the media," he said, with resignation, he thought, even as he said it.

He noticed her scrutiny, as if she were trying to sort out his opinions to decide how to respond. She didn't; she merely smiled lightly, then turned toward the bath.

Soon the room glowed with honeyed light from a fire. Outdoors, shadows fell behind tall spruce trees and pines. He switched on lamps to either side of the sofa, one over the kitchen sink and, last, the chandelier over the dining table.

Then, from the refrigerator, he removed the quiche he'd baked the night before and placed this on the counter. After preheating the oven, he stood at the sink, looking through the window into coming darkness, and wondered, *What now?* when he heard Senga's, "Is this you, Sebastian?"

She must be standing before the photograph collection in the hallway, he concluded.

"Ah, yes, I am afraid so, among others," he called back. "You see, my uncle and aunt never had children, so we nephews and nieces were given special attentions. I hope you like quiche, Senga. I made it just yesterday with eggs, cream, spinach and cheese."

She nodded, smiling, as she continued to study the photos. He continued.

"They invited each of us, alone, every few years, to travel somewhere with them. It was always such adventure."

"How wonderful . . . where did you go?" Senga asked as she peered into each framed picture, ". . . and who is this?"

When she inhaled he knew she'd guessed.

"Oh, Sebastian . . . it's your wife, isn't it? What was her name? If you don't mind my asking—"

"No, of course not, and I had quite forgot you knew she had died. Yes, that is Elsa—I always think of her in the present tense—I'm sure you can understand."

He remembered having told Senga about his Elsa on that day nineteen years ago, when he and his father had returned to the falls to retrieve the flask that had fallen out of his pocket. He also understood that Senga was not waiting for him to disclose more at this time. She returned to the photographs.

"And my last voyage with Aunt and Uncle was to Mexico."

"Ah," then, "She's very beautiful, your wife," Senga said. "Children?"

"I have a daughter—and a granddaughter now. May I pour you a glass of wine, Senga, or would you prefer something else?"

"Oh . . . sure, wine would be good and, thank you," she said, glancing once more at the photo of Elsa and him, taken in Copenhagen. "I love this sculpture . . . *The Little Mermaid*," she said, looking over to him then back to the image. In the background, the mermaid perched on her boulder in the harbor, waiting for the mandatory tourist photograph, and her prince.

"What happened to her, Sebastian?"

"Oh, I will tell you, but not yet, please, if you don't mind; let's simply be here, now . . . could we, Senga? I would like only to sit here with you, before this lovely fire, drinking this lovely wine."

"I think that's a good plan." And Senga took one last look at the photo of him and his long-deceased, beloved wife and crossed to the sofa and table, where he'd placed her glass. She lowered herself onto the soft, gray leather. He returned with a small bowl of nuts and a dish of Kalamata olives.

"Would you like to know about the front door?"

"Yes, please," she replied, and Sebastian enjoyed watching the woman draw her legs up under her and tuck herself into the sofa's comfort.

Doors. *Which one are we passing through?* he wondered.

The first time Sebastian saw the round-top door was also nineteen years ago. Aunt Karen (his father's sister) had designed it, and there was to be a celebration planned around its installation. Sebastian's uncle had set about learning the art of forging metal; iron, in this case, to fashion the hinge straps, and these leaned on the side of artistic license.

The strap, attached to the door jamb, was simple enough, but those attached to the door itself bloomed in a pattern simulating a river's delta, or the stark winter silhouette of an oak tree turned on its side, an open hand, only more ornate, given the etchings and designs engraved onto the metal itself. Aunt had designated certain runic phrases to be thereupon inscribed, but Sebastian held back on disclosing these, and Senga didn't ask. Her stillness, and present posture, reminded him of Eriksen's mermaid in the harbor of Copenhagen.

Senga studied Sebastian as he turned back to the flames after telling her about the door. He'd looked at her curiously for a moment. It was an odd feeling, to be regarded this way. She took a sip of the excellent Pinot Noir, then carefully replaced the long-stemmed glass on the long, low table and reached for a small handful of mixed nuts. She hadn't seen this person in nearly two decades and yet, here they were in this intimate setting, giving one another solace in a snowy landscape. The nuts piqued her appetite and she realized she was hungry.

Between her recognition of the falls and recognizing Sebastian's name and voice in the gallery, some great wheel had turned; a seismic shift. She felt lighter. Barring more dramatic circumstances, how had she come to be here? She allowed these notions to float, unexamined and untethered, like the Indian ignoring her from behind his tree (where she kept him for now).

Sebastian Hansen held himself with such grace, she thought, with an athlete's posture and purpose. She knew nothing about him, save what she'd unconsciously absorbed after Emily's fall. His sensibilities at the time may have saved her sanity, she'd later consider. He was made like a climber of mountains; his build, sinewy; muscles, lean—his step, springy, recalling the self–possession of the buck from her window. . .

Shape shifters of mysterious origin. Interlopers in time.

The hairs on the back of her neck tingled. She reached for the glass of wine, drank and held the glass. Sebastian reached for an olive. His hand and forearm drew her attention, the sweater's sleeves pushed back to his elbow, and she remembered why: the arm grasping her daughter's body, but mercifully sans emotional context. She turned quickly to his profile, to an expression still sorrowful, a clear, blue-eyed sadness. The light from the fire bounced off his irises now; he'd cut his eyes toward her when he sensed her gaze. There was the melancholy smile, Senga thought; *It recounts the history of the world.* Two deep, vertical lines had been etched between his blond brows. She hadn't noted their presence before.

"So I think we could toast to something, Sebastian; I mean, you don't run into someone after so long and ignore the magic. Could be bad luck, or—" she lamely finished. Then she smiled.

He had turned to her again when she began the stream of words, then he took a breath and, letting it out, smiled again, and she liked seeing the one eye crinkle at the corner. *There is hope in that,* she heard.

"Absolutely, Senga; you are correct—let me think . . . hmm . . . ah! To 'all things beautiful;' to 'loved ones;' and to—"

"To 'a snowy autumn evening in the Hills,'" she finished, to which she raised her glass and he followed. They each drank. Then came a confused memory of his proffered flask of medicinal whisky as she held his eyes now, and she knew they'd fallen; were *still* falling.

"Does it count as 'staying in the present' if I ask *why* you made the photo of the falls?" she asked quietly, still regarding him after a moment.

"I anticipated that question," he answered and turned back to the fire. "And, yes, it does. Senga, I made those photographs the day after, ah—the accident. My father returned with me, as he wished to pray for you and the child there. My father was a . . . how shall I say it? A friend of God. So, we set out early, for good light. I knew what I wanted to do, and the day dawned clear. We hiked in—of course. . . I carried my tripod this time and, while the sun shone low through the trees, I made the pictures.

"I have not returned to the place since, my dear. We wished to forge a kind of peace with it, my father and I. . . We helped one another, but we also knew you were suffering so very much—how could you not? It was peaceful there, I remember, despite the force of the water, and no one else happened by. So we were able to . . . well . . . the following day we returned to Denmark."

"Thank you, Sebastian, and your father. He has passed away?"

He nodded. Senga wanted to continue, but let it be. Just then, the bell dinged to indicate the oven temperature had been reached. Sebastian rose and Senga followed as they crossed to the kitchen.

"That looks wonderful!" Senga praised the quiche, wishing to transit previous subjects with some grace; it was time. Moreover, she could sense his moving easily with her, as if they were aboard the same ship crossing space . . . and dark memory.

"Thank you. One of my favorites." He carefully slid the dish into the oven. "What do you think, about ten minutes?"

"Yes, that should do it. I can't wait."

Would she like to see the rest of the house? She agreed. But first, she watched him cross to a CD player on a small table in the foyer. A low drone of pipes filled the air. *Good acoustics,* Senga observed. Sebastian adjusted the volume. A lovely, if mournful, tune followed.

"What is that?" asked Senga.

"It is called *The Emigration Tunes,* by Loreena McKennitt's band. I sent this CD to my aunt some time ago. Beautiful, no?"

"It's *sad,* Sebastian."

"Mm, yes, quite sad, leaving one's country of origin and settling elsewhere. I am of the opinion that sad tunes help us cross such expanses . . . and this one I love. Wait until you hear the entire piece, then tell me what you think." And he nodded in the direction where they'd begin, accompanied by strains of music. A procession.

CHAPTER 32~SANCTUARY

"Carter," the sheriff greeted, when he entered the medical clinic waiting room, earlier that afternoon.

"Sheriff," replied Carter.

Larissa and Tanya were engrossed in a children's book. The sheriff looked at the woman and child, frowned in consternation, glanced back at Carter and approached the receptionist at the check-in window. Carter couldn't hear what was being said. Larissa glanced at the sheriff, then to Carter—her face betraying nothing. He smiled at her in reassurance, but it was the sheriff who inspired confidence, Carter had always thought.

When the sheriff returned, Carter stood and introduced the woman and her child, who remained seated.

"Sheriff, this is Larissa Ivanovna and her daughter, Tanya." Francesca had repeated the pronunciation for him. "Larissa, this is Sheriff Miller."

She reached for his hand and he carefully took hers.

"We're sorry this happened to you, Miss Ivanovna," the sheriff said, ". . . The folks here will take good care of you and your little girl. Do you understand?"

At this Larissa smiled, if somewhat crookedly, and said, "Thank you, Sheriff."

A nurse appeared and asked Larissa and Tanya to follow her.

Carter and Sheriff Miller remained behind, the sheriff removing his hat and hanging it on the rack by the door. He looked pointedly at Carter, who removed his. Carter spoke up, "It's bad out there, Sheriff."

"What's bad, Carter? The weather? The road? The sushi? Be specific, will you?"

"Um, I meant, the situation up at the old Berry place. . . That's what Charlie, uh, the Chief, calls it, anyhow. Sorry . . ."

"Well, write it up when you get back from the shelter. . . They're expected, right?"

Carter nodded, adding quickly, "Yes sir."

"And take your time, but not too long, with that report. Confer with Chief Mays. I talked with him this morning. We're working on a warrant now, so I'll need your paperwork sooner than later, and the roads *are* still bad up there. The problem is—if we plow, they'll know we're coming, won't they?" This to see if he was paying attention, Carter thought.

"Um, yes . . . and I was thinking, if we get a warrant, we'd need to pull some bodies in to help—maybe from next door?" Meaning the next county.

"Yes, I expect so, Carter. Good thinking."

Carter realized the sheriff had probably already thought of this and was merely being kind—or instructive. He took a breath, blew it out and stood up to stretch his too-tightly wound muscles, hat in hand.

The nurse returned and asked to speak with the sheriff, alone. Her large blue eyes conveyed concern.

"There's no one else here, Julie; go ahead and say what you need to—Carter's on the case."

She closed her eyes for a moment, opened them and joined them, the sheriff having stood when she appeared. She sat down and they followed suit. A file lay in her lap; she opened it and began to read her notes with an effort to modulate her voice, Carter thought: a list of injuries, several obvious for their visibility and others, more insidious.

"They need to stay overnight for observation, Mark. I don't like the look of some of the bruising and, while I don't think there's internal bleeding—it would've shown up by now—the woman shows multiple past fractures in her arms—um, the same one, actually. I ordered an x-ray. Whoever did it is . . ." Julie stared at the file for a moment. The sheriff and Carter sat by quietly until she resumed.

"Okay—I'm . . . okay. It's just—I've never seen this much damage—it's . . . it's disturbing, to say the least. They were both, ah—mistreated; tortured wouldn't be too strong a word."

"What do you say in your report, Julie?" the sheriff gently asked her.

"Multiple arm breaks . . . and the woman's been repeatedly raped and sodomized, judging by my exams. Her genitalia is, ah, hamburger. The little girl—"

"Julie, I know it's hard—we'll get 'em—what about the girl?"

"Her mother didn't think they'd raped her, but they used her, and in front of her mother. The bruising is from her trying to squirm away, she told me . . . well—in so many words . . . it would've helped to speak Russian, but she used sign language. You said they were out all night in the blizzard?"

Carter spoke. "Yes ma'am. The wrangler up at The Blue Wood found them yesterday morning lying in a snow bank. . . It sounds like the staff did a good job of it, not being able to bring them in and all."

"Those folks deserve praise. They did just fine . . . saved their lives. I'm just surprised they survived. Look—I've changed my mind; I'm going to recommend they stay two nights, maybe three, before they go to Jamison's, and I'll see if Mental Health can send someone over; no, I'll insist. So . . . do you think the person, or persons, who did this, will come looking for them?" she asked.

"Now, that I don't know, but tell you what," the sheriff spoke to her and his deputy, "I'll have Carter stick around. He can do his paperwork at the hospital as well as in the office, at least for now, and, meanwhile, I'll visit with the Jamisons. It's pretty secure out there—that fence and all."

Jamison's place, a shelter, lay at the edge of town, two minutes (by car) from the Sheriff's Office. Surrounding the three-acre property was a tall chain-linked fence, complete with barbed wire along the top of an outside-pitched section, sacrificing attractive appearance. In the last several years, the couple had planted shrubbery to camouflage it. A locked gate into the property, with modern keypad, discouraged the casual or unwanted visitor. In recent years, the need for such measures had doubled.

Two dogs of mixed breed patrolled the grounds, gifts from a past resident, in appreciation for her and her son's care. The dogs had been trained at her expense and were presented to the Jamisons—a retired nurse and her retired law enforcement husband who offered sanctuary for victims of domestic violence. But this was beyond abuse, Carter knew.

After exchanging their work schedules and "so longs," they parted, with Carter returning to the office to grab his paperwork and a quick bite to eat. He returned to the hospital after another stop at the café to buy two more sandwiches, two orders of fries and two milkshakes for Larissa and Tanya, hoping they might be able to enjoy them.

He was led to a room, where the television was tuned to a cartoon. Tanya lay on her stomach, riveted. Larissa smiled at him and said, "*Car-ter,* back so soon? What you have in bag?" He noticed the strain was fading from her face. Her gaze had softened. The abrasions on her eye had been dressed again and butterfly strips covered the cut below her brow. They couldn't stitch it now, he supposed; *too late—she'll be scarred.* Her lip and cheek were still swollen but, on the whole, the woman seemed in better spirits.

"I brought you and Tanya some lunch, um, or early dinner," he amended. He looked at the nurse in question and she nodded:

"That's fine, Deputy. They haven't eaten yet. I'll leave you, but make it short. I'll set a chair out here for you—I see you have a clipboard. Good. You're all set, then," and she smiled at him, turned and left the room, then stuck her head back in the doorway, "You're welcome to stay in the room tonight; that chair next to the bed reclines," and without waiting for an answer, she left.

Larissa and Tanya ate slowly, with as much pleasure as could be taken in their circumstances. Larissa's mouth still looked tender.

Carter marveled at their resilience and fortitude; then he remembered they were Russian. He'd studied the country's history at the University. Russians were nothing if not resilient. They'd been invaded for thousands of years and suffered further depredations after those of World War II, even more so than Jews by Hitler, Carter recalled. Joseph Stalin stood personally responsible for millions of deaths, "and of his own people, the extraordinary thing," his professor had claimed.

Carter looked at Larissa . . . *ah, "Lara," like Dr. Zhivago's,* he remembered. He'd seen David Lean's masterpiece. But Julie Christie this woman was not, he noted. This was a *Russian* woman; strong, proud—and pissed off, he amended. Of average height, Larissa looked thin to him; large bones gave her a gangly appearance.

His cell phone beeped.

"I'll take this outside," he told them as he walked through the door and closing it behind him. It was Charlie from Sara's Spring.

"Chief Mays, what's up?" he asked and listened. "Oh, shit—sorry—*really?*" Carter said, then, ". . . The sheriff wants me to fill out this report and stay here at the hospital—I'm outside their room . . . so what are you going to do?" he asked Charlie. "Okay, got it. Uh, you've spoken with the sheriff then? . . . *Roger,* I'll be here. . . Yes sir, they're all right, well, as well as can be expected. . . The woman's arm's been broken, so that's got to be worked on, and the shrink, I mean, psychologist, is coming over sometime.

"She's had some horrendous shit done to her, Chief," he spoke quietly into the phone, immediately regretting it. "Okay . . . let me know, will you? Later." He pressed "off."

"Damn it!" he cursed under his breath. *That was privileged information, you idiot.*

Carter returned to the room, where Larissa and Tanya were just finishing their meal and stuffing wrappers into the bag.

"Here, I'll take that," he said, dropping it into the waste basket. "Can I get you anything else before I go?" he asked.

"No, *Car-ter.* You are good man and we thank you . . . say *thank you* to the police man, Tanya."

"*Spaciba,*" Tanya smiled, but her mother raised a forefinger and her eyebrows, and the child said, "Tank you—it was good."

Carter felt a flush of well-being thrum through his body. He smiled and turned to walk out the door, saying, "You are welcome . . . and I'll be right here," he added as he pulled the door closed behind him. He sat down to begin the tedious paperwork, but not until he mentally sorted the chief's call.

The wrangler at the guest ranch had driven the tractor to the old Berry place with the intention of plowing their road; in effect, taking matters into his own hands. When he arrived at the turn-off, a single lane had already been plowed, after a fashion, and he proceeded to the homestead and old sawmill.

It appeared abandoned. He'd climbed down from the cab with the rifle strap slipped over his shoulder. The snow was deep. Reaching the house, he knocked several times, then stepped to the back of the place. Spotting a sooty indentation in the side "yard," surrounded by black-speckled snow, he made his way toward it and discovered a pit of recently burned debris with a queer smell about it. A plume of sluggish smoke rose. There remained some unburned lengths of plastic tubing, tubs and "just a lot of plastic," the wrangler had told the chief. Then, spying the trailer, he slogged over to it—the door stood open and he stepped up into it. It appeared to have been cleared out, but was nonetheless a wreck. The bedroom at the back of the trailer held items of female clothing in the closet.

A lone vehicle was parked beside the house. The Army-green, flat-bed dually. He'd gotten the license plate information. A snow blade hitched to the truck's front appeared to be listing to the left, as if it had hooked on something. The wrangler reported he'd called out repeatedly— he hadn't wanted to surprise anyone.

Crime scene or not, Charlie told Carter, the guy had meddled where he shouldn't; but, in the long run, he may have done them a favor. The man on the snowmobile that morning had asked the wrangler to come by with the tractor—if he could—that he didn't know if their outfit could handle the job. The wrangler told Charlie that he hadn't known if he'd be able to, so he hadn't mentioned it earlier.

Hunh, Carter thought, *now that's a crock. . .*

Charlie didn't think the subjects would return any time soon—citing the dogs' absence. He had the plate number of the only other vehicle on the premises. Meantime, they could sift through the garbage, the burned material, house and trailer, when, and if, they got the warrant.

There's enough probable cause—and it's admissible. Carter took a swig of his drink and propped the clipboard on the thigh of his crossed leg, clicked his pen and began his paperwork.

CHAPTER 33~MERMAIDS

Light knocking woke her. Confused, Senga opened an eye to see a room awash in shadow. Not her own cabin then, she realized, remembering where she was.

"Yes?"

"I have coffee for you, or would you like to sleep longer?" came Sebastian's voice through the door.

She'd assiduously avoided these particular waters and wasn't sure how to proceed. "Um, I'm coming—"

"I can leave this on the table next to the door, my dear—it will stay hot for a time," he said, but she wanted to see him and called out.

"No—wait . . . *please?*"

After leaving the impossibly warm and comfortable bed, she wrapped herself in the silk robe he'd provided, one of his aunt's. The fabric felt sensuous on her bare skin—*like warm water*, she thought.

Last night, they'd discussed her leaving and she easily chose to stay. Sebastian showed her the spare room where he used to sleep on visits. He'd since moved to his aunt's room, and, in the short time spent sorting the household, Senga thought the place already reflected him—given their discussions. Perhaps his aunt, uncle and he were enough alike to ensure a seamless transition.

She opened the door to him. Nodding a greeting, he presented the tray and stood quietly.

"I *could* have rinsed my face, at least, before you set eyes on me," Senga said lightly.

He looked at her and groaned.

"That bad?" she asked while reaching for the silver tray with cup, small sugar bowl and creamer and a bright silver carafe that reflected the hall light.

"Uh, no, Senga. . . . That *good.* You look wonderful and rested. I hope you slept well?"

She nodded, smiling, then, "Come in, come in, while I, um, luxuriate a while longer." She carried the tray into the room and set it on the bedside table. Sebastian crossed to the window and pulled back the drapes.

"Too much?" he asked as sunshine bounced off the snow and into the room.

"No, no . . . the walls soak up the light. But this down comforter . . . I felt like a baby sleeping in a crib, I swear. And it's so heavy! Is it from Denmark?"

"Yes. Aunt always loved our linens, so Uncle made an effort to procure them regularly."

"*Procure?* Really, Sebastian, no one talks like this. We 'buy,' or 'get.' Sometimes we 'purchase' or 'acquire,' and those are suspect; still, I am charmed, I'm sure, by your vocabulary. It's been a long time since I heard The King's English, hunh, if ever. . ."

"Now you mock me." He feigned distress as he pulled a small chair to her bedside.

She'd climbed back into her veritable nest and was busily fluffing the duvet and extra pillows around her. Then, she reached for the coffee, but it lay just beyond her grasp.

"Shall I pour you a cup? I wouldn't want to disarrange your work."

"That's not a word—'disarrange,'—at least I . . . don't . . . believe it is. . ." The bemused look on his face told her otherwise. ". . . But it could be," she admitted, ". . . and yes, I'd love a cup, thank you, then I'll be fettled. Cream and two sugars, please. Have you been up long?"

"Hours. No, I jest. I woke about three-quarters of an hour ago. 'Fettled: a positive emotional or physical state.' How is the coffee?" Then he winked at her.

"I am impressed, on both counts." She winked back.

Senga had taken several short sips. The caffeine began to clear away mental cobwebs and dilate blood vessels.

"Wonderful; perfect; *just right*—I feel like Goldilocks, which makes you a bear."

Sebastian chuckled. She hadn't heard him express amusement. Was it the laugh of someone who seldom had occasion? Or rather someone who'd learned you may as well laugh when you can? The latter, she decided. And, that it was achingly beautiful; free—not forced or contrived. Natural. A soft-spoken man's response to amusement would match, wouldn't it? Yes, it was a "piece of cake" chuckle, she thought, remembering Papa.

They continued their unorthodox meeting, with one interruption, when Senga rose to visit the bathroom. She washed her face and cleaned her teeth with the new brush Sebastian had provided. After working to arrange her long-long hair, she finally gave up; she could braid it when she dressed.

The night before, they had talked until two in the morning, about everything, about nothing, restricting little. Feelings, opinions, observations and enthusiasms stretched to include their wounded and painful places. Family—past and present—all introduced and sorted.

The quiche was consumed, followed by a green salad and, last, purple grapes.

Her morning toilette mostly completed, they met in the hallway at her door. Sebastian carried a plate on which he'd arranged slices of Pumpernickel, made with raisins, smeared with butter; a tiny jam pot and small silver butter knife beside.

"*Mmmm*, that looks inviting," she said, pointing to it.

"I could say the same of you," he teased, but she sensed his sincerity. His brand of humor required attention, the paying kind. Intelligence plus humor equaled irony—why she appreciated Shakespeare.

Sebastian waited for her to pass into the room before him, then he laid the plate on the tray and sat down. She stood, arms crossed.

"Breakfast in bed? Now here's a novelty."

"I want to spoil you this morning, my dear; you will have to climb back in."

She did.

"Um, do you always call almost-strangers 'my dear,' Sebastian?"

"Actually, no. You are the only one. . . With my daughter—well, I use the Danish. *Kære.*"

She waited to see if he spoke sarcasm here, but no; he fiddled with the bread, his attention on spreading the jam—raspberry—just so. So he was serious, she thought.

"Do you harbor evil intent by me?"

At this, Sebastian became still, then turned to meet Senga's sober eyes and considered her. In turn, she watched him carefully, reading him as well, as he seemed to be deciphering her motive, method or madness—whichever deemed appropriate. He sensed—or so she thought—that she wasn't joking.

"What is this, Senga? Why would you ask such a thing?"

"It's a fucked-up world, in case you haven't noticed, and I only use that expression when I really mean it, Sebastian . . . which is often. . ." She gave him a wry smile.

"Yes . . . well . . . ah, I see . . . but to answer your question—I assume you expect me to answer it—so, no, I do not. And, perhaps more important, I forgive your asking it of me . . . my dear."

It was here that Senga's shields dropped and she fell to pieces. She'd tried so very hard to hold on, to behave normally, to accept this most lovely man's hospitality; even his tentative affections, which she desperately wanted to accept and to return. She replaced the cup of coffee on the tray and lay back on the pillow, turning her face into it. A mewling rose as she turned back to look at him.

"Senga . . . How can I help?" he asked. The bread replaced on the plate, he lifted one of the small linen napkins and held it out to her with tenderness; her tears burst anew at the gesture, but she was alarming him, so she took a deep, choking breath and worked to regain her composure.

"Y-you are so *kind* to me—" She hiccupped, pushed back the duvet, and moved to sit on the side of the bed, wiping her eyes with the cloth. Sebastian sat, and reached with his right arm to pull her into his shoulder.

Love and death are the two strongest forces in our lives, she heard; *you have shared both. It is Time.*

"I—I'm not used to people doing for me, Sebastian . . . it feels strange. I don't know. . . Anyway, I won't analyze . . . it feels trivial to me, you know—hollow?"

"Yes, yes, I know the word. Please, proceed—"

"But . . . if something feels true or *real* to me, I catch myself expecting it all to fall apart, you see—it has happened. . ."

"I don't wonder, my dear—and may I call you this? It seems I can't help it—you are . . . so very *dear* to me, you see."

She did see, perceiving the truth in him, again, and plainly this time, especially now her *what if's* and fears had been verbalized, as though the light of day had accomplished it. Had uncovered the thing.

A *chick-a-dee-dee-dee* interrupted them. Sebastian smiled at her, then, standing and pulling her up, said, "Come and see."

Through the window, early morning sunlight on the bright, copper-sheeted roof of a bird-feeder flashed like a beacon, like that reflected from the tractor mirror yesterday morning. *Only yesterday?* The feeder topped a post about ten feet away in the— *back yard? Apparently*—or so she thought. Several trees had been crushed by the heavy snow. . . *So the storm damage was extensive.*

The back yard abutted a steep hillside. The fenced enclosure may have served as a flower garden. It too was covered in snow. Wind chimes hung in several places, including a large one, whose deep, sonorous bell could be heard, even now, through the closed window.

She remembered a silent church bell in Montana long ago, the suggestion of light, and another great gear turned, a mechanism easing into its proper place, and an experience followed in her body with a *clunk!* Several chickadees flitted away, as if they heard it too.

"I think they are telling us something," she heard Sebastian say. "I wonder what it could be?" he asked as he glanced down at her quickly, an eye twinkling and, just as quickly, returning to the feeder. Crows' feet framed his eyes, and strong lines—his face. His tone reflected actual wonder, nothing more. He was utterly transparent. Her opposite.

As they watched the chickadees return, Sebastian drew Senga to him. He stood tall, about the same height as Papa, she thought. She had felt safe in his presence too, as if he were a towering, protective tree.

"Make love to me, Sebastian," she said, keeping her gaze on the birds, then, turning to him, she repeated her entreaty in case he hadn't heard her, "Make love to me."

He had heard. And with another groan and intake of breath, he leaned over and swept her up, the front of the silk robe falling open to reveal her breasts; her nipples—hard with need.

"*Oh Gud*," he muttered, and he met her mouth with such fervor she thought he'd swallow her. Wrapping her arms around his neck, she burrowed her face into his shoulder, desire calling from her depths, and Senga felt herself rising to him as if she were the mermaid from the harbor of Copenhagen, swimming up from an abyss of loneliness and pain, where time and space had converged and congealed.

Sebastian laid her on the bed, where she untied the robe, and he helped her out of the sleeves. A current of eel-like electricity charged through her and, with terrible yearning, she undulated and swam closer and closer. He regarded her as he undressed, with equal parts fascination and longing, yanking the teal sweater over his head, and then the blue t-shirt. She inhaled the clean scent and sight of him as he unbuckled his belt and removed his jeans and underwear. Her eyes drank him as she squirmed and made mewling sounds, seeming to breathe water in her stertorous impatience, and finally he spread himself over her, covering her body with his, which smelled sun-dried. Still. He kissed one breast and the other. "*Senga—*" then suckled them greedily. She pressed his head to her, and made such cries as she'd never made, and he entered her, bracing himself on either side of her shoulders. Past thought, past words, past reason. She grasped his forearms, then hoisted high her pelvis to receive him, the slick and wanting mermaid's vent sought and found.

"*Ow!*"

It stung for a long moment, and she winced. "A fucking-price-of-admission," she quipped, accompanied by silent questioning from Sebastian, and she reached for his buttocks to pull him in deeper, to feel him subsumed into her very cells, until she'd received him wholly. All senses merged into this one confluence and she felt all flow into Itself.

He cried out just the once and they lay entwined, floating, while they recovered, and gently drawing his cock from her, Senga felt herself held aloft on a running wave, the vault of sky arcing high above. Silky, warm water caressed her, and her pelvis tilted to the salty air, to be kissed by sun and breeze, licked by a curious sea otter and nudged by a passing seal. As Senga rocked on this sea of emotion, Sebastian cradled her head in his large hand, to keep her head above proverbial water, and with the other, he reached down to her and she rose again to meet his movements and, after a short time, she floated beside him, riding the siren's salty wave to a shore that had waited for so long.

She cried. She laughed. She cried. Sebastian lay still beside her, spent as well. He held out his arm and Senga moved into the crook of his shoulder, wet now with her tears.

"Are you cold?"

"No. Are you?" but she reached down anyway and pulled the duvet over them, for its heft. *It is good, and it feels good. Timing.* "*It has its own reason and its own meaning.*" *If Sebastian is time, then I am surely space.*

At last, he spoke. "That . . . was—" He pulled away his arm to turn to the wall and she saw his shoulders heave.

"Sebastian?"

She heard a low cry and moved against his back; her body cupped his and she rested an arm on his thigh. Heat radiated from him.

"Have I . . . made a terrible mistake, Senga?" he asked, choking once.

"Mistake. What mistake? No, Sebastian . . . the opposite, if anything. But . . . how do *you* feel about it?" she asked, not entirely certain she wanted to risk the reply.

He turned over and used the heels of his hands to wipe his eyes. *Like a little boy, a precious little boy,* and Senga reached behind her for the linen napkin and dabbed his lids. "There, there," she said.

"How do I feel? I cannot tell when you joke, Senga, not as yet. How do I *feel? Truly?*"

"Well, yes; I need to know . . . I *want* to know."

He took a deep breath and held it as though he were underwater. After a moment, he blew it out.

"Ah, I see," she said, and he looked at her, brows furrowed. "No, really," Senga continued, her tone just above a whisper. "I understand, Sebastian. Me too. I've been living with my breath held and now . . . I can let it go. It's as if I've been holding back the tide. Is . . . that about right?"

"Senga, you have an uncanny ability to cut through so much, ah—"

"In English, we call what we're cutting through, 'bullshit,'" she whispered, as she lightly brushed her fingertips back and forth on his softly furred forearm.

"No, no . . . that is not what I want to say—"

"Mmmm. Well, I think I know what you mean. . . Caroline says—Oh! I have to call her. She may be wondering what's happened. Please don't let me forget. . . She says much can be said without the extra words; don't you think? Um, as in now, you may be thinking." Senga reached under the duvet, her eyes on his, and taking his spent cock, she gave it a light squeeze. He jerked, then moaned and she continued to hold him, gently.

"In the West, there's a word for someone who talks all the time, or talks about themselves a lot. Windy. I'm windy when I'm rattling on about herbs, for instance, or, food. . . I'm hungry now. Are you? But your cock's trying to get our attention, I think."

Sebastian put two of his finger tips to his lips, then tenderly pressed them to Senga's to silence her. His appetite was indeed piqued with the help of this creature's ministrations. This word, "creature"; in his own country, it held a less alien nuance. The word suited her as no other, and yes, he had fallen, he knew. They had both fallen, but now, each lay splendidly caught and saved here together, in this bed of his youth and later visits. He'd seldom returned after the tragedy in 1994. His aunt sorely missed him during the long absences, but he had paid a visit before her illness rendered all unfamiliar to her, and all difficult.

This creature called Senga. He knew the name was "Agnes," spelled backwards. The first time she told him her name, nineteen years ago, he recognized it. It was common across the water in Scotland—and he wondered how she came by it. He and Elsa had been acquainted with a woman by the name who had married one of his colleagues. Last night Senga had mentioned Scots in her background—could be that influence. And yet "creature" did sound unkind. Perhaps not when paired with wonderment, fairytales, beguiling possibilities—all these were Senga.

They had become (better) acquainted last night, and nothing, save Elsa and Emily, was off limits. Such a sense of freedom Senga expressed, despite the obvious pain behind her eyes. Did one pay for the other?

Put plainly, Senga was wine, feast day and banquet, and he would show her how much he wanted to dine at her table. And lie in her bed. His rational side asked how one could know so much about another in so short a time. A quote attributed to Einstein occurred to him, about the rational mind serving the sacred, intuitive mind. . . But he had known her for nineteen years, he countered, and, besides, it didn't matter. Last night he told her that not a day had passed, in all the years, without a thought of her. Had he, likewise, occupied a hidden corner of her mind?

They were older now. He was fifty-five and Senga, forty-seven. Time enough, he hoped, to love one another well in the time left to them. If only she might consider it.

During his silent reverie, she lay unmoving. He turned to her and earnestly declared, "Senga—I love you and I do not wish to live without you." Then, without waiting for a response, he traveled to the end of the bed and worked his way up, from nibbling her toes, to massaging her calves—eliciting groans of pleasure—to devouring her most hidden place, which (he was pleased to note) completely unhinged her, proceeding to her mouth, dessert, whereupon he placed a most determined kiss, returned in equal measure, and she drew him into herself once more.

After, in regarding her supine form (which no longer vibrated with hunger), he told her she most assuredly resembled someone well-loved. Her lips curved up at the corners.

CHAPTER 34~CURIOUSER

Caroline had tried to call Senga after the blizzard. No answer. Rufus told his wife she was being fussy.

"She's all right, Caro. Probably got to working on something and forgot. I could send Gabe over, if that'd make you feel better."

"Yeah—do that, would you? It's not like her, hon."

"You know, we could put in some kind of intercom to Gabe's room. Think he'd mind that?" Rufus said as he hoisted himself up from the kitchen chair, grabbed his cane and limped toward the door. He plucked his hat and coat off the hook.

"Yeah, I expect he *would* mind. Writers don't like to be interrupted, from what I hear. Has he talked to you about what he's working on?"

"Nah."

Caroline was cutting up a chicken to fry for their Sunday dinner. Gabe had told her how his Mama used to soak the "whole mess" in buttermilk for a couple of hours before rolling it in the flour mixture. Caroline would never let on she fried chicken especially for him—*a little taste of home*, she thought of it. She'd also called Senga to invite her to dinner. Caroline liked to serve it on Sundays around 1:00.

"What time's the game, do you know?" she asked Rufus as he was stepping into his overshoes. They enjoyed the Denver Broncos.

"Uh, I think it starts at 2:00, but I'll have to check."

The telephone rang. "That's probably her now," Rufus said as he opened the door and stepped out.

"Hello?" Caroline didn't recognize the number—a Spearfish exchange, she noted. She put the phone on speaker so she could continue to work.

"Hi, Caroline, it's me."

"Where *are* you? I've been trying to call—you stuck in Spearfish?" Caroline asked, then, "Wait a sec, hon—" She wiped her hand on a towel and opened the door to call Rufus back.

"Okay, I'm here. Rufus was gonna have Gabe drive over."

"I'm all right. Sorry to have caused you worry, Caroline. I drove over yesterday to sell some apples and pick up a few things." Pause. "I saw someone I met a long time ago and stayed at his home." Pause. "Everything's fine. . . How about y'all?"

Caroline frowned, not quite knowing what to say.

"We're good, Senga—now. . . But yesterday, after Gabe plowed, Sadie stepped into the car gate—"

"Ohhh! Is she—*ohh* . . . is she—?"

"She's good, hon. In sick bay for now. We got her out—don't ask me how, but we did; she's stiff—probably pulled a tendon or two. Gabe's doctoring her fine. Poor man blamed himself, but Rufus set him straight. Uh, now *who* did you say this person was you stayed with last night?"

"I didn't, but I've invited him to come over this week, and you can meet him then. I need to go, Caroline, and I'm so glad Sadie's all right. How are you? It must have been horrible. I can't imagine. Do you need me to pick up anything while I'm here? Liniment?"

"No, no, we've got what we need; we're all good. Nothin' a little nip couldn't help, Senga. All right then, we'll see you later. Be careful and 'bye' now."

Caroline once more wiped her hand on her tea towel and pressed off, forgetting to let Senga respond, a habit she knew infuriated her neighbor. Now she was curious, and she knew it would gnaw until she met the man.

Hell, I'm already dressed to go out, Rufus figured, so. . . He slid open the heavy barn door a foot and stepped into the aisle, then pulled the door closed. Gabe was busy running a stream of cold water down Sadie's hind leg as she stood haltered between two leads, these fastened to either side of her, on the wall. Her hind leg was poised in a bucket. She nickered at Rufus' approach. He stepped over to the can of grain and small bag of apple-flavored treats, picked out two and hobbled over to feed her both.

"*Patron*," said Gabe, then he stepped to the pump and shut off the water. He lifted Sadie's hoof, moved the bucket away and gingerly set the hoof down. Taking a towel, he rubbed her leg to remove excess water. Then he moved to comb out her tangled mane.

"It's full of burrs," he mentioned. "But she's eating well though—I think she kind of likes being pampered."

"Don't all females?" Rufus said. He wanted a smoke but resisted; he never smoked in barns. "Senga called. Sounds like she stayed in Spearfish last night, with someone. . . A man . . ."

"Is that right?" Gabe grinned.

"Someone she knew a while back, she told Caro. Any ideas?"

"Uh, no, boss. Senga and I don't much discuss the past. She's talked with Francesca, I know, but . . . well, Francesca keeps her confidences—she's like that, you know. . ." This followed by a grunt. When the comb passed easily through Sadie's mane, he reached for the bute on the shelf and gave her a dose, then grabbed the curry comb and began behind her ear, working in small circles, down along her neck to her shoulder and on to her flank. Rufus reached for a nearby stool and sat, but this hurt, so he stood back up and leaned against his cane, feeling decrepit.

"Just wondering . . . maybe she'll stop by. Say, those Berry place folks—"

"Rufus, man, now you're riling me. . . I just want to brush this sweet girl and tell her how wonderful she is, and not have to think about any BS. Would you mind? It *is* Sunday, if that makes any difference. No offense, boss, but I'd just rather let it be for now."

"Nah, Gabe, you're right. Hell, I'm just feeling sorry for myself. Pathetic, ain't it? I'll leave you two alone. Dinner's at 1:00 remember." He started to walk away.

"Boss?"

"Yeah?"

"Say, I just remembered . . . I've finished a story and wonder if you, ah, if you'd mind looking it over—for errors, you know?"

"Christ, now *you're* feeling sorry for me, Gabe. . ." Rufus adjusted his hat and looked away.

"I am not. And *quit* that—I can't stand it. So . . . would you?"

"Hunh. What's it about?" He was intrigued, and thought it funny that Caro had asked him only this morning if he knew what Gabe was writing. . .

"I'm not saying. Caroline can look at it too if she wants. I, ah, would appreciate it," he said, adding, "If you see anything off, just make a note in the margin. And don't worry, I'm used to critique, though it's harder from this side of the desk," he said with a snort.

"Well, if you're sure, Gabe—you bet."

Gabe set down the brush and walked to his room, ignoring two kittens at his heels. He returned with a manila envelope and handed it to his friend.

"I don't usually do this—show my work—but I describe a situation that needs an expert eye, so it'd be helpful to me. And thanks." He turned back to Sadie, reached for the curry comb and resumed the task.

Rufus slid open the large barn door, stepped out, slid the door closed, walked several paces from the barn, turned and muttered, "Thank *you*, Gabe."

CHAPTER 35
~CAROLINE'S LAMPS

The fried chicken turned out *so good*, thought Caroline. *Good idea—using buttermilk like that*, she reflected as Gabe also showed her how to break off chunks of the cornbread, add it to a cold glass of the sour-tasting milk and, "eat it all up with a spoon." He told her it was "more an Alabama thing," adding, "But Southern *is* Southern."

After Sunday dinner, he returned to the barn to attend to Sadie and spent the rest of the afternoon in his room, writing—at least, that's what she thought he said he was going to do when he stepped off their front porch, balancing a plate of leftovers in one hand for his supper and a Bud Light in the other.

Rufus was settled in his chair, heating pad in place, two beers within reach and a freshly rolled cigarette just put to his lips, when he turned on the television to wait for the game. Caroline had washed the dishes and told him she'd join him, "after a bit." Rufus had shown her the manila envelope containing Gabe's story, that she was welcome to read it— Gabe had said so. Rufus was waiting until the game was over. She'd wait until he had, as this seemed only fair.

Her thoughts were colliding like bumper-cars, ever since Senga's run-in last week, then Sadie's. What was it Senga's Grannie had told her? About Time, and the *right time* for things? Whatever it was, some burr had landed under Caroline's saddle and she needed to root it out.

"I'll be downstairs if you need me," she called to Rufus, and she gathered up a basket of wash at the basement door. A pretext, though she *could* add the clothes to the washing machine. She wanted to be alone where it was quiet—bar the noise from the washing machine. She rather liked the sound— the rhythm of a beating heart.

After loading the washer, she crossed to the old horsehair chair that needed to be reupholstered and settled into it. The springs were "sprung," as Rufus said, and she squirmed to find the right spot for comfort. *Now that's a burr. . .*

Furniture she no longer wanted upstairs furnished this spare room. She'd created a nook in the back corner of the warren-like space, where an old round-top occasional table squatted beside the chair. On a tatted doily (likely worked by Rufus' grandmother) stood a Tiffany lamp, and this she lit now by twisting the paddle knob a quarter turn.

Warm light glowed through leaded glass, called "confetti," for the specks of color. The shade's floral design included warm purple irises and red poppies; leaves and stems, of cool greens. The shades of both lamps (this was one of a pair) curved outward from the finial then rolled back under, like a cresting wave, their edges deckled, incorporating the flower pattern.

They were—exquisite.

Caroline reserved the adjective solely for her lamps. They stood eighteen inches high, from finial to the bottom of their bronze bases, which reflected the soft patina of age. She suspected they were valuable, but had never had them appraised. Shortly after receiving them—as she examined their intricacies—she discovered the stamps of authenticity on the base of each lamp. The pattern on the base could've masked the stamps, she thought. *But surely he didn't know. . .* However, there it was: "Tiffany Studios New York," and a number.

She'd told no one. Sixty-two years had passed.

The lamp's fraternal twin now graced Gabe's writing desk in the barn. Pearl-colored and pink grape clusters, with leaves on a more translucent background, made it a better choice for a working desk.

"Are you sure, Miss Caroline?" Gabe had asked when she positioned the lamp on his table's surface. Rufus and Gabe had just moved the table into his room near the new window. "I don't want anything to happen to it," he'd added, and, "It

looks like a *real* one to me. Tell me about it," he'd said, and
Caroline saw Rufus turn away and pretend to be about
something else. She'd brushed off Gabe's interest, saying "It's
just an old lamp, Gabe," as she patted his forearm. "And this is
the place for it."

Rufus Strickland had loved Caroline since their one-room
school days. He was a year older and had graduated when this
sorry business with Henry Peterson began. News of Caroline's
behavior had reached him, but he'd ignored it, expecting she'd,
"eventually be chased around the round pen by callers,"—he'd
told her after they married—*Until you tire of the meaningless
exertion*, she'd waited for him to add, but he hadn't. It was
understood.

Caroline was sixteen years old in 1951. She was sole sister
to four brothers, and Teddy, the eldest, had always looked after
her—keeping her on a tight rein—until he went away and
didn't return. Her favorite, and her champion, was lost in
Korea.

As the family ranch lay far north of Sara's Spring, Caroline
boarded in town during the school year. She and her brothers
had attended the rural country school through eighth grade,
usually riding the distance to and from the ranch, enduring
heat, thunderstorms, cold, snow and other hazards associated
with the experience—often stereotyped too truthfully, she'd
later muse.

Earlier that spring, on a chilly Sunday evening, the lamps
arrived through the nephew of her landlady. He'd seen them in
the window of an old second hand store in Denver and had
thought of Caroline. She was delighted, thanked him profusely,
and gave him a peck on the cheek. He smiled, told his aunt
goodbye and said he'd return in a few weeks.

Her parents urged Caroline to return the lamps, her mother
telling her, "Things like this are never free, Caroline."

Henry Hollis Hannity Peterson, or "H," as he was known,
had just graduated from Vanderbilt Law School and was a new
hire in a "prestigious" law firm in Denver (his word). Henry
enjoyed escaping to the hinter-lands—how he considered
Wyoming. Caroline saw through him the moment she was

introduced—his over-blown attitudes, his air of superiority, a windy self-regard. Older and wiser Caroline now recognized in these traits a profound sense of inadequacy, but back then, she'd enjoyed the attention he lavished upon her, so it became a game. And a reckless one in the end.

Following long-standing tradition, the Stricklands hosted a yearly barn dance—the aisle in the barn wide and welcoming. The string band staged themselves at one end, and bales of hay along the stalls offered seating, with colorful quilts thrown over to prevent chafed posteriors. Two mares, a gelding and the Strickland's quarter horse stud were led to outdoor paddocks for the duration. Normally, the dance was held in late May, to coincide with branding season; some years, in early June.

School was still in session, but Caroline was home for the weekend. Henry was visiting his aunt in town and, as the barn dance fell to word-of-mouth open invitation, he decided he'd attend. Later his aunt admitted to everyone she'd told him it wasn't a good idea, "seein' he wasn't from these parts and all," but her sage advice went unheeded.

Anvil-shaped clouds had grown all day to the south. As the dance was indoors, the possibility of rain did not deter the neighbors as they parked their cars and trucks in rows, where, in the past, buggies and wagons had pulled up on fresh-mown prairie.

Caroline and her family arrived—she and her mother carrying covered dishes for the potluck, and guarding their footing on the pasture's uneven ground. In the barn, two makeshift tables of plywood on sawhorses groaned beneath pots and dishes. They added their contributions and went their separate ways to visit. Caroline saw Rufus and grinned. Her family's ranch lay about seven miles from his, as the crow flew. They hadn't seen much of one another lately.

"How's Caroline?" he asked her, in the odd manner folks had of asking after someone, using their name. *Folks like to hear their name, is all*, Teddy had replied, when she once asked him about the custom.

"Oh, she's swell. You?"

"I'd be just fine if you'd dance with me tonight," Rufus said in his self-deprecating manner.

She smiled again, and noticed how Rufus looked especially fine this evening—*If only he wasn't so darn quiet and dull all the time.* . . Tall and lanky, he was a hard twist (doubtless after some brand of chewing tobacco), with sinew and veins roping firmly under his skin. Rufus Strickland knew how to work. Unless his help was needed elsewhere, his heart was with the horses and his father left him to it.

His face radiated well-being, and people tended to look upon it a bit longer than necessary. This evening, it appeared already bronzed below his forehead, given the constant shade of his hat, and the hazel eyes shimmered like pools on a hot summer day.

Caroline noted his crisp white shirt, sleeves rolled up, his light tan leather vest and pressed jeans, but no kerchief and no hat. Most of the men left off wearing both tonight.

"Why, Rufus—you even polished your boots!" she blurted, immediately regretting it; it implied too much and she added quickly, "Of course I'll dance," as she turned to look for someone else, in case he'd shown up.

In those days, Caroline's appearance advertized the fashion of the day, something she'd give up in her twenties. She styled her brown hair in a long pageboy, trying to imitate Jane Russell, and she usually wore western-style dungarees, boots and yoked shirts when not in school. Her mother sewed her shirtwaist dresses and skirts, but Caroline's favorite was the popular Poodle skirt from the Sears Catalog. Saddle oxfords and bobby socks completed her uniform. For the barn dance, she'd restyled a yellow gingham dress her mother had sewn last year, updating the neckline by lowering it and adding two flouncy petticoats, so the wide lace trims would show when she twirled.

The band was playing, the dance in full swing, with kids chasing each other, younger boys terrorizing girls as usual, when Caroline, then dancing with Rufus, glanced toward the door to see Henry Peterson standing beside one of the tables. Glaring at her, unsmiling.

"Doesn't that boy know it's impolite to stare?" said Rufus.

"Well, I think I'm the only one he knows here—I'd better go greet him, Rufus. Do you mind?"

Of course he minded, she knew, but he dropped his arms to his side and walked off.

Henry could dance, "but not to *this* kind of music," he told her. They managed two slow tunes and Rufus cut in on the second, "The Tennessee Waltz." Henry handed her off with good grace.

"Caroline, are you and that guy, um, you know, together?" Rufus asked, his dark brows furrowed. He was clearly in pain.

"I don't know what you mean, 'together,'" she said.

"Well, there's talk, is all."

And at this Caroline stopped dancing, walked away and left Rufus alone. She strode over to where Henry was standing, took up his hand and led him out of the barn. This did not go unnoticed by the crowd, and Rufus shrugged his shoulders then wanly smiled.

Outdoors, she and Henry made their way to the back of the barn, against the wall, where tall grasses and nettles grew. Caroline heard nearby high-pitched squeals and snorts— neighbors engaged in the same activities. Henry produced a flask from his back pocket and offered Caroline a swig, which she took with alacrity. The string band music could be heard on the other side of the wall, the vibrations thrumming through the wood. This tickled Caroline, and she began to wave her sylphlike arms in rhythm. Henry reached for her and they were soon wrapped around each other, grappling, kissing or, *smooching*, as it was called. They slid to the ground, careful to avoid the stinging nettles. He cupped a hand over a breast, then moved his hand under her dress. Caroline extended an arm, saying, "Uh-uh. Sorry, buster," then she smiled, her eyebrows cocked to add weight to the apology.

A nearly full moon peeked behind the ominous clouds. Henry watched as Caroline rearranged a moon-lit breast into her brassiere and smoothed her dress, and then, saying nothing, he reached into his front shirt pocket and removed a pack of cigarettes. Lucky Strike, she recalled. He put one to his lips and lit it with his Zippo. Sensing her interest, he raised the pack to her. She drew one out and, while lighting it for her, he said, "You usually have one of these . . . well, after—"

Caroline inhaled, immediately coughed and tossed the cigarette during a spasm. Henry offered her another swig from his flask. They stood up. She brushed off the back of her dress, arranged her hair with her hands and examined his face for telltale lipstick. Stepping over a prone couple, they sauntered back to the front of the barn, where Caroline introduced him to several interested classmates.

She told her parents Henry would give her a ride home after the dance. Her mother gave her a look—one of sadness, Caroline remembered, not frustration. The dance broke up around two in the morning, not to last all night as often happened; thunder had begun to drown out the music.

As Rufus told it, he'd awakened around four in the morning to distant thunder and smelled smoke through an open window. His father called both the Volunteer Fire Department in Sara's Spring and a nearby neighbor who owned a water truck, but it was too late—the fire too hot, and too much fuel in the old Strickland barn. Little rain had actually fallen and a lightning strike was suspected. After the dance, Rufus had returned the horses to their stalls. All perished.

Rufus, his parents and several neighbors had witnessed the conflagration, hearing the screams of the horses piercing the air over the roar of the flames. Rufus distinguished the cry of the stud and rushed in to save him. A whoosh of fire exploded to his right from the pitchy timbers and the acrid smell of smoke dried in his nostrils as burning flesh and straw mingled. Loud crackling popped all around him, *like someone chopping a hole in ice,* he'd said. *No. Like a frozen river in spring thaw—the way it pops and squeals.* . . He mentioned too how windy it'd seemed inside the barn.

He'd dropped down and crawled on the floor of the barn toward the stall, but a burning roof truss fell on him. Rufus pushed this off before he lost consciousness, smelling burnt flesh, his own. His father, having made his way in, was able to drag him out, still unconscious, by the ankles.

The left side of his beautiful son's face was burned away, including the ear. His left hand was burned too, but it healed. Rufus spent two months on a burn ward, to eventually require multiple skin grafts—an arduous and painful process. . .

Caroline would go on imagining Rufus as he appeared that night before the fire, much as she still regarded herself somewhat frozen in time, despite the vagaries of aging.

Henry Peterson traveled north to Wyoming less and less, and when he did he didn't get in touch and she utterly forgot him. His aunt said little. Someone who'd seen Henry smoking outside the barn that night accused him of having started the fire and, accidently or not, it was a serious matter. Recouping from the losses took the Stricklands several years, hospital costs aside.

Rufus and Caroline married in 1953. They lived in an old camper on the ranch until their first child arrived two years later. After the new barn was raised, with generous help of neighbors, the ranch house underwent renovation to accommodate Caroline, Rufus and their baby, Haley.

Caroline always suspected her cigarette. . .

She sighed and reached over to turn off the lamp, rose from the chair with some difficulty to put the laundry into the dryer. She had no energy to carry it outside today. Besides, it was Sunday, and she never liked to do housework on Sundays, except the cooking.

"You were somethin' to behold," she muttered. She hadn't thought of that night in an age and wondered what had prompted the memory. *Not the lamps*, though they were still on her mind for some reason. She'd managed to disassociate them entirely from Henry Peterson. Senga liked to say things come to you for a reason—*or some horseshit like that*, Caroline silently added.

As she climbed the steep steps to the kitchen, pulling herself up by the banister, a thought occurred, *Why didn't I sell them to help the Stricklands?*

"Hunh," she muttered aloud, ". . . guess that's not what they're for . . . but what?" She was thinking aloud and paused near the top.

Why, I don't know . . . I just don't know.

Crossing into the living room, she saw Rufus intent on the football game and shouting at a play. She studied the pale, smooth side of his cheek and jaw, where grew no whisker, where skin taken from the inside of his thigh had patched him up. The graft now stretched—scarred and taut—across the prominent left cheek bone, pulling down his left eyelid. He hadn't lost his eyebrows, now beetled and white. No surgery had been able to mend the ear. Rufus had adopted a longer hair style to cover it. His scalp had also suffered burns, where his hair would never grow back. What he did have was still thick and white. Ever conscious of disturbing people by his appearance, Rufus turned to address them from his right side, making no other allowances.

Caroline's guts turned to soup—not at the sight of her husband—but at the force of the recollection, and she drew breath as she slowly walked over and kneeled before him. He moved his torso and head from side to side so he could see the television.

"What do you want, Caro?" he asked, annoyed, looking around her to keep his eye on the play. Smiling, Caroline said, "A piece of you," her eyes riveted on his, tracking his waving head with hers, and she reached for his belt buckle, unbuckled it, unbuttoned his jeans, pulled down the zipper and reached in.

"Christ, Caro—you pick the damndest times! . . .Oh! . . . *ahhh*, oh. . . *oh my.*"

How I love this man—was all Caroline knew and all she wished to remember.

They returned to the game just after half-time. The Broncos were a second-half team anyway, she reminded her husband.

CHAPTER 36~SKEEDADLED

Francesca needed to pack for Italy, but it was proving difficult this year. Gabe. The difficulty. Last year this time, they'd parted fairly easily, as though it were simply an item to check off. She procrastinated now. Hadn't even bought her plane ticket.

"What day did you say you're leaving, Francesca? I'll need to tell Jim," said Mary, when they met in the commons on Monday morning.

"Ah, Mary, I don't know. I have not booked a flight. . . I am lazy."

"You are never 'lazy.'"

"Ah, Mary. Okay. I will tell you. I want *Gehb* to meet my— my family. I think he is—*come si dice?* 'The One.'"

"Oh! Well, I had no idea, Francesca . . . does *he* know this?" Mary, interested, sat up now. Between them on the table, a pot of coffee, a pitcher of steamed milk and a small bowl of various sweeteners. They had just sampled Lupita's blueberry and pecan scones, which needed no butter. Francesca would miss this aspect of Lodge Life.

"*Gheb*—no, he does not know. But, I am going to speak with him this evening—on the way to Senga's, actually. She is mysterious about someone she met, or met again, as *Gheb* says."

"Well, *do* let me know," Mary crooned, "And, when you'll need a ride; or will Gabe take you to the airport?"

"I want him to come *with* me to Italy, but he must stay through November for the, ah, hunt, and Rufus—he needs help, especially this year, because of his—" Francesca pointed to her hip.

"Hip."

"Ah, yes, *heep*."

"We'll have hunters here too . . . spread out, but we'll be busy. I'll be glad when December rolls around. . ."

"Ah, Mary, do not wish away your life—my Papa always said this to me when I was young."

"You're right, Francesca." Mary stood to straighten the throw pillows on the sofa. "Guess that blizzard and all spooked me more than I thought. What do you hear about the woman and child, or have you heard?" She changed her mind about the pillows, gathered them and set them beside the lodge door. "We need different colors now—these are too summery," she declared, resuming her seat at the table.

"*Jeem* said he spoke with Charlie—the police from Sara's Spring—and the woman has to be in hospital longer. They had to break the arm again and, ah . . ."

"Reset it? Oh, the poor thing. . ."

"Yes. The police are looking for the men, *Jeem* said."

"Jim said what?" called a voice from the back of the hall as Jim stepped into the room.

"Speak of the sun and all that jazz," quoted Mary. "Good morning, Jim. How are things?"

"All right, I guess. Got those horses up from the lower shed. They were hungry. How are you two?"

"Fine, thank you," Mary answered for both. "What do you hear about Larissa and Tanya?"

"They'll be going to the shelter tomorrow. I talked with Deputy Carter last night and he's tight-lipped, but he mentioned he'd be in the area today—I think he meant the Berry place." Jim rearranged two logs on the fire. "Might drop in. They must have gotten a search warrant. That's all I know."

"So they all 'skedaddled,' as we say down South," said Mary. Francesca noted the word.

"They'll be back. The truck, for one. . . Where's Lee? Still at the house?" Jim asked.

"He's buried in some bookkeeping. Got it in his head to offer a three-week camp for kids next summer. A 'trial run,' he says. Hasn't he talked with you?" Mary asked.

"Oh, now and then, but I didn't know he was going ahead with it. We'd need more kid-broke horses. . . Well, they're all kid-broke to me, but even gentler ones. And I told him he'd need a nurse or some kind of first aid-trained staff for sure. My horse-doctoring won't cut it. Parents are sort of particular when it comes to that, you know—well, some parents. . ." Looking around, he asked, "Where's Lupita?"

"I sent her to town with a list after she baked these." Mary lifted the scone from her plate. "She needed to get out, but she'll be back for dinner around 6:00. It's leftovers or pizza. Get a cup, Jim. Have some coffee . . . and these scones are scrumptious."

Charlie Mays and his officer arrived at the old Berry place turn-off. Another deputy had accompanied Carter from the Sheriff's Office, search warrant in hand. They were equipped with bags, gloves and two thermos bottles of coffee. Charlie had thought to bring sandwiches from the café. He was considerate that way, though it wasn't all altruism.

They carefully approached the house, wearing their vests, with guns drawn. Charlie had Carter go behind the house, while he and the other two stepped onto the porch, the deputy and officer hanging back on either side of the door. Charlie reached out his hand and knocked loudly, calling, "Sara's Spring Police—search warrant!" This he repeated, and when he was satisfied no one was coming, he tried the doorknob, found it unlocked, turned and raised his eyebrows to his team. "Well, let's clear it . . . be smart now." He wondered about booby traps.

They found no one home.

The list Jim had supplied—what he'd spotted in the pit as it smoldered—would keep them busy for a while, Charlie thought. Maybe they could split up and search the house, trailer and pit at the same time.

"Okay. Carter, you and . . . what's your name again, son?" he asked the other deputy.

"Kelly, sir."

"That first or last?"

"Last, sir; Nathan Kelly."

"Carter, you and Kelly work through this pit—and be careful, please; I brought a rake and two shovels—they're in the back," he nodded to the SUV.

"Cal and I will start in the trailer first." Cal was a Sara's Spring kid who'd joined the department last year. "And keep your ears open—they could return anytime. Remember those dogs . . . shoot the bastards if they come at you. . . I mean the dogs, Carter." This to Carter's look of surprise.

The team settled in for an afternoon of filthy, cold work, with no interruptions by dogs or returning residents.

Company for supper was rarely on the menu at Senga's. She was both nervous and excited about the evening. Busy with a task, she slipped off the rails into daydreaming, finally giving up to fix a cup of tea. Purple Bergamot flower tops bloomed in the just-boiled water. Lifting the cup, she inhaled the tart aroma and her mind settled. Taking it to her chair, she again tried to focus, turning the kaleidoscope to a different quarter. She'd been making notes for an upcoming workshop at the health food store in Spearfish, but it was no good; she couldn't concentrate. *And how could you?*

"Grannie," she spoke aloud, "Lend me your Glory Robe, would you?" she said.

There's no lending it, dearie; it's hanging in that hidey hole you call a closet. . .

She needed fresh air, she decided. She'd walk to the mailbox. The Postal Service only delivered mail three days a week and today was Monday. Senga finished the tea, straightened her papers on the table, stepped to the calendar that hung beside the door and checked the workshop date—to be sure. She'd lost time somewhere. Stepping outside to see if she'd need a heavier coat, she thought not; the air was warming again. Snow still lay on the ground, but much had melted in the last two days. She stepped back inside, sat down to lace up her boots, put on her jacket, scarf and hat, then grabbed Friday's mailbag and her walking stick.

At the mailbox sat a large box. The mail carrier had set it on a flat stone to keep it dry. Senga looked at the return address: one of her cousins in North Carolina. They hadn't kept in touch. Intrigued, she nevertheless continued to walk up the highway for two miles.

It felt good to be moving her body again. One car passed.

I am sole consciousness of all I behold, she silently declared—if self-consciously and probably incorrectly, she amended. Her thoughts drifted to the Indian. The walking did this, as though the jostle of placing one foot before the other mimicked in the brain, and notions popped up mechanically. An idea sprung, like a stick poked between spokes of a bicycle wheel: *look for it—the arrow's shaft will be long gone, but not the point.*

"Hmmm. . ."

Overhead, the roar enveloped her—a disintegrating rush of noise. Senga recognized a B-1 bomber making a run through the Powder River training area. *More accurately*, she corrected, *only the sound following the plane.* She looked up and spotted the sleek, black aircraft in the distance. The roar dissipated and she steeled herself for the second. They flew in pairs. *Gigantic arrowheads*, she mused, then grimaced at her metaphor. She waited. Nothing yet.

She would search the ground where the buck had stood, then thought of Sebastian and yesterday morning's encounter, as tingling pulsed the tips of her fingers and flooded her pelvic region. She had to purposefully mind her steps in order to reach the mailbox. "Girl, you got it bad," she said aloud, her classmate's long ago comment. *What am I—a doe in estrus?*

Senga replaced today's mail bag with an empty one and lifted the cumbersome box. Not too heavy, it measured about eighteen-inches square. She couldn't imagine what it might contain. Shaking it, she heard Styrofoam peanuts. Trudging back to her cabin, she wondered what her cousin had mailed to her.

Uncle Will had passed away years ago. It was he who'd saved the house and property in North Carolina from being sold. After writing to him, to say where she and her baby were living (breaking the news in this way), she heard from him only once, to say her cousin Colin had moved into the house with his wife and young son. Senga had replied that she and Em were well-settled in Sara's Spring. She thanked him for everything he'd done for her and sent him her love. What had become of Grannie and Papa's things, she didn't know. *May still be there*—she wondered, with a twinge of regret for having never returned.

Senga shook the box once more before setting it down on the table. "Hunh," she muttered. Jacket, scarf and hat replaced on the hook, she removed her boots, stoked the fire and peered at the box again. Noise overhead startled her. The second plane. She glanced out her south-facing window in time to see it bank to the east, chased by a roar.

The log in the woodstove caught, so she closed the door and crossed to the refrigerator for a bottle of cold water. Then, pulling out her pocket knife, she cut open the box and lifted the cardboard flaps. White peanuts greeted her, and these she began to scoop out, onto the table. She recognized Grannie's small cedar box.

The Lane Company once created miniatures of their cedar chests for high school graduates, and her grandmother had employed hers, "to keep things apart," she'd explained. It was locked, but a key was taped to the bottom. *As if it hasn't been opened. . .* Senga suspected, followed by, *I grow cynical. . .*

She spotted her old diary. This was locked too, but no key included. A tiny thrill, like butterfly wings, ruffled her heart. Senga used her knife to cut the leather band that folded over the pages, but a thread of metal wire interrupted her blade. She opened a tool drawer for a pair of needle-nosed wire cutters to pinch the wire apart. A musty smell arose, and Senga brought the open diary to her face and inhaled. *Boxwoods*, she recognized. Another scent from her youth.

Next, a large manila folder. She opened it carefully and pulled out two photographs: an eight-by-ten black-and-white, and a four-by-six color. The black-and-white showed a dilapidated house. She sat down.

The metal roof had always looked worn, but the photo showed it rusted through in some places; it appeared the house hadn't been painted in years. It looked gray, with peeling strips of wood hanging horizontally from the clapboard siding. The front porch, choked with vines, and the yard completely overgrown, put Senga in mind of an old grave yard. *A ruin.* Broken windows winked and great holes yawned from the flooring of the front porch. *God knows what the interior looks like*, and she shuddered. On the back was stamped, "Gerald's Photography, Blowing Rock, NC," and the date: "September,

2013." She set it down, feeling disconnected. *Io sono frammentati.*
I am fragmented. She lifted the second photograph.

It was inscribed *Colin, Julia and Willie Cowry, March, 1985.*
They were standing outside the house wearing what looked like
"Sunday Best." *Maybe when they moved in,* Senga thought in
passing; there the house appeared as she remembered and she
sighed. Behind her cousins hung the sweet-smelling, lavender
bunches of trailing wisteria. Forsythia bushes, whose blooms
announced spring, framed the steps in front of the house.
Senga remembered the bright yellow sprigs Grannie arranged
in a vase each spring.

Her cousin and his wife looked happy, Senga thought; their
little boy was squinting into the sun with a pained expression.
Senga wondered why they'd moved away, and why the house
was falling down. *A house needs purpose.*

In the folder, she found a business-sized envelope. It was
addressed to "Agnes Munro," from Colin. She set this aside for
now. Standing, she reached through the pesky packing and
finally upended the entire box onto the floor, peanuts
everywhere, and two more items fell onto the rug. She
recognized her herbal notebook—the blank book Grannie had
given to her—for drawings and notes from their walks, talks
and her studies. Beside it lay a photo album that looked to be
filled with prints. This she reached for hungrily as she lowered
herself to the floor, cross-legged. She set the album in her lap
and opened the cover.

Her journey through the images began in the past. Senga
recognized her great-grandparents, the Mac Kays and the
Cowries. And here was her father's family, the Munros; he
must've been around ten in this picture, she thought—how
sweet; how *earnest* his face. She peered into the face of her
grandmother, Maria Teresa, to search for a likeness, and
finding none, she moved to her grandfather David Munro. *No,
not there either.* Her father, Andrew—*Andrea,* or Andy, as he was
known—took after his Italian mother.

The photographs were black-and-whites, and contrast lent
intensity. Maria Teresa had been striking in her youth, Senga
noted. She remembered her presence as *round* and soft, her
bosom like a violet-scented pillow whenever Senga cuddled in
her lap. And here was another photo of Maria Teresa, or

Nonna, just before she returned to Italy—her Grandpa David having died shortly after Senga's father was killed in Viet Nam.

How horrible, Senga lamented, and the belated awareness stung.

Youth had inured her to the suffering of others—or had some capacity finally been met?

Some inoculant—ingeniously administered by means of evolution, to insure the continuation of the species. . . Senga considered this, then shook her head in her manner to ward off a patent excuse.

Almost forty years ago, she realized with a start. Nonna called her son Andrea, she recalled now. *She'd be about ninety now—if living. . .*

She turned the page. Papa and Grannie on their wedding day, she guessed. No white wedding dress. She remembered this photo. It had hung in her grandparents' bedroom, above Grannie's bed-side table.

Senga wondered who'd compiled the photos. Colin? Her uncle? *Yes*, she suspected it was Uncle Will. *But when?* She searched Papa's face now, missing him, then—"Ahhh, *there* I am."

An hour passed. She'd never seen several of the photos of her mother. In one, she and Grannie stood before the stone wall of an overlook, the hazy Smoky Mountains ranging in the background, the horizon receding farther and farther back. They seemed to be enjoying a picnic, given the open containers at their elbows. Both wore glad smiles. Senga lifted the photo from the page and read on the back, *September 1960, on road to Frontier Nursing School in Kentucky.* Her mother had been thirteen or fourteen. Senga knew Grannie had attended the school for a period of time, and also knew she'd left. No reason given.

Another photo was dated two months later, taken at a carnival (Senga deduced, by the visible edge of a merry-go-round). It showed her mother in a different light. *A cornered animal,* thought Senga. The eyes seemed vacant, yes, but with an aspect of pain or terror behind them. *What?* A shudder rippled down Senga's spine. Her mother's hair hung limp; *dirty,* she noticed, her make-up, garish.

"Oh Mama. . ."

Aware her mother had suffered, Senga had only felt the aftershocks. Having overheard Grannie's description of Lucy's mental break, on the heels of burying her father that morning long ago, Senga wondered now how humanity ever evolved at all, *inoculations or no.* And weren't vaccines composed, in small part, of the very ailment one hoped to resist? *Yes; so there it is,* she decided. *What doesn't kill you does make you stronger,* she added, if glibly, but acknowledging the gift of resilience.

She flipped the page, hoping to find another photograph of her mother, wherein she recognized her. And there it was—

Thank you. . .

The 1976 Thanksgiving Pageant. Someone had taken photos of Senga dressed in her Indian Princess costume, complete with noble turkey feather, standing before the fireplace and mantel. *Who?* Her mother. She'd lovingly braided Senga's two plaits with great care; even ritually, Senga remembered. . .

She'd just taken a shower and combed out her hair, when her mother tapped on the bathroom door and asked if she could help with her braids. "Um, okay, I guess," Senga answered. The pageant wouldn't begin for another three hours, and the drive into town was long, so there was little time. She had sat in the warm kitchen, the smell of cornbread sweet, as her mother's hands deftly worked the pattern, all the while murmuring how well she was going to perform her lines, and how proud of her they were. . .

Senga moaned as she tucked away this new, precious memory into its drawer.

Another photo showed her family; Papa, Grannie, Mama— and her—posing in the school lunchroom before the potluck. She examined the image of her mother, whose face beamed with pride. "*Ohhh*—" and the corners of Senga's mouth turned down, into a trembling smile, then came the tears as the album slid from her lap onto the rug and Senga wept until she was spent, until her eyes and head burned with the effort, and when recovered she began again, the jag this time reaching deep into her throat and pulling out a latent scream that pierced the air around her. Her throat grew hoarse, and finally choking on the cry, she forced a swallow, then settled.

When she opened her eyes, Senga saw a shimmer of movement in the fabric of the cabin's atmosphere. She wiped her eyes and nose on the sleeve of her sweater.

Dropping her gaze to the floor, covered with the white packing material and scattered memories, she observed with eerie fascination, how the shimmer, wave-like, rose from the rug and dissipated into a deafening silence—like a weight, and then weightless. And there she sat, listening to her body's intermittent heaving sighs, and feeling the warmth of the crackling fire. She inhaled old fragrances, gazed—stunned—at images, tasted salty tears and felt—

What do I feel? You never explained that well—the difference between feeling something inside and experiencing something outside. Like the cold or, this fire's warmth; or the touch of a loving hand and the silky brush of fabric. What the hell? No, you never did. . .

'Useful,' dearie; don't forget feeling 'useful. . .'

After several moments she felt restored. Her cousin's letter could wait, she decided. She surveyed the mess she'd created, gathered the packing material into a pile and, standing up, brushed it into a bag. Then, she neatly arranged the items into a nook on a shelf, leaving the unopened letter on top.

A plate of appetizers, corn chowder, cheese and homemade bread, all prepared earlier, awaited her guests. Sebastian had offered to bring wine and Francesca, a dessert. Gabe joked, "I'll bring Francesca." All that remained was to change her bedding and sweep the floor, and this she did. After, she washed her face and lay down. *But only for a minute,* she proposed, before sinking into oblivion.

CHAPTER 37~BLINDSIDED

That Hulett rodeo may've been my last. . . You know I turned thirty-eight this year? Kinda old for riding bulls, wouldn't you say?" Gabe was speaking to Rufus rhetorically. Rufus guessed this and blew out a plume of smoke. It rose straight up. No wind.

They'd learned to anticipate one another, to cut out superfluous speech. This bordered on superfluous speech, they both knew. *Nerves?* Rufus wondered. Earlier, Gabe had brought out a softer lawn chair for his boss to bask in early morning sunshine. The open doorway of the barn wasn't technically "inside," so he could smoke. The temperatures were back in the fifties.

"I don't spring back like I used to," Gabe continued, ". . . I'm selling my gear—put an ad in the store—unless you could use it. Can't think for what, though." And here he grinned at Rufus, then turned back to tending Sadie. She was still stiff, but moving better, Rufus thought. The vet was coming out after lunch.

"Whatever you think, Gabe, and no, I don't think I could use an old, sweaty bull rope, but thanks for asking. . . Keep the gloves though—they're handy. *Ha.* But say, liked that story of yours. . . A real turn you gave us. Uh, Caroline read it too. And I really don't know why you needed me to check . . . you got a handle on all that just fine. Hell, you were raised on a ranch, weren't you?"

"Well, yeah, but, you know, sometimes when you take something for granted you can't describe it well—at least that's been my experience. I appreciate your reading it, boss."

After waving away the sentiment, Rufus asked, "When are you leaving for The Blue Wood?"

"Senga's expecting us around 6:00. Thereabouts, anyway. So I guess I'll head out around 3:00. If that's all right?" He walked around to Sadie's head and gave her the anti-inflammatory.

Rufus nodded, coffee mug at his lips. He set it down.

"Caroline'll be champing at the bit for details about this guy, so pay attention. . . Guess I'll get on back. I'm supposed to be doing these exercises—"

"I know, I know. . . They're a pain in the ass; been there, but they're worth it. Sorry—you won't get an excuse from me."

"Didn't expect to. Well, see you later, son."

"Later, *patron*," he heard Gabe call after him as he slowly made his way back to the house, hitched up the steps, let himself in, poured another cup of coffee and eased down into his chair. *Screw the exercises.*

"Where *are* you?" he called for Caroline. The house was too damn quiet. Gabe quitting bull riding weighed on him for some reason. *Damn. Well, at least he got 'im a buckle from the local one.*

Tradition called for rain on one of the two days of the rodeo, and this year was no exception. Gabe qualified on Saturday, on a white bull named "Blast," to earn Sunday's ride.

He had a cheering section: the Stricklands, Francesca, Senga and several others from the close communities turned out to watch him in the finals, hauling lawn chairs and coolers of beer and soft drinks. Gabe wasn't so much a novelty anymore as one of their own, and Rufus sensed the difference. He wondered if Gabe did. Rufus' occasional public praise of his "good hired man" trumped fear, he'd told his wife a while back.

A public service club provided a barbecue lunch, and slices of homemade pie always sold out first. By afternoon, the sun shone again and the hillside serving as one of the grandstands had filled up.

Overnight rain had left puddles in the arena, and these had been smoothed out. There'd be muddy cowboy shirts and jeans by the end of the day. Part of the spectacle. The

Northwest Ranch Cowboys and Wyoming Rodeo associations sponsored the annual event. More a ranch rodeo, it was good practice and fun, as smaller competitions often were. Gabe had maintained his memberships, as well as his PRCA permit— whose insurance had come in handy back in 2006.

He drew a good bull on Sunday.

"And next up, Gabe Belizaire on 'The Whip'!" called the announcer, who mentioned Gabe's being a "Black cowboy, one of the very few in these parts. . ."

Senga rolled her eyes at Rufus, then yelled loudly, "Go Gabe!" She looked at Rufus and asked, "Will they never learn?"

Caroline sat on his right and Francesca below, on a folded blanket.

Rufus patted Senga's arm, as if he were settling a nervous horse, his eyes riveted on the chute.

When Gabe was ready, he nodded for the chute to open. Rufus held his breath and kept his eye peeled on his friend. Caroline had her left hand gripped tightly on his thigh. She hadn't attended a rodeo since the one in 2006, when Gabe was injured.

The crowd watched respectfully, the pickup men paid attention and the clown watched as the bull burst from the chute, turning and twisting. Gabe rode in a perfect mix of timing and elegance. *Counting to eight takes longer in a tornado*, Rufus decided. The horn sounded and Gabe came off one side as the bull trotted off toward the end of the arena, where he was smartly roped and escorted out. Gabe stood up, tried to brush off some mud and received his smattering of applause— more enthusiastic from his corner—but the spectators recognized a good ride when they saw one, between visits with their neighbors, often the case.

He remained near the chutes after his ride to assist if needed and, when scores were tallied, it was announced he'd won the event.

"I've never seen anything like it, Gabe," Rufus heard Senga say afterward, when Gabe brought the winner's belt buckle over to show them. "I meant the ride, not *this*," she amended, when he held out the buckle. "Have you ever heard of Mithras?"

He and Rufus exchanged glances.

"Well, I expect I have," he answered coolly, looking directly at her. Francesca leaned in to give him a peck on the cheek in congratulation, having to first remove the western straw hat he'd bought her earlier in the day. She wore it proudly, if a little self-consciously.

Gabe, Francesca and Caroline walked toward the barbecue for a plate; they'd bring one back for him. Senga grabbed an apple from a sack and sat down beside him. They watched kids cavorting and were enjoying the atmosphere, when he grunted. She looked at Rufus. His face had gotten too much sun, he knew—and he needed a haircut. He suspected his appearance looked worse for wear today. *Oh, hell with it*—

"You know, Senga," he began, "*you're* the one trying to make Gabe the same as everybody. Well, he *ain't*—to use the vernacular. And he knows he's different. *I* happen to think he's *better*," and, at this, Rufus peered at Senga until she felt compelled to twist toward his fearsome countenance. He nodded once—to place heavier emphasis on his point. He'd meant to elicit understanding from the girl. When he felt he'd achieved this he turned his attention back to the hillside and arena.

For once the girl didn't have a smart-ass comeback, he thought, but he sensed her nearby molecules disintegrating. He loved Senga, but, damn, she sure could be blind sometimes.

After a long moment, he heard her speak to Francesca, who'd returned with a plate for him.

"Um, I'm feeling puny," she said, ". . . I'll talk with you later," and she left, with no other leave-taking. Francesca took her chair.

"What is wrong with Senga?" she asked, as she watched her friend negotiate the hillside.

"She's just had a turn is all—something she ate, probably," Rufus told her before he bit into his hamburger.

"Thanks for this," he said, lifting the hamburger with both hands in her direction. Then, he put it down, adjusted his hat brim against the slanting sunlight, and handed the plate back to Francesca. He stood, to turn his chair away from the sun, chiding himself for failing to ask Senga for more salve against chapping and sunburn. He sat and got settled again. Francesca handed him back his plate.

He sat, lost in thought. *He rides the bull so we don't have to. . . Wonder if she'll figure that out one of these days*—"Well . . . I'm not telling her," he muttered aloud.

"*Scusi?*"

"Oh, nothing, hon. . . Say, you look cute in your hat!"

On that day, he was awarded one of Francesca's bright, flashing smiles.

When Caroline walked into the living room, she saw Rufus asleep in his chair, a hand mirror lying in his lap.

Oh, hell. Not again. Lightly, she stepped toward him, lifted away the mirror, and was half-way back to the bathroom when he stirred. The last time he'd brought it out, he told her about pickin' that bone with Senga, that he'd never blatantly used his injury in such a rotten manner, and he understood—with sickening realization—that he knew exactly how Senga had felt that day.

"*Puny* doesn't begin to describe it," he'd told Caro. Some months ago, Senga had spouted an old Chinese adage, "Everyone you meet is your mirror." He'd seen what Senga had seen: the full force of that night's fire; the smell, the horror and the pain; the wretched, screaming deaths of the horses; his father's utter desolation. But most cruel of all, his son's loss.

"That you?" he muttered to Caro. "Where've you been?"

"Folding clothes downstairs, why? You okay?"

"No. Come here, will you?"

"What's the matter?" She wanted to return the mirror, and stood unable to go forward or back.

"I'm sick of this, of everything," he said, in a tone she recognized with dismay. Never feeling sorry for himself as much as just plain tired.

"Oh, hon—it'll pass. . . It always does, you know." She walked to the dining table and left the mirror there, then went to her husband. He needed a haircut, she noticed. They'd let it go too long. While Rufus didn't usually fret about his appearance, he preferred to look as normal as he could. Tidy hair went a long way. She'd trim it tonight, before his shower.

"Are you hurtin'? Want a couple of those pills the doc prescribed?"

"No, they . . . you know they constipate me, and that's worse, but yeah, how about a couple Tylenols, and would you plug in the heating pad? It's unplugged and I was too lazy to get up again."

Caroline returned with a glass of water and the pills. Rufus took them and swallowed the water. She plugged in the heating pad and turned it to medium.

"I was thinking about Gabe's ride back in June. . . Sure was pretty, wasn't it?" he said. "Says he thinks he's done riding bulls. Maybe that's what's got me down."

"Why's that? He's lucky he ain't been hurt worse, Rufus. Be happy for him."

"Yeah well—"

The telephone rang. He reached for it on the side table and answered. Caroline saw his eyes light up, like just-lit candles, and a crooked smile formed on his face.

"Jake! It's good to hear your voice, boy. It's been a long time."

Caroline's eyes opened wide and she mouthed *Jake?* Pointing to herself, as in *our Jake?* Better than Tylenol then, she thought. Better than Jim Beam and the stronger medication too, and she sat down on the sofa and watched as Rufus looked amazed at whatever his grandson was telling him.

CHAPTER 38~YOUR COMPANY

Sebastian motored through the quiet countryside on the little-used highway to Sara's Spring. He regretted having ignored the beautiful drive in all the years he'd visited his Aunt Karen. A different route had once led him to the giant stone called Devils Tower. *So long ago now.* He remembered how impressed he'd been by its singularity, its massive assertion amidst the softer surrounding landscape.

The road dipped and twisted, pulling his attention back. *This would be marvelous in the roadster,* he thought, as he accelerated through a curve. Aunt's old Volvo handled it well enough. He passed through a narrow canyon of red sandstone and roadside boulders, the creek on his left, bordered by the occasional burst of red, finally recognizing them as Wahoo, a crimson shrub his aunt had particularly liked. Yellow and ochre remained the principal fall colors—gorgeous, despite recent dampening snow and sad evidence of the blizzard's damage. At the summit, through what was known as, "The Bear Lodge," roadside aspens leaned into one another, their black and white bark stark against the snowy background.

Beside him a canvas bag containing several bottles of wine clinked when the weight shifted through the curves. He arranged his muffler among them. Beside the bag lay a tissue-wrapped bouquet of white calla lilies. It had been an eon since he'd presented flowers to a woman other than his daughter. He looked forward to meeting Senga's friends.

Rufus and Caroline—those are their names. They were clearly dear to her. The man had been horribly burned while trying to save his horses. He was only nineteen, Senga had told him Saturday evening. *Then, this Gabe, and his Italian friend, Francesca.* Sebastian had little acquaintance with Blacks, having so few in his country. When he said this to her, Senga laughed, adding there were *precious few* in this pocket of the world as well. She cited a recent public radio interview with an oil-field worker who expressed no interest in settling in the state. She thought he'd blamed the cold, but she had forgotten the reason. Most likely the utter isolation.

They hadn't pursued the subject and he anticipated meeting the man and the woman. Tonight at dinner. *And a writer*—Sebastian recalled; *the isolation might work to his advantage.* That the man rode bulls—or had ridden them (he didn't know if this was still the case)—either meant he was foolhardy, or adventurous. He expected to know which by the end of the evening.

Italians, he found entertaining and warm—not to place them in a box, but there it was. Then, his thoughts turned to Senga, and Sebastian narrowly missed making a tight turn.

"*Now old son,* pay attention," he said aloud in Danish, slowing the car.

Senga's directions led him through Sara's Spring. It was not without its charms; the old-west façade of the café to whit—someone having employed decorative corbels. The presence of a small town here seemed an afterthought, given the mostly unpopulated landscape he'd just crossed. He hadn't been able to put a finger on it. There simply wasn't enough evidence for means of livelihood.

Yes, that was it. . . What do these people do? And then, he spied the saw mill against a hill, and then the school, a grocery store, another café and bar, the post office, a few more businesses—including a medical clinic—and he revised his thinking. But he was still bewildered.

He spotted the road sign for the correct highway and turned north, feeling further sense of abandon, as if he were casting off more and more trappings of civilization with each mile post. *At least there are those.*

Arriving at Senga's mailbox as described, he was glad to see it. It heralded a kind of relief to him, as in: *It's all right now; she sends and receives communiqués from the outside world.* He slowed and turned in, driving the short distance to park near her garage. There was her automobile. . .

After switching off the engine, Sebastian gathered his items and stepped out of the Volvo. He stood for a moment to get his bearings. It appeared as she'd stated. Primitive, but in an *odd* way; a complement to the home of his aunt. Mysterious, but serene. Yes, this was clearly where Senga lived.

Could he think of her as "his" Senga? *So soon? We aren't growing younger, are we,* he thought, as he continued to survey the grounds. "Ah, the orchard." A pity it had to be surrounded by such a fence, out of necessity, he knew. Still, the trees looked somewhat satisfied and smug in their way. *Well-tended.* Two stacks of limbs and twigs lay neatly piled. He noticed a small garden where stood the past season's tomato bushes and bean plants, with squash or pumpkin vines weaving in and out of the standing dry corn stalks, and trailing onto adjacent grass.

Farther along the path, he was abruptly startled by the twinkling appearance of what appeared to be a living art installation: a tall juniper, lit by strings of fairy lights. Sebastian chuckled, captivated.

On the conifer's thick trunk, about two feet from the ground, a face stared out: the pair of eyes, a bulbous nose and smiling mouth greeted him. *And what is this?* He bent to discover the naked Danish troll dolls, popularized in the sixties, their long wooly hair dyed in impossible colors. He heard a door close and turned to see Senga stepping off her small porch, a large grin on her face.

"Sebastian. You're here," she said. "Welcome."

Joy rose in him. He always believed the first ten seconds of reuniting with a loved one brought an interlude of grace, where the joyful quality existed in its most raw and precious state. It was the principal thing. *The only thing.* Of course, he knew this depended on several factors—the state of the relationship, for one.

She stood before him somehow different than he remembered her—in her own surroundings, of course—but did he imagine anguish behind her eyes now? *Has she been weeping?* She was dressed in jeans, a dark green turtleneck sweater, hair brushed into a braid, no make-up; a flush colored her cheeks. Her eyes sparkled, though, in greeting, and he felt welcomed.

"Senga."

He strode to her, beaming, and she exclaimed, "Gifts? You come bearing gifts? But *you* are the gift!"

He held out the bouquet, all the while consuming her with his eyes—her face, her hair, but especially her eyes—infusing her presence into his.

Senga peered into the white tissue, her face reappearing with yellow pollen on the tip of her nose, and, laughing quietly, Sebastian used his thumb to wipe it away, showing her the yellow smudge. She smiled. "Come in, come in. . ."

Inside, she reached for a pitcher on her shelf, filled it with water and carefully arranged the lilies, then, she took the bag from him and lifted out the bottles, placing them on the counter.

"The lilies are magnificent, Sebastian—thank you," she told him, as she set the flowers on the table among the place settings. Then, they turned to one another. Sebastian opened his arms and Senga moved into his embrace and they stood long, and they stood as one.

Gabe and Francesca left The Blue Wood and had just turned toward Sara's Spring, when Francesca spoke. He asked her to repeat it, thinking he'd misheard.

"I said, *Gehb* . . . will you come to Italy and meet my family? And you *heard* me."

He glanced over to see Francesca scrutinizing his expression as unspoken response. He looked at the road, then back to her, his brows knitted.

"Stop staring at me, woman," he said, turning his eyes back to the road. "Uh, what's on your mind, Francesca?" He hadn't seen this coming. . . And yet? He heard from the part of his brain where inklings of the obvious resided. . . "Meet your family, that's what you said?"

"Yes, *Gehb*, you know, as people *do*," she demurred, face toward her window while she waited.

"Does this mean you want to meet my family, too?"

"*Assolutamente, caro mio*," and now she turned and smiled at him.

Just a whisper of a smile; she isn't being coy . . . hesitant—yes—in case I don't feel the same. Oh Lord. . .

"I love you, *Gehb*," was all she said; it was all she knew she needed to say.

Gabe noticed a turn-out, slowed and pulled in. He left the truck running and twisted in his seat to face her. He spent a moment looking, saying nothing. Francesca looked by turns nervous, relieved, finally impatient—which he knew was coming. He smiled his wide, laughing Buddha smile.

"*Imbecille!*" She flung her glove at him and he caught it mid-air with his left hand. Then, she pressed her lips together, but it proved too difficult to hold and she grinned.

"I love you too, Sweet Francesca, but, well . . . you already know that, don't you? When?"

"When what?"

"When do I meet your family?"

"Oh! Ah . . ."

Now he wondered if she might be having second thoughts, her response sounding vague. He shifted in his seat and looked out the window to give her room. *Damn, this is too much like gentling a horse*, he thought, regretting the comparison.

"I go—then you come later," she proposed, the exquisite brows lifted in question.

Gabe studied her, trying not to be obvious. He wanted to determine her state of mind; so much depended on simple frame of mind, he knew. He could write a thousand words one evening and the next have to toss them all, having underestimated the effect of consciousness. It was a crucial ingredient to most anything, he had learned. *Thank God*, he hadn't had to learn the hard way too often. The Sisters of St. Joseph had instilled prevention in that regard; *prophylactically*. He smiled to himself. *Is that even a word?*

"Why do you smile?"

He looked at her, "Well . . . because you love me," and he reached for her face with his hands and kissed her mouth. Gabe felt her response in kind and it seized him in a paradox of desire and satiety. The elusive satisfaction of longing.

He put the truck in gear and drove onto the highway. Out of the corner of his eye, he saw her inhale and shiver once.

"Are you cold? Here, I'll turn up the heat."

"Ah, *Gehb*, no. You don't have to. I am warm . . . down to my toes," and she took another deep breath and let it out. "So . . . hunting ends at the end of November?"

"Yes—why, would that be a good time?"

"Mmmm," Francesca affirmed. "Before the *pazzo-crazy* of Christmas."

"All right. I'll get to work on it. I'll need a passport—and Francesca, ah, why exactly am I meeting your family?" He needed to be certain in this regard.

"Oh, well, you know, you and I are, ah . . . *ah, beh, mamma mia!*"

At this, Gabe screeched the truck to a halt, sliding a short distance on the roadside gravel. Francesca jerked forward in her seat, the belt holding her fast. She shot a look in his direction. It was time, even if not how he'd envisioned it— *Come to think of it, I've never in my life envisioned this,* he thought; *well, some things are done by ear,* he reasoned. *Or, by the seat of one's pants. . .*

"Francesca—*Sweet* Francesca," he began, shifting in his seat again to face her.

"Yes?" (Eyes wide.)

"Please . . . will you be—no, that's not right; will you *do* me the honor of being my wife? Will you marry me, Francesca?"

Her wide eyes blinked once, twice, and her face broke into a wide grin. She removed her seat belt and scooted over, saying, "Yes, yes, I will," and Gabe noticed her statement ended not with an exclamation point, but with a period and he was glad. He didn't trust exclamation points. She laughed, then he laughed and they laughed together.

He said, "Well, now that's resolved, guess we'd better get on down the road to Senga's. Are we telling her? And uh, we can look for a ring. . . I wasn't prepared. Do you mind waiting, Francesca?"

"Oh, *Gehb*, I don't care about a ring, and yes, let's tell Senga and her friend. We will celebrate with them, no?"

"Yes; yes, we will," he said, and he drove on to Senga's in a state of mind entirely foreign to him, feeling at once exhilarated and fearful, but he did spot a plausible analogy: *like riding a bull,* and he sighed. A mere eight seconds seemed short. Francesca was humming the melody of an Italian aria whose title escaped him. But she was from Lucca, of course, where Puccini was born.

Senga stirred the chowder and replaced the lid. She'd forgotten Europeans don't eat much corn, so she asked Sebastian if this was going to be acceptable. "Of course," he'd said in his gentle manner. Everything about the man spelled gentle, Senga thought—and tender. *Painfully tender. Now there's a paradox. . .*

"Here, would you put these on the table?" and she handed him the butter dish and a pot of chokecherry jam. She stared into the refrigerator, wondering what else? She'd made a green salad, but would leave it until needed. Sebastian opened two bottles of wine, a *Vernaccia* and a *Pinot Noir.* They were enjoying a glass of the white with potato chips.

She watched Sebastian as he perused the room, and she waited for questions. It was as though she were viewing her life through new eyes. She'd mentioned the box from her cousin, pointing out the photo album, diary and herbal notes resting on her bookcase, but he didn't press to view them. She also mentioned the letter she had yet to open. And, she told him, that, yes, she'd indeed had a crying spell earlier—after viewing photos of her mother. Sebastian had pulled her to him and held her, his hand cradling the back of her head.

Blessed are they who mourn, came to her, *for they shall be comforted. . .* The man's capacity for rendering comfort knew no bounds, Senga decided, and she allowed the full measure, not pulling away, nor resisting. At the same instant they relaxed and stood apart, both sated.

Senga would wait until Gabe and Francesca arrived before slicing the bread, lest it dry out. Francesca had only visited Senga's home once, and not for long. This soirée was a departure for Senga. *What next? A garden party?*

"This is a wonderful piece," said Sebastian, breaking her reverie. He held up the black pottery bear that she had returned to a shelf.

"Yes, isn't it? It's the perfect size to hold in one's hand. It brings me clarity—when I allow it to."

"Mmmm . . . Senga, I've taken the photograph of the falls from the gallery. Would you like to have it? I brought it with me."

This took her aback, just when she thought her equilibrium was returning. "Ahh . . . I'll think about it. Thank you."

He spied the Ashford spinning wheel just inside her bedroom, and marveled at its simplicity, then he browsed the titles of her books. She knew he'd glean more insight into her person this way, and she didn't disturb him as he scanned her collection. She hadn't enjoyed the same advantage at the house of his aunt, but he had told her they (his aunt, uncle and himself) were similar in their interests and sensibilities.

"I wish I'd known her," she'd told him, meaning his aunt.

She took a moment to visit the bathroom to freshen up. She washed her hands and face again, then, placing a few drops of oil on her finger tips, she massaged these onto her face, paying attention to her neck as well. She questioned her image in the mirror, then returned to Sebastian.

"Would you like to see the orchard? The light's still good, and Gabe and Francesca should arrive any time."

"Yes!" After shrugging into their wraps, he handed her the glass of wine and turned to open the door, but Senga had to show him how to lift the latch. He noted a small painted sign, *Starwallow*, above the door; he would ask about it. They stepped into the gloaming, light enough to see, but only just.

CHAPTER 39~OF FIVE CHAIRS

Y ou just missed the turkeys. . ." Senga and Sebastian stepped into the pale, blue light of early evening, bundled against the chill, glasses of golden wine in hand. The air was still. She explained the birds had flown up into their roosts for the night just before he arrived.

"Pity," he replied. "Next time, then."

She heard the word, pity, not as glib response, but as true sentiment. It spoke in his face.

After circling the orchard, she showed him where Emily's ashes lay buried in a Walker's Shortbread cookie tin—her daughter's favorite brand—at the base of the old juniper, the very one glowing with fairy lights. It stood away from the porch, a long, green extension cord to be plugged in beside the cabin door every evening at dusk, like the votive candle it was.

Sebastian, transfixed by the sight, whispered, "It is extraordinary."

"Apples are susceptible to Cedar Apple Rust," she began, "It's a fungus—causes blight.

Cedars and junipers are related. . . I had to dig out a few seedlings of each species from the orchard area, but this one— well—it must be far enough away, on the other side of the cabin . . . besides, I just couldn't. . . It spoke to me."

She saw him smile, then look at her and say, "I knew it was a fairy tale. . . Did you know it is customary to plant junipers near our doors in Europe? Keeps away the witches, it is believed," and he winked at her, turning again to the tree, from whose rough trunk stared the features of a face.

"A peaceful countenance," he remarked, "but merry." He squatted down to better see. Beneath the lower boughs, next to the trolls, he studied a tiny fairy village. Snow still clung here and there, half-covering diminutive benches, tables, and chairs. An arched bridge, painted turquoise, spanned a miniature river, created by a winding line of narrow mirrors, the river "banks" bordered by cast-off costume jewelry necklaces. Fairy figurines sat or stood, some perched above on limbs, others with snow still atop their heads, and for a split- second Sebastian found himself wondering why they didn't just get out of the weather.

Rising, his blue eyes sparkled as he looked at her, then back to the tree. From dozens of branches hung loosely tied blue ribbons—several in shreds, doubtless picked apart by birds; two, newly placed, judging by their shiny state. The juniper was a study in texture.

"Every ribbon's a prayer, Sebastian."

"I know, my dear," and she knew he did.

The tree's limbs, leaves and twigs were further festooned with decorations of all kind, an impossible array of whimsy and imagination: bird houses, wooden Christmas ornaments (glass bulbs broke in summer hailstorms, Senga had learned), trolls, wind chimes, metal stars, moons and suns; multi-colored yarns woven into spider webs, mermaid figurines; little dolls suspended by elastic thread; and, finally, dozens of tiny mirrors, in shapes of diamonds and circles, glued back-to-back, these also suspended by elastic thread, to bounce and to capture light, whether starlight, moonlight, sunlight, fairy light—to illumine Emily's and her mother's way. A sturdy, child-size wooden chair, painted red, the color chipping off the legs, sat tucked beneath the juniper's protecting lower branches.

"*For Emily-Who-Loved.*" Sebastian read aloud the dark blue inscription on the chair back. He brought his hand to his mouth as he stood in reverence, or incredulity, at the sight, Senga couldn't tell which. *Both?*

Extending her arm, she poured out a few drops of her wine to the ground before the face. "To the guardians of this place," she whispered, "and our Emily." Sebastian followed her example, then lightly clinked her glass. He brushed her forehead with his lips.

Both turned when they heard the truck, its jouncing headlights casting long beams onto the hillside behind cabin and garage. Senga smiled at Sebastian and, quickly reaching up, she pulled his face down to hers with both hands and kissed his mouth; then ignoring his reaction, she walked to the orchard's gate, left open, and waited for her lover to follow.

I have a lover . . . I see my love and my love sees me, she recited silently as she considered Sebastian, gazing at the tree. He turned to join her. He looked back once, still captivated.

I love my love and well he knows; I love the ground whereon he goes; and if my love no more I see, my life would quickly fade away. . . The lyrics of the old mountain tune echoed in memory and Senga perceived the perfect timing: the time of day—betwixt and between; she and Sebastian near Emily once more; and, just arriving, Glorious Life in the persons of Gabe and Francesca. Senga had never met two people who so embodied Life as these, her friends. *Past, present and future, all here at once . . . and so, It Is.*

She latched the gate to the orchard after Sebastian stepped through. Gabe and Francesca were just descending from the truck—Francesca holding a small grocery bag.

"*Ciao, Senga! Come sta?*"

"Uh, *bene?* Okay, English now—how are you? It's good to see you!"

"We're dandy," Gabe answered for both, "Hey, y'all," he added in his southwest Louisiana drawl.

He walked around his truck and stood beside Francesca. *They dressed up,* Senga noted. *Oh my. . .* One of Gabe's "fancy shirts," as she called them, reserved for bull riding, peeked from under his jacket. This one a subtle shade of lavender. He'd shaved and trimmed his large mustache. But the grand smile trumped all.

"Damn, Gabe, don't you look good!" Senga said, then she looked at Francesca, whose face mirrored Gabe's happiness. "And so do you! All right, spill it—right now. What's happened?"

"We will say after you pour us some wine, *cara mia,*" Francesca said, her brown eyes flashing toward Senga and Sebastian's nearly empty glasses.

It wasn't lost on Senga that Francesca had taken pains with her appearance this evening—which would entail little effort. How could the woman look even more stunning? She wore well-fitting black jeans and tall boots and, under her brown Italian leather jacket, Senga spotted the off-white silk blouse Francesca claimed was her favorite, a feature of which was the placement of the first pearl button—directly between her ample breasts. A shade of creamy café-au-lait, their soft, *Rubenesque* shapes pressed together invitingly above the shirt's neckline, this accented by a narrow band of ecru lace. Nature had been generous and Francesca shared the bounty, Senga had decided some time ago, and she appreciated these sometime-appearances of the splendid breasts of Francesca. Her body proclaimed *Woman* in every language, and happily, the woman was completely at ease in her skin. As was Senga.

She glanced furtively at Sebastian, noticing the playful gleam in his eye, and that was that. *We may have an extra guest (or two) for dinner.* Smirking at her provocative thought, she remembered herself:

"Oh! Gabe Belizaire and Francesca Albinoni, may I introduce my friend, Sebastian Hansen? Sebastian—Gabe and the *sweet* Francesca. . . Does *dolce* go before or after nouns?" she asked the Italian.

"'*La Dolce Vita'?*" Francesca said, quirking a brow.

"Ah, yes, before." Anita Ekberg had nothing on *La Dolce Francesca.*

They shook hands, then Senga stepped up to hug her friends. Gabe had worn scent tonight, she noticed.

"I love it here, Senga," said Francesca as they made their way toward the cabin. "*Ahhh, bellissimo!*" she cried, seeing the lighted tree and stopping to inspect it. Gabe spoke quietly to Francesca. Her expression altered as she processed his words and she turned to Senga with a heart-rending look, then she took a breath and regained her prior sensibility. She approached Senga, who waited at the door for them, kissed her on the cheek and looked into her eyes. No words. Senga smiled her gratitude.

Indoors, they hung their jackets on hooks behind the door, and Francesca set the bag on the counter.

"Gelato. It must go in the freezer. I am surprised the market in Sara's Spring has it," she said as she lifted out a box of vanilla wafers and a bar of dark chocolate.

"Oh joy!" Senga said. "*Thank you.* Now, white or red? Sebastian brought both."

Gabe called out, "I'd like a glass of the white first, please," and Francesca agreed.

"How's Sadie?" Senga asked Gabe.

"She's doing well. . . *That* was crazy; do you know I believe she understood her predicament. But poor Caroline . . . it's all good now. It'll take a few weeks—or months—to loosen up those muscles and heal the tendons. Doc came out this afternoon."

Senga pulled up her wing chair to serve as the fourth seat, placing a pillow at her back in order to sit up. Sebastian sat in the captain's chair. The ladder-back in the bedroom was appropriated and another, from the porch. It was close in the cabin, but not crowded. *Intimate,* Senga thought. She recounted Sadie's near catastrophe to Sebastian as they settled around the table, but she wasn't sure he grasped the improbability of the happy outcome.

Cut-up vegetables, pickles, sliced salami, olives and crackers filled a plate in the center of the table, the lilies Sebastian brought having been admired and moved beside the window. A fire burned warmly in the woodstove. Senga had lit several candles, but left the light on over the sink. The room was infused with the varied ingredients of soup: garlic, caramelized onions and *herbes de Provence* chief among them. She liked to cook with a lot of herbs—roots and flowers as well. "Seems obvious," she'd explain.

"Your wine is poured; shall we make a toast before—or after—you say what you are going to say now," Senga looked pointedly at Francesca and Gabe.

"Well," Gabe said, "I think we could toast all night. To lots," he added cryptically, resettling in his chair.

"All right," Senga said, "You first."

Gabe considered Francesca, Sebastian and finally, Senga. "To present company and absent friends, and, to Sadie," he proposed as he raised his glass while looking at each in turn.

"Absolutely," answered Sebastian, and they drank.

Francesca's eyes grew wide after tasting the wine. She smiled.

Senga wondered if Gabe knew who Sebastian was; she couldn't remember having told him all the circumstances of that day. His name wasn't common, and this man's accent *was* Danish. If Gabe suspected Sebastian's identity, he might be inwardly reeling for her—his friend—yet he appeared unconcerned.

"Yes, to absent friends . . . and my Emily. . . Gabe, Francesca—" Senga began and then paused. Sebastian rested his hand on her forearm. He looked on her with compassion. Senga returned his gaze, as though drawing strength. Exhaling, she continued:

"Sebastian and his father were there when my Emily fell."

Gabe let out a short groan. Francesca made a sound.

"They saw it . . . And he—Sebastian—was holding her in his arms when I climbed down. She was gone. His father hiked out to get help." Pause. "Isn't life strange? I haven't seen this man in nineteen years." She spoke calmly with no hint of distress, her eyes on Sebastian's, and the corners of her mouth quirked slightly in an intimation of a smile; then, she lowered her head.

"*Ai, cara mia. . .*"

Senga covered Sebastian's hand with her other one. He said quietly, "We are fortunate to have found one another again." A simple statement, demanding no response, and, more important, one delivering moon and stars into the palm of her hand.

"Well." Gabe leaned back in his chair, his expression strangely blank, thought Senga. He leaned forward for a cracker and a piece of salami, held these up to Francesca, who took them from him, then, making one for himself, he popped it in his mouth and sat back again, accomplishing all while holding Senga's gaze.

What is he doing? She wondered. *He's trying to read me. He needs to know I'm all right.* Sebastian moved in his chair.

"Senga." Gabe spoke only her name. No emotion, save intent in his eye.

She smiled, rose from her chair and walked behind him and, bending over, she crossed her wrists over his chest. Then, into his ear she whispered, "It's all good, Gabe—really—I love him." Gabe raised his hand and she saw the yellow bruising on

291

his dark knuckles and the healing abrasions. He grasped her forearm for a moment and released her. She brought her cheek to his, squeezed him and turned to the pan on the stove to stir the chowder, glad for the mundane task.

To the stillness Francesca asked brightly, "More wine anyone? And, this is *very* good, Sebastian. Italian! A *Vernaccia*—where did you find it?" She proceeded to pour out the remainder of the bottle into Gabe's and her glasses.

Sebastian visibly relaxed. "I'm glad you like it, Francesca. . . My aunt and uncle collected wines, and I confess to looting their reserves. There it is. And, Gabe—"

"Hey, it's cool—but Senga's an *amie*; she's *chère* to me too, man—just so you know that," and Senga recognized her friend's protecting spirit, perhaps in warning, and she loved him for it.

"Yes. I see," said Sebastian. "This is evident, Gabe, and I am glad . . . no worries there."

After another awkward moment: "Senga tells me you write. Are you *raconteur* or do you prefer non-fiction?"

"*Raconteur*," he said, chuckling, and Senga heard ease return in his voice, "I haven't heard that word since I left Louisiana. Yes, I like to tell stories." He turned in his chair to Senga at the stove, "Uh, I brought you the latest one, Senga. Don't let me forget—it's in the truck."

"Oh! Thank you, but, ah . . . I don't think this is what you were going to tell me—us—after we plied you with wine . . . and you've now been plied," she said with a grin.

Gabe turned to Francesca, leaned over and touched her head with his. Senga saw her Papa and Grannie making the same gesture. *Ah, at the pageant. . .*

Francesca lifted her chin to Gabe, indicating his story to tell.

"I've asked Francesca to marry me. She said 'yes'—"

"*Ohhh!*" interjected Senga, grounding the charge in the room.

"And, I'm going to Italy to meet her family—" A pregnant pause.

Francesca sat quietly, her eyes on Gabe speaking volumes.

"And—" Senga prompted him.

"Well, and . . . well, hell, Senga, guess we'll see. . ."

Senga detected a sour note. Enthusiasm tempered by doubt, or, experience.

Oh no, you don't, Gabe Belizaire. "They're going to love you, Gabe," she said, guessing his concern. She held his eyes longer than necessary to confirm his understanding of this simple fact. She didn't drop her gaze until he had.

"Congratulations. I am *so* happy for you both," she said.

Francesca's mood indicated *something* was imminent and she laughed out loud like a school girl, throwing off any doubts as to what she believed—with all her heart—would happen. Sebastian struck his glass lightly with his fork (*ting!*) and raised his glass once again:

"To Gabe and Francesca . . . for a safe journey, *clear* seeing and all happiness."

Perfect, Sebastian, thought Senga, while they clinked glasses and took sips. Gabe and Francesca radiated happiness.

Toasts are purely prayers, Senga realized, *christening wishes from good fairies.* . . Then Gabe reached for the smooth hand of Francesca with both of his; the contrasting shades, a chiaroscuro of shape and gesture. Raising her hand to his lips, he closed his eyes and kissed it with devotion, and when he reopened his eyes, Francesca leaned over and kissed his mouth.

"*Ti amo, cuore mio,*" she said just above a whisper. I love you, my heart.

"Um, I need some air," Senga said as she rose. "Anyone as warm as I am?" And she stepped to the door, pulled up the latch, and placed a piece of kindling between the door and the jam. She stood in the draft, allowing its current on her face and neck. *Damn nuisance, hot flashes. So that's what these are. . .*

Francesca looked up at her and smiled knowingly. *Just you wait,* Senga thought, smiling back—like a catbird.

Senga brought the homemade loaf of artisanal bread to the table on a cutting board with a knife, and asked Sebastian to slice it while she handed out bowls. She replaced the dish of appetizers with the pan of soup, placing the ladle handle on the edge, and presented an assortment of cheeses: Camembert, Gouda and a Jarlsberg—the Camembert nearly oozing.

Sebastian opened a second bottle of Pinot Noir and, rising from his seat, he refilled their glasses and returned to his chair.

"Senga, this looks delicious," he said.

"What is this soup? It is pretty," Francesca said.

"Um, it's called chowder . . . mostly corn and cream, and potatoes, to help thicken it. Hope you like it. I make it often—it's hearty . . . Gabe, would you ask a blessing?"

"Why sure," he said, "but first, I forgot to ask earlier—what's that red cloth on the tree across the ravine? Too dark to see it now."

"Oh . . . It's just something I wanted to mark—a measurement, actually," she dissembled and, glancing at Sebastian, she noted his scrutiny and lowered her eyes.

"Hunh," said Gabe, then he crossed himself. He expressed gratitude for the evening, for "these friends," and blessed the meal. They ate with good appetite, with laughter and noises of appreciation. By turns they regaled one another with anecdotes.

Gabe asked Sebastian what he did and Senga exclaimed, "Makes wonderful pictures!"

Sebastian smiled at her and explained he had retired from an ad agency in Denmark after thirty years. For the last three years, he'd explored the more creative, hence, rewarding side of photography—"Personally, if not monetarily," he joked. But Senga knew he earned "well enough," as he'd told her.

Gabe mentioned bull riding and his post at the university, now preferring the rhythm of writing and ranch work. Adding it proved less painful. Francesca and Senga recognized the masculine dynamic, necessary when two men were becoming acquainted, and they listened respectfully, after Senga's initial exclamation.

Backgrounds established, Francesca told Senga and Gabe that the Russian woman and her child were still at the hospital, and that Jim had visited them on Mary's request.

"Mary, she tells *Jeem* to go see them because she knows *he* wants to. She is a wise lady, Mary," Francesca said. "I like this woman."

Jim had reported that Larissa and Tanya were doing well, but they weren't sure when they'd move to the shelter. "Maybe Wednesday," Francesca said. Larissa's arm was in a cast and her face less—and here Francesca broke off. Gabe outlined the circumstances to Sebastian, but Senga's experience at the grocery store—he left to her discretion. Rufus thought there was enough evidence for an arrest warrant, but the Berry place people had apparently taken off. Someone had left behind a truck, so they might return.

"They *skee-daddled!*" said Francesca, and all laughed.

After serving the green salad, followed by cheese and more bread, Senga asked, "Would anyone like coffee? Or, do we just want to continue drinking this great wine? And, would you like to wait a bit for dessert?"

"I could wait, but that was so good, *chère*," said Gabe, and the others made similar sounds.

"I'll make coffee anyway and keep it warm on the stove," said Senga, after which she cleared the table. Francesca offered to help, but Senga put up her palm, saying, "No, thank you; just sit and shine," and she took the French press from the high shelf, filled the electric kettle with water and plugged it in. As she was doing so, her eye fell on the photo album, with waiting letter on top. She stepped over and drew out the album, placing the letter aside, then waited for a pause in conversation.

"In the mail today I received some things that've been moldering in the house where I grew up, in North Carolina. Photographs; my, ahem, *diary*, um, *childhood*, which will make for fascinating reading, I'm sure; my herbal notes and drawings . . . but there's a wonderful photo of my Italian grandmother, Francesca; would you like to see it?" And Senga turned the pages to the photo of Maria Teresa, placing it on the table before Francesca and Gabe.

"This woman *here?* She is your *nonna*, Senga?" Francesca's finger touched the photograph. Her voice had risen an octave.

"Yes, she is. But I, um, take after my grandfather. . ."

"What . . . is her name? No—let me ask you, Senga—is her name Maria Teresa Barone?"

CHAPTER 40
~THERE BE WOLVES

I need some air—I've had enough of this shit," Jacob Brady growled to no one in particular. "Come on, Dale," and he jerked his head toward the door of the mom-and-pop motel in Belle Fourche, South Dakota, where the four of them, and Duke and Daisy, had stayed in one room for the past two nights. Stir crazy referred to more than jail time, Dale knew.

Jacob gathered his wallet and keys from the bedside table. He gave himself a once-over in the mirror, grunted and Dale did the same. The younger man emulated nearly every tick and gesture. This drove Jacob to distraction and Dale knew it, but he couldn't help himself. He had other compulsive habits. Shooting his mouth off, for one.

When he told George and Jacob about the crazy woman in the store on Thursday, it was they who'd talked him off the proverbial ledge.

"I'm gonna blow up her fucking house, and then fuck her," he'd ranted. "And I don't give a shit if she *is* the one who knows survival medicine and all. . . She pulled a *fucking knife* on me!"

He swore compulsively, as well.

"You wouldn't get to if she was dead from the explosion," had been Jacob's bored observation. Dale continued to rant for an hour. Forgetting what had once landed him in prison: assault and battery with a rather large knife.

When the cops pulled up on the mountain, George had to practically sit on Dale to tell him how it was going to be. They couldn't afford any second looks, *and did he hear what he was saying to him?* Dale knew George was pissed when he called him a "little cock-sucker." But then, George called him that a lot, so what else was new?

In the motel room, George Canton was sitting up against the grungy headboard, eyes glazed-over, as he watched a program on television about catching crabs in Alaska. He was either ignoring Jacob or hadn't heard him. Hard to tell which, Dale thought. The old man was a relative of Jacob's, but how was lost to once-removed confusion.

Joey, the image of dejection, lay on the second bed thumbing through a hunting magazine. He'd taken his first deer last year and had looked forward to hunting again, but it looked like that wasn't going to happen now. Dale hated being around disappointment. He'd already lived that hell once. Dejection corroded your insides, he knew. Left people with an angry hole.

He checked for his wallet and they grabbed their coats. Then, without saying goodbye or when they'd return, Jacob opened the door and they stepped out, pulling the door shut. Then, Jacob opened the door again with the key and told George and Joey they'd bring back a pizza or something.

"Beer too," George piped up.

"A Coke?" Joey asked.

Jacob grunted as he shut the door again and turned toward the car.

"Cops might be looking out for us," Dale said as he got in the car.

"Don't worry about it."

Jacob drove across the river to the end of town, and turned toward Montana. He'd come this way last year, he told Dale, and knew of a road house where they could relax for an hour or two and be out of that box of a motel room.

They didn't talk as they drove into the sunset, a narrow band of pastels on the western horizon. Pretty much all it was out here, Dale reflected—sky and snow. *And sagebrush . . . a few antelope, probably.* He'd always liked antelope. Seemed African, somehow. They looked strange, like things do in Africa. He noticed Jacob was driving faster than usual. But then, there wasn't a whole lot of traffic on this road. . . He studied Jacob through half-closed eyes slanted in the man's direction. The man had been ruggedly handsome once, but meanness had made inroads. It was written all over his face, Dale decided. Then he corrected himself. Not meanness, as much as a, "get-'er-done," mentality. A hardness. *Yeah*. Personal hygiene aside, something none of them paid much attention to, Dale admired the man's physique, never mind what he did with it. He turned his eyes back to the coming darkness.

They passed through Colony, Wyoming, where the bentonite mine lights came into view, its long berms of blue-gray clay, even snow-covered, like split-open whales *or something*, he thought. He was glad to be out of that stinkin'motel room though, glad Jacob had asked him. That proved something, didn't it?

Jacob spoke, but Dale didn't hear.

"What?"

"I *said*—I wonder what happened to Larissa and the girl." Jacob's face was screwed up with speculation.

"Oh."

"What do you mean—'Oh?' Don't you ever *think* about anything at all? Ain't you the least bit curious? *Jesus*, Dale. They could've been carried off by some bear. . . Or, ain't there supposed to be wolves out this way now . . . migrating from freakin' Yellowstone? And if someone *did* find them, which is possible, that guy on the tractor, I bet . . . hell, I don't know . . . but if she's talked, or the guy plowed the road and took a look around, then they're looking for us. No doubt."

Dale yawned. No, he wasn't interested. In fact, he was glad the woman and kid were gone. Jacob had been frenzied by Friday noon and had him and Joey nearly gutting the trailer, by throwing out contents and supplies to be burned. That fire—how it'd stunk! he remembered. He was to keep feeding it crap they were hauling over and stir it around with a shovel, but he'd had to wrap an old flannel shirt around his face to do it. And, even with the fire, it was damn cold. His feet about froze. At least George and Jacob had waited out the blizzard and he was glad for that.

Jacob turned toward him and snorted.

"You're a piece of work, you know that, Dale?"

"Yeah, been told that some. . ." His stomach growled. "Man, I could eat."

"It's coming up," Jacob said, and they soon turned into a parking lot, large enough for tractor trailers. It was dark now. Dale stretched when he stood. *Not much here*, he thought: a gas station and convenience store, another bar, a post office. He glanced at the sky to the few stars coming out. A waxing moon had risen, just on the southwest horizon. *A quarter-moon in a ten-cent town*, went the song.

"Ha," he said, and then, "Hunh," kicking away a chunk of melting ice behind a wheel.

Jacob went ahead of him, toward the door. Dale rushed to catch up. *Gathering wool* came to mind. He hadn't thought of the phrase in years. His grandpa used to say that about him. *Well, whatever. . .*

Inside, Dale saw Jacob nod to the bartender who nodded back, and Dale wondered if they knew one another.

"I've got to hit the john—go order us beers and I'll be right out," Jacob told him, and Dale wandered into the room.

It was spacious, with deer mounts and beer advertisements hanging on the walls. Two pin-ball machines sat side-by-side and a video shooting game, opposite. A television tuned to CNN, with sound turned off, hung high from the dark wood paneling to the right of a long, polished vintage bar. This was made in the Old West style, with carved shelving and turned posts, of a reddish wood; maybe cherry, Dale guessed. A mirror ran low, across the back, placed so people on stools could see who was coming up behind them without having to turn round. He congratulated himself on figuring that out, or maybe he'd been told once; *hell*, he couldn't remember. . .

He sat down on a stool, having his choice of any. An older couple sat at one of the tables nearby. A slow Monday night. The bartender, who'd seen some miles, hitched over to him, towel in hand, drying a glass.

"What can I getcha?"

"Two Coors—my buddy will be right out.

The bartender looked at him, trying to decide if he was old enough.

"I'll need to see some I.D., son," the man said. Dale was annoyed, but he retrieved his wallet and fished out his driver's license. He was twenty-eight, but looked sixteen some days and forty-eight on others.

The bartender grunted, then nodded, and turned to get the beers.

Jacob arrived and sat down.

"You serve food?" he asked.

Without a word, the barkeep reached under the bar and brought out two menus, printed on a piece of paper and placed them in front of his newest customers.

"Says they have pizza, Jacob—" said Dale.

"We'll order one before we leave . . . it might stay warm enough. I'll have a cheeseburger and fries. What do you want, Dale?"

"Uh, the same, with everything on it."

The barkeep said, "Okay, coming up," and, after taking down the order, he turned and went through a door at the end of the bar.

Jacob sat quietly nursing his beer, not in the mood to talk, Dale guessed, so he did the same. He looked in the mirror at the two of them sitting there like best buddies, like they were livin' large and did this thing every night, going to a bar together, shootin' the bull; only they weren't shooting any bull tonight. He made a face in the mirror for the hell of it. Jacob swung his head around and gave him a look that warned, "Stop, or else." Dale removed his coat and decided to sit on it rather than hang it up. He'd gotten in the habit of, 'exhibiting his ink,' as he called it, and had worn his sleeveless, collarless shirt.

The barkeep returned with a tray of salt and pepper shakers. He set this on the bar.

Dale saw the man's thick, gray eyebrows knit together in seeming concentration as he busily filled the shakers, two places down from him and Jacob. He'd glance over every few moments, to where Dale sat hunched over his bare arms, beer in hand.

He's checking out my tats, and Dale sensed the familiar surge of adrenaline that accompanied this knowledge. It was a game with him. The barkeep gave him the slightest upturned corner of his mouth and Dale thought, *Bingo; got 'im.* Then, he swiveled on his seat to face the couple at the table. A rancher taking his wife out to supper, he decided.

The rancher was wearing his cowboy hat. The woman looked tired. Her backside spilled over the chair in every direction as she leaned over her plate, her left hand poised in front of it, guarding the last of her food like it was her last meal. *Wouldn't want to try to clear her table*, he thought; *she'd bite off my hand*, and he smirked. He wheeled back around and took a long swallow of beer. After several moments of this sitting and drinking, Dale slid off his stool and turned in the direction of the restroom. When he returned, the hamburgers were waiting, steam rising off the bun and fries and he almost drooled. Jacob had ordered another round. Dale sat down and dug in.

After several minutes, the rancher stepped up to the cash register at the end of the bar. Dale watched (in the mirror) as the man then helped his wife up and out of the chair; she seemed wobbly, he thought, and he watched the woman smile at the man, who faintly returned it. The man glanced at the table, sighed, took some bills out of his wallet and left a tip. Dale saw them move toward their coats and the exit and then they were gone. He thought it'd been like watching a movie, seeing it all in the mirror like that. The woman reminded him of his mom.

When the barkeep stepped into the kitchen, Dale quickly sidled over to the table, picked up four of the five dollars in tip, stuffed these into his pocket and was spinning on his stool just as the barkeep reappeared through the door.

CHAPTER 41~THAT GOOD

"Sebastian?" Senga looked around and frowned, "Ohhh, not again. . . Sebastian? There you are," she said to his cup of water. She took a sip. "Oh my . . . must be the wine. I felt woozy . . . sorry; what were you saying, Francesca?" And she saw Sebastian shake his head slightly in Francesca's direction.

"No-no . . . what did you ask me? Something about my *Nonna* . . . Tell me."

"Senga, are you all right?" asked Gabe.

She sat up and shook her head in her fashion, then nodded; *and what was the fuss?*

Francesca spoke quietly in a low, measured tone, reaching for Senga's hand, to ground her. "I believe I know your grandmother, *cara*, in Italy—"

Senga's eyes narrowed as she tried to digest the statement.

"Yes, this is . . . *pazzo*—crazy . . . I know. Maria Teresa Barone lives down the street from me—from the home of my parents in Lucca. This photograph is old, *sì*, but I am not mistaken. Maria Teresa has, how you say, a *way* about her."

"Yes," Senga croaked, "Lucca. But I thought *Nonna* must have, um, passed away by now; we haven't been in touch. You are sure, Francesca? Maria Teresa Barone Munro? She could have dropped Munro. . ." She started to rise to turn off the heat under the whistling kettle.

"I've got it, *chère*; just sit," Gabe instructed.

"The coffee—it's above the sink on the shelf," she reminded him.

"How long have you known Maria Teresa?" Sebastian asked Francesca as he inspected the photograph, having removed it from the sleeve to inspect the back. Her name and a date: *August 15, Feast of the Assumption, 1975; Lucca, Italy*—all in Italian.

"Oh, she and Mamma are friends a long time. I grew up with Maria Teresa. She is like a *nonna* to me—" She broke off her sentence, then said, "but this is so *crazy*, no?" A pause. "Senga . . . you must come to Italy with Gabe when he comes, yes? It is *perfect*. Maria Teresa will be so happy to see you! She is old-old now. Wears dark all the time, like a little *strega; a weetch,* do you know? But her skin, ah, a miracle; always smooth . . . so—will you come?"

"Olive oil," Senga interjected, ignoring the question. She took another breath, gave Francesca's hand a squeeze, let it go and stood. She needed Sebastian. Reaching for his hand, she looked him in the eye; he stood. *Loomed*, she thought, and she led him to her bedroom. Francesca whispered something to Gabe, and Senga called from the bedroom, "I just need a good ole hug—so y'all can relax now."

Gabe choked and Francesca giggled then began to describe Maria Teresa to Gabe. *Background noise.*

In the tiny bedroom, Sebastian enfolded Senga in his arms, moving his hand up and down her back. She clung to him. "I'm all right . . . it's just been a day is all—a week, actually," she said. "I'm glad you're here, Sebastian. So glad."

He cupped her face and kissed her mouth tenderly and with such intent that Senga felt the life force rise from the earth, through the floor into her toes, and continue to rise until she gasped. Reflecting for a moment afterwards, she chortled.

"That bad?" he asked, repeating her question from. . . *Was that only yesterday?*

"No, that good," and she reached up and kissed him back, the absolute power and peace of it, a complete mystery to her. One she would allow.

When they returned to the table, Gabe poured their coffee. He'd set out Caroline's thick cream and sugar. Francesca was serving the gelato and had placed cookies and pieces of dark chocolate on a plate.

Gabe spoke after Senga and Sebastian were settled. "Well, now . . . this is a rare evening. I am never surprised by the lengths which God—or however you wish to name the ineffable—goes to grab our attention, but *this*, well, I am going to have to think about this . . . and I want to say that I am so proud to have witnessed this wonder . . . and you, Sebastian—I am most happy to have met you."

"Italy?" Francesca reminded him.

"Senga," Gabe addressed her. "Come with me. I'm planning to go after hunting's over, sometime in early December. Think on it, will you?" he said, adding, "It takes about this long to get passports, and Sebastian, I mean you too, to come—"

Sebastian smiled after swallowing a spoonful of gelato. He made a sound of pleasure.

"I would love to accompany you on this, ah, *odyssey*, Gabe—and Senga—but circumstances call me away. I have not yet told you, my dear," he looked at her, "I return to Denmark in two weeks to complete some business, but I plan to come back to my aunt's . . . well, it is difficult calling it mine . . . You see, my daughter, son-in-law and granddaughter are coming to pass the holidays."

Everyone cried "*Ohhh*," in unison.

"How wonderful for you, Sebastian," said Francesca.

Senga looked on him and grinned, sensing her heart's boundaries and capacities enlarging with each loved-one's mention.

They ate their ice cream and sipped their coffee pensively, each lost in thought, then Gabe said, "Francesca and I are hankering to do a little dancing this evening. . . It's no *Fais do-do,* but there's a decent jukebox at Earl's, if y'all want to join us. We thought we'd go for a bit anyhow."

"Yes, *come* with us. . ." Francesca pleaded, ". . . and we can discuss your trip to Italy with Gabe, yes?"

Senga sighed, and looking at Sebastian said, "I think we're in for the night, ya'll, but thanks for asking. I asked Muriel for the morning off, so I don't have to get up too early, but y'all go—enjoy yourselves. . . And congratulations again. I am really happy for you."

"Thank you, *chère.* It was just wonderful, all of it," Gabe said upon rising. "I'll get that magazine—" And turning to Sebastian with his hand extended, Gabe repeated, "It's good to meet you, Sebastian."

"You as well, Gabe, and please let me know if I can help in any way with the arrangements, or logistics, for your trip. Please?"

Francesca wrapped her rose-colored scarf around her neck and put on her jacket after handing Gabe his. She kissed Senga on both cheeks then stood on tiptoe to reach Sebastian's face. He bent down. *"Un piacere incontrarti*, Sebastian," she said, and he told her it was his pleasure. They bade goodbyes on the porch of the cabin, the light of the juniper casting shadows behind them. Gabe soon returned and handed Senga the magazine. He grinned, and she opened wide her mouth, shut it, then whooped. She extended her arms and gave him another hug.

"I am in awe," she said, releasing him. Then, "Okay—go! Be careful, and let the good times roll for us too." *Us* echoed in her mind.

I am an "us."

They watched the truck drive away and turn north toward Alzada. Then, Senga bent down to unplug the fairy lights. She blew a kiss to the tree and they went back inside.

"Senga, what does the red cloth on the tree signify?"

CHAPTER 42~CURSED

Dale was almost finished with his excellent hamburger when he heard the door open and close. He wanted to twirl around on his stool, but he made himself watch from the mirror, as another couple entered the diner. *Well, I'll be—,* he thought, and he elbowed Jacob in the ribs. His idol jerked his head over to him, annoyed once again, and Dale lifted his chin in the direction of the mirror. Jacob complied and saw a black man come in with a woman—who was not black. But she was something else, Dale thought, and he searched for the word . . . *Uh, yeah, 'bodacious'; that's it.*

Jacob reached for Dale's forearm and put his hand over it for a quick second, and Dale said, "Yeah, yeah. . ." The barkeep sidled two paces over and asked if they needed anything else. He'd put some music on the jukebox. *Oldies,* Dale noted.

"No—yeah—we need a—hell, what kind of pizza do you think they want, Dale?"

"Oh, George—he likes about anything. . . Joey too, for that matter. Make it a pepperoni and sausage, with lots of cheese," Dale told the man, who was examining his neck tattoos now, Dale saw. The 88 and the zigzags. The barkeep smirked. Dale smiled back.

"All right; all on one ticket then?" the man asked.

"Yeah, and we'll need a six-pack of Coke and one of Coors," Jacob said, ". . . and another round here."

"Okay," said the barkeep, writing it down. "Be with you in a second," he called to the folks who'd just come in.

"Uh, you really gonna serve *that?*" Dale piped up, throwing his thumb behind him.

"*Dale, shut the fuck up,*" Jacob rasped.

The barkeep looked at Dale, smirked again and said, "Gotta make a livin', man," and turned away. Dale thought the guy had a limp. *Ha, a wimp with a limp,* he rhymed in his head.

He consulted the mirror. The man was familiar. . . *Shit! It's the same one was in the store,* and he turned to Jacob and repeated this revelation in a low voice. Jacob stared into the mirror then turned on his stool to get a better look.

"*Damn,*" he said under his breath.

Dale heard him and wondered if he meant the woman or the situation. Jacob turned back around and took a swig.

"*That ain't right, Jacob. It just ain't ri—*" he repeated in a hushed tone, making it all the more obvious he realized, so he swallowed the last syllable.

"Set tight, Dale, and shut up," Jacob said now through gritted teeth as he continued to view the newcomers in the mirror. They'd taken a table near the entrance. The black guy sat facing them, the woman to his right. He was helping her with her jacket.

Dale hadn't seen a woman like that in, well, he'd *never* seen a woman like that, he realized, *except in the magazines, or on calendars,* he decided. She was the woman of his dreams, curvy in all the right places, and spilling out of her top like she was— *Oh god,* he was *feeling the feeling* again. His foot started tapping wildly on the foot rail, his calf bouncing up and down to some discordant music only Dale could hear.

"*Would you relax?*" Jacob whispered. "We've got to get out of here with *no* trouble, do you understand that?"

"Mmph, well. . ."

"*Dale!* Get a *grip,*" Jacob spat, and went back to eating his last few fries.

Earl, owner and operator of this little piece of heaven since 1986, took the pizza order to his partner of thirty-some years, Mae, and told her it was for a *live* one at the bar, their code for possible trouble, and that Gabe Belizaire and his girlfriend had just come in. Mae asked him if everything was all right, and Earl told her he hoped so—but the quicker she could make the pizza the better. Earl wouldn't have stayed in business as long as he had if he hadn't a nose for trouble. It's what persuaded him to buy the place all those years ago when he'd wanted to find a way to leave trouble behind. At last.

An old biker now—by virtue of his still riding a Harley into his sixties—he'd survived an accident when he was thirty-one, but had lost his left leg below the knee. A prosthetic made it possible to ride, but not as far, nor as often. They could make it in this slow corner of Montana, him and his old lady, on what they made during the summer, particularly due to income earned the weeks prior, during, and following the Sturgis motorcycle rally in August, when the stretch of highway was heavily traveled. Their place was a popular watering hole.

He and Mae preferred the quieter months, like now. Earl was sixty-five and Mae fifty-five. They'd had enough excitement for a life-time. Just wanted to coast now.

Earl moseyed to the back of the room where Gabe and the woman were seated. Gabe had told him Thursday when he was in with Rufus Strickland that he wanted to bring a friend in sometime, and so here she was. *My god . . . a goddess*, he thought, but he didn't smile as he approached the table. That would've been irreverent, but he had another reason. Gabe narrowed his eyes, pursed his lips under his mustache, and started to say something, but Earl cleared his throat, and with a slight jerk of his head to the side he indicated his intent. Gabe remained silent.

"What can I get you folks?" he asked, then he laid down copies of the menu with a sticky note attached to Gabe's that read, *White supremacist bullshit at bar, just so you know*, and he'd drawn a happy face under it. Gabe crumpled the note then grunted.

"Uh, we'll each have a glass of that red wine and an order of your sweet-potato fries. Please," he told the man then smiled. And then he introduced Francesca.

"Earl, I'd like you to meet my sweet Francesca; Francesca, this is Earl . . . and man, she knows *all* about you," and he looked at his friend as if to say "Your move."

Francesca smiled and held out her hand. Earl squeezed it and said, "Happy to meet you; it's a real pleasure," he added seriously, wondering what the hell was going to happen now. *So this is how he wants to play it. All right*, he thought, adding aloud, "I'll be right back with your wine."

Returning to the kitchen, he gave the order to Mae.

"Gabe's girlfriend is named 'Francesca.' A beauty. And they aren't going to make it easy on me, as in leave. . . Can't say I blame him. Okay, I'll go keep an eye on these guys." Mae gave him one of her looks, then grabbed a bag of frozen sweet potato fries from the freezer.

When Earl returned to the bar, the two men were still nursing their beers. *It's really bothering him, the poor dumb kid,* he thought. The kid looked nervous, as if he might implode.

"The pizza'll be up in a couple minutes," he casually told them. They'd seen Gabe being friendly with him. This might get sticky. He wished Gabe had played it differently, but he understood.

He said he'd keep an eye on them and didn't think they were carrying. *Hard to tell.*

Earl lifted a bottle of Woodbridge Pinot Noir to the bar and opened it handily. He took down two wine glasses from the rack and poured them three-quarters full, then carried them out to Gabe and Francesca. The song on the jukebox ended, making the room too quiet.

"We're celebrating tonight," Gabe said, leaving off his friend's name. "I'll need some bills for the jukebox," and he handed Earl a five-dollar bill to change.

"That machine takes fives," Earl said, grinning. "Congratulations, then." He didn't know whether to engage them further, or wait until the two at the bar left. *Oh, what the hell. . .* "Okay, I'll bite. What're we celebrating?"

Francesca spoke. "Gabe has a story in an important magazine, *and. . .*" he heard her pause for effect, ". . . we are engaged. He will travel all the way to Italy to meet my family, after hunting is over."

Earl heard the obvious pride in her voice, and caught the look on their faces as she turned to Gabe. A moment of sheer goodness and grace washed over him. He began, "That's *just gr—*" when out of the corner of his eye he glimpsed the form of the kid at the bar swivel around and pull back his arm to throw something. The other guy's hand shot up and grabbed the beer can.

Then the kid shouted, "*We must secure the existence of our people and a future for white children!*" and he started to come off his chair as if he'd been wound to a string and released.

The older man grabbed his arm and yelled, "Dale! Knock it off! I mean it, quit! Go get in the car and wait for me—" The man pressed keys into Dale's hand and, pulling him back, he grabbed up the coat and shoved it into the kid's arms. The door to the kitchen swung open and banged against the wall.

"What's going on out here?" Mae came out with a boxed pizza. She looked over at Earl, her eyes wide. She set the pizza down in front of the customers at the bar and squinted down on them. The older one stared back, then turned to the one named Dale who was trying to pull on his coat, the sleeve of which had been pulled inside-out. It was humorous.

"You wanted regular Coke?" Mae asked the older guy, her eyes still trained on Dale who now resembled a crazed cartoon character.

"Uh, yeah, that's fine," he said, distracted, and Mae walked over to the cooler and pulled out a six-pack. Earl returned to the bar. He shot a look over his shoulder to Gabe, who nodded.

From behind the bar Earl cleared Dale's plate and beer can, which the older guy had set back down, half full. Earl was pouring out the rest when Dale said, "Hey! I wasn't finished with that!"

"Yeah, you were," Earl said, and he proceeded to scrape the other plate and put it in a tub of soapy water. *The kid is actually vibrating*, Earl thought, and he told the older man that he hoped he was done.

"I'm just waiting for the six-packs of beer and Coke, and to pay the bill . . ." he said, then to Dale, "Go on, *git!*"

"Oh, right," said Earl.

The kid named Dale walked toward the door but had to pass by Gabe and Francesca. Earl slowly moved to the cash register after handing Jacob the check, and Mae came out with the beer and placed it and the Coke in a paper sack. She waved at Gabe, who raised his hand. It then appeared to Earl, almost in slow motion, that the kid simply burst a gasket and was bleeding a torrent of *nasty* verbal abuse all over Francesca. Gabe had just risen from his seat and was pulling a right fist when Francesca picked up her nearly full glass and tossed the red wine into the increasingly apoplectic face of Dale. Gabe lowered his arm but stood by. The kid, sputtering and stupefied, stepped back, stumbling, and brought his coat sleeve to his eyes. He looked at Francesca with fury, and a strangled noise began in the back of his throat. He was winding up again.

Earl saw Francesca reach now for Gabe's glass and raise it in warning, holding the kids' eyes with hers. This time she'd hurl the glass as well, those eyes warned. Gabe stepped back, ready if needed. Clearly, he wasn't. And then Francesca proceeded to return Dale's rant, only in Italian, and with interest. It seemed to frighten the kid, Earl saw with amusement. Dale's eyes grew wide and he backed up toward the exit as if he'd been cursed. Earl knew the kid had already been cursed with racism and hatefulness. He picked up Francesca's *Disgraziato*, Disgrace, it sounded like, but *oh*, it was a classic tongue-lashing, a real *beaut*, and Earl counted it privilege to have witnessed it.

Glancing from Gabe to Francesca and back to Gabe, Dale started to say something, but Mae interrupted with a loud "Hey!" and when they turned, she was standing behind the bar holding up a twelve-gauge and gesturing with the barrel the direction of the door. Earl calmly handed back change to Dale's buddy at the bar and said, "Enjoy your pizza, but don't come back." Then, stepping back and crossing his arms, he waited for the man to go.

The guy laid down two twenties, picked up the bag and box of pizza, walked by Gabe and Francesca, never once looking at them. He nudged Dale in the back with the pizza box, and they left.

"And don't let the gate hit you in the ass when you go!" yelled Mae, as she lowered the gun. No one moved for a moment, then Gabe jumped up and hurried to the entry, to see a Bronco accelerating east. Mae and her shotgun arrived to make sure both men had indeed left the premises. Earl caught up.

"What was that bullshit the kid yelled?" Mae asked Gabe.

"Oh, that. . . Somebody named David Lane created this fourteen word manifesto that's become a rallying cry for this bunch. It's . . . well . . . I pretty much ignore it—you have to, man," this said to Earl. Mae made a sound as she broke the shotgun open and turned to go in.

"Humph," grunted Earl, then, "Your lady's a real beauty, Gabe. I'd say she thinks you hung the moon, dude," and he snorted. Gabe thanked them for their help and they reentered the room.

Gabe walked by Francesca and Earl watched him wink then hold up a forefinger, as in "wait a second." He asked Earl if he could borrow the phonebook which included the northeast Wyoming counties. After apologizing to someone for calling so late, he told them the Berry place folks, at least two of them, had just left Earl's in Alzada, heading toward Belle.

"The cop in Sara's Spring," Gabe explained, covering the mouth piece.

Charlie Mays would call the sheriff, who would then alert authorities in South Dakota. They'd watch for a car matching the description and check motels in the area. It was only a matter of time, Charlie told Gabe before he hung up, and Gabe relayed this to Francesca and Earl. Then, he sauntered over to the jukebox, inserted a bill, and spent several moments choosing music. The first was the Eagles' "Desperado."

Gabe turned to Francesca and smiled.

The woman rose from her chair, hips swaying, and not taking her eyes from his, she sashayed over to him. He held out his hand; she took it, and he pulled her body close to his. They began a slow 4/4 waltz. Earl watched. He tried not to; it looked too—personal. A perfectly-timed performance. A ballet. Exuding sex. He hoped he wasn't being crass, but he became aroused just watching them. He wished he could have bottled it—whatever *it* was. *Oh yeah, love. . .*

Earl finally averted his gaze and retreated to the kitchen, and when the song ended he took Gabe and Francesca two more glasses of wine and the large order of sweet-potato fries.

In the kitchen Mae informed him, "You know, Earl, you don't limp as much when you're all fired up," then she walked out to meet Francesca when they returned to their table.

"Happy to make your acquaintance, miss, and *whoo-ee*, you *are* a pretty thing," Mae said, extending her hand. Francesca, taking it, blushed through her olive complexion.

"My pleasure—ah—?"

"Mae. My name's Mae."

Earl arrived. "I love the way you talk," he said, "but we're so sorry for the . . . the—"

"It is fine, Earl . . . we forget about that," she said, waving her hand dismissively. "We dance now. Gabe is a *good* dancer, do you know? We celebrate tonight."

And they did. And a good time rolled.

CHAPTER 43~THEE IMPLICITLY

The clock in the cabin read midnight. For someone accustomed to being in bed asleep by 9:00 or 10:00 p.m., at the latest, this marked a departure. Senga cleared the table and washed the dishes, while Sebastian dried and put them away on a shelf to the left of the sink. She wrapped the bread and cheeses, covered the pot of chowder and placed it, and the cheese, in the fridge. Last, she replaced the lilies on the table and put water in the kettle to heat. Her nightly tisane.

"Would you like a cup of tea or warm milk? It's from Caroline's cow. Sometimes, I put a splash of brandy in mine. Not tonight though . . . I drank a bit of wine," and she blew out her cheeks.

"Tea would be perfect," said Sebastian, hanging the towel from a hook. "Any kind you have, my dear." He stoked the fire in the woodstove, then arranged his chair to face the flames.

She studied his face, the mouth turned down slightly at the corner; she didn't know if he simply held it that way. Not yet—*had only three days passed?* He wore his russet sideburns long and his sandy-white hair fell to just below his collar. From this angle, the upper lid to his right eye folded deeply. She knew his left eye was dissimilar, as most people's eyes are different. His left eye held the twinkle. The right cast a more sober tone.

"I enjoyed Gabe and Francesca very much," he spoke, breaking the silence. "They are brave *and* loving—a particular, and *peculiar* combination. She is lovely. Brilliant, actually. And I would like to read his story after you, if I may."

"Of course. He told me what it's about—after he submitted it. Do you want to know?"

"No; I think I'd rather read it, ah, with no preconceptions? Do you say this?"

"Yes, we do. All right—I won't spoil it for you."

Senga smiled while reaching for the bag of coffee to check its contents for the morning. Satisfied, she left it on the counter, French press beside, and the pan with water.

"If you wake early. . ." she said, and he nodded. "The cream is in the pint jar, and here's sugar." She slid the dish toward the press.

"Will you travel to Italy with Gabe to see your grandmother?"

"Would you mind?" she asked with a tentative inflection. "I mean, would this bother you, Sebastian?" She read his face as he turned toward her. His left eye twinkled, yet she wondered.

"No, Senga. I would dearly love to go with you if I could, but I am committed between now and Christmas—as I said. And . . . you must be there for Gabe, as I see it—and to see your grandmother. It will be marvelous. I'm not jealous by nature, my dear—perhaps a bit envious of Italy showing you her treasures without me; it has been decades since I was last there."

She hadn't thought about Francesca's revelation again until now. It unnerved her and she shook her head the once. Then, turning to the shelf, she brought down two mugs and crossed to her jars of herbs. She chose linden flower and placed two tablespoons into the wire basket of her tea pot. She'd add ten drops of skullcap tincture against headache to hers.

"Do you think you might have headache in the morning?" she asked.

"I hope not—why?"

"I'm adding another herb to my tea, in case I do . . . oh, that wonderful wine, Sebastian!"

"I know a possible cure for headache, Senga," and he cocked a brow—the one over the twinkling eye. *Naturally*, she thought.

"Mmmm, I expect you do," she said, returning his gaze, in kind.

Senga had wondered if Sebastian was uncomfortable with intermittent silences. He didn't fill them with idle chatter.

What exactly has happened?

When the water boiled, she filled the tea pot, set her timer for seven minutes and excused herself. Sebastian glanced up and smiled, then returned to contemplating flames.

In the bathroom, Senga leaned against the back of the door and closed her eyes. She inhaled to a count of four and exhaled to six, repeating it once. She wouldn't question a gift, but she'd ask how. *How* had this occurred? In her high school French class, she'd learned a love-at-first-sight experience was called a *coup de foudre*, or a "thunderclap." She'd been acquainted with Sebastian; *but not truly*, she countered, and yet, possibly more than she'd supposed. Some unconscious molecule in her person (but conscious in and of itself) had taken his measure during those terrible moments after Emily's fall. He'd revealed himself to her. And she to him.

No, no *coup* necessary.

Had Em's death represented an interface? A membrane stretched between their singular universes? *No*, she wouldn't distill her daughter in this way. The wonder and mystery of their present circumstance had merely been postponed. . . An exigency of time.

This has nothing at all to do with 'late blooming,' dearie. Senga's eyes shot open. *All things bloom in their own good time—even Love. Even you. . .*

The timer in the kitchen began to beep and Senga took one last, deep breath, gathered herself up by the scruff of her own neck and returned to join the fray. *Well, it's as good a word as any.*

Sebastian was fumbling with the mechanism. He handed it to her as if it were a crying infant. She pressed a button and all was quiet again, save the hissing of the fire and the Ecofan whirring from the back of the woodstove.

Senga poured their tea. "This is linden . . . hope you like it."

"Ahhh, tila, or *tilleul,* we call it at home. It is usually drunk after dinner. Popular. Why do you like it?"

"It's good for the heart, for one thing; anti-inflammatory, promotes resilience, and it tastes good . . . important for medicine, yes?"

"Do you have a problem with your heart, Senga?" he asked, frowning.

"Mm, well, nothing that can't be helped with common sense and common herbs, but don't tell my doctor," she teased. "I've had some anxiety and angina, but they've both abated. And, I did stop smoking several years ago."

"You smoked?"

"Oh, yes, I did. And I enjoyed it, until I didn't. Began when I was, oh, around fourteen, right after my Papa died—my grandfather. It was just Grannie and me. Papa raised tobacco, as I've mentioned—not that I ever tried those leaves . . . there is a curing process, you know. But cigarettes are inexpensive in North Carolina—at least they were then. You could say I was experimenting, but store-bought cigarettes are drugs, not just herbs. The tobacco and papers are interfered with too much in a lab. But you know this. Sorry."

Sebastian waved his hand.

"Tobacco, in essence, became a friend," she explained, "an ally—calming me when I felt wound up, winding me up when I felt down. You know—a regular drug habit. Grannie could smell it on me and told me I was foolish, but she let it go. I gave it up when I realized I was actually considering the things company. . . Did you ever?"

"Ah, yes. When I was young and, yes, I take your meaning about company. But it was also something my friends and I did together. A sacrament of sorts, yes? Communion—like breaking bread. It is merely a habit, but a hard one to break . . . it was for me. Our bodies require oxygen; I do know this," he said, as he spied the magazine on the table and picked it up, then he looked at Senga and spoke in a voice—a *tone*—the timbre of which she now found needful; its resonance—part and parcel of his being.

"You have a *strong* heart, Senga dear; you are resilience itself," and she heard this as a statement of belief. An incantation of sorts. And she believed him.

"I am intrigued by Gabe's story," he said after a moment, changing the subject.

Senga took the magazine from him and opened it to the table of contents. There it was: "The Carnival Horse," by Gabe Belizaire.

"It's not too long. . . Sebastian, would you read it aloud? I want to hear it in your voice," and she flipped the pages until she came to it, holding it up to him in entreaty.

He groaned. "It's late, Senga."

317

Her expression pleaded and he said, "For you." He reached for his tea, raised it to her, took a long sip, said "Mmmm," and began reading. "'The Carnival Horse,' by Gabe Belizaire—

"Jim Mason had promised his six-year-old son Micah, and four-year-old daughter Bridget an afternoon at the carnival. They had spotted the garish poster tacked to a wall in their small town's grocery store, and diversions such as these seldom visited their parts. Jim secretly hoped his kids would forget about it, but no, every day it was mentioned, either at breakfast or at dinner. His wife Wanda had to tell their children that enough was enough; that if they kept on about it, it just wouldn't happen.

Jim had a bigger stake in their forgetting the date—some friends were planning a fishing trip for that weekend and had included him. It was a big deal. He rarely went anywhere with his buddies anymore. But the day arrived and both Micah and Bridget hurried down the stairs to their breakfast, excitement palpable and overflowing. It was almost better than Christmas.

'Oh, Lord, I've got to take them, don't I,' he groaned to his wife, who was busy frying up bacon and eggs.

'Yes, sir, I expect you do, Jim,' and she turned a sardonic eye in his direction. 'You just plan a different fishing trip, that's all, baby.' This did not allay his acute disappointment.

They were going to eat lunch first and then go. His wife had made other plans, but then it was not she who had told the children she would take them to a carnival. . .

Jim drank a beer with his sandwich—a usual Sunday habit—and then one more for the road. Wanda did not witness this as she had already left the house. She would have given him the old stink-eye.

In the car, he squirreled away the other three beers at his feet, and they drove to the large lot outside of town, where the Ferris wheel could be seen from blocks away. Micah and Bridget had rolled down their windows and blaring carney music floated into the car, a Pied Piper's siren song. Micah was jumping up and down in his booster seat in anticipation, with Bridget soon joining him. Jim popped another beer and chugged it before arriving at the parking area. He was tight, he knew, but it was only a carnival, wasn't it? There was always the back road home.

Beside the car, he squatted down to Micah.

'Now. You need to hold your little sister's hand all the time. You hear me?'

Micah nodded—an earnest look on his face.

'I'll hold onto yours,' Jim said. 'Okay, let's go.' And they turned toward the entrance.

The air crackled dry and dusty with summertime static electricity."

Sebastian paused, saying nothing, and not leaving the words. He seemed to be digesting them. Senga shifted in her chair, then rose to add more tea to her cup. He raised his cup to be refilled while their eyes met. He drank, set the cup back on the table and resumed his reading, the ending waiting to be picked, like an apple.

". . . 'It's time to leave, mister,' a young Jimmy had overheard the carney say to his inebriated father. *So sadly*. Grown Jim remembered how he'd wrapped his little hand around his father's as best he could, the other clutched his sister's, and he'd pulled them away, toward the exit.

'I—I only wanted to get you that horse prize, baby girl,' Jim remembered his father saying, as his little sister leaned into him to correct his balance.

'I just want you, Daddy,' his sister had muttered, looking up with longing. . .

Micah shouted up at him now, 'Dad! I'm here! Where *were* you?'

Jim startled and looked down at his son. *He looks so much like his mother*, he thought, dazed. Jerking aware, he remembered Bridget and turned abruptly, but she stood next to him, eyes gazing upward, her chubby hand raised and latched onto his pocket as though she were a baby opossum.

'Where were *you*?' Jim asked Micah, whom he thought he'd lost in the crowd.

'I was just waiting for you, Daddy. . . Can we get some cotton candy now?'

They did. Jim didn't mind the god-awful sticky mess he'd have to clean up when he got home. At least he'd have it to clean up, he thought, the image of molasses filling his sobering senses."

Sebastian rubbed his face and lowered the magazine to his lap, indicating the story's conclusion. He made a sound.

"Mm-hmm. . . Think it's a memory?" asked Senga.

"If it is, then it is a universal one, I should think—if you substitute where it happened. . ."

"The setting."

"Yes. This reaches deep inside, I think," he said, lifting the magazine.

"Um, did you notice Gabe leaves race out of it?"

"How do you mean?"

"Nowhere does it mention the color of the characters' skin and the sad part, if I'd not known that Gabe was Black—or African American, if we're politically correct—I wouldn't even be discussing the notion. That's strange. That's implicit bias in reverse—maybe. But yes, he wanted to tell a universal story, as you say."

"Implicit bias?"

"Um, if something is 'implicit,' it's unconsciously implied, right? Like . . . like learning a classmate's family had a maid. . . In the South where I'm from, we naturally expected the woman to be Black. I don't want to give you the wrong idea— where I'm from *no* one had a maid. We were all pretty much in the same boat. Poor. Neighbors helped one another if a need arose. But, if you could grow your own food, put it up and sell a crop—even tobacco—you were better off than many. Papa even sold moonshine for a while . . . you know, homemade whiskey?"

Sebastian nodded. He finished his cup of tea and set the mug on the table, then covered a yawn.

"Anyway . . . if Gabe had written the characters as Black, well, it'd lend another negative bias, and he may have wished to avoid this, given, as you say, its already *universal*, ah, poignancy. It's simply cross-cultural. Aches across the board." Was she was losing him with idioms? Maybe not.

"Yes. Indeed, it does . . . and yes, I believe you have rooted out his intent, though in my experience, when I have spoken with an author about his or her work, many times, the author was not aware of underlying symbolism, or even allegory; those remained unconscious. Did you know? It's true, Senga—when some reviewer writes something regarding this or that, often the author is nonplussed to hear it. Insight comes through anyhow it can, I suppose—my point. . .

"And speaking of black, my dear. . . I believe your friend is quite possibly the blackest man I have ever seen."

"He does *gleam*, doesn't he? Like obsidian." She smiled. "My 'obsidian friend.' Now *that* sounds—"

"No-no; that's simply a descriptor. And poetry. My countrymen—and *women*—" he gave Senga a courtly nod, ". . . by contrast, are among the palest of the pale, like creatures discovered on the bottom of deep sea trenches. What would be the opposite of 'obsidian?' *Oh, bother!* To bed, my dear. I can barely keep my eyes open."

"Was your teacher of English from England?"

"Actually, she was and she had us read from *Winnie the Pooh* often. I am quite indoctrinated; you have been warned."

After a long naked embrace under cool sheets, they took comfort and pleasure in the close to the surface, firing nerve endings of bare skin, and by falling asleep together to the hypnotic whirr of the stove fan and the crackle of fire in the next room.

Come ye, daybreak was Senga's last conscious thought; that, and *Pooh*. . .

CHAPTER 44
~ALL ABOUT CROWS

*C*orvus brachyrhynchos. The Latin swam to consciousness as jeering cries woke Francesca; one caw answered by another in the distance. *Two then—that is good,* she remembered from her personal mythology. She'd always enjoyed the sight and sound of crows—their particular idiosyncrasies and reputations notwithstanding. Comical birds, if aggravating, as all comics could be. Wasn't that their job? The "satirists" of the bird world, crows. To wake us. To make us uncomfortable.

The night before, Senga had described the origin of *scare crow*: a dead one was hung high on a gibbet in a garden to discourage others. Sensing her guests' discomfort, she told them she preferred the more conventional straw man, or woman, in her case. . .

Hermione (she explained) was spending the cold season in the back of the garage, doing double duty. If someone happened to come sneaking around they'd earn a scare. Senga admitted she fed the crows—away from her small garden. Unsalted peanuts. They left trinkets. She brought out her collection.

Beh . . . decided Francesca: *She is related to Maria Teresa for certain. . .*

She liked Senga's friend, Sebastian. Gabe had whispered to Senga upon leaving that he (Sebastian) was *simpatico. Sì. That is the word.*

Francesca lay against the strong, lean back of Gabe in his hired-man bed, her arm draped over his waist as he clasped her

322

close. She raised her head. Dawn lit the window and shone dimly through the colored lamp shade on Gabe's desk. Glowing purples, pinks and greens. She lay her head back down and breathed in his scent. The spicy, orange-cedar fragrance mingled with the sweet and sour of last night's lovemaking. She moved her hand from under his arm to stroke his belly over the tightly curled hair. The springy texture woke the nerves in her palm. Gabe groaned, waking.

"*Buon giorno, cuore mio,*" she whispered, moving her hand to his groin, "*Ciao, Teed-beet,*" she crooned.

Gabe grunted.

Eight miles away (as crows flew), from Senga's bed, Sebastian heard loud caws echoing against the hillside behind the cabin. No provincial rooster for his Senga, he thought. She lay asleep beside him, turned toward the wall, quietly snuffling. He slowly rose on his elbows and twisted round to her. He had loved to watch his Elsa sleep, a source of great peace. Thinking of Elsa now brought his daughter to mind, Erika, and Jytte, his granddaughter, then his son-in-law Peter and their plans to return with him from Denmark to spend the holidays.

He had yet to tell Erika about Senga.

He lay back down, content to let morning seep in slowly, even if it meant the gears in his mind would begin their machinations: a show in Copenhagen, beginning November 18, to run through mid-December; legal arrangements to sort regarding his Aunt Karen's estate, and other considerations—in light of his decision to spend time in the United States. He had two more weeks in the Hills. And it seemed likely Senga would travel to Italy with Gabe to see her grandmother.

Extraordinary . . . but (perhaps) not so surprising, given Senga's—what? he wondered. *The woman invites magic. Isn't this what we're supposed to do?*

The crows cawed again. An entire flock must have flown over, he thought. *Good.* He studied Senga's bedroom. A small window faced east just to his right from where he lay in the double bed. The pane threw gentle light across the room to the west wall, where a mirror perfectly reflected the source, thus doubling the effect. Practical magic. Her clothing hung willy-nilly from various hooks on the wall. A small dresser stood under the mirror, painted in several colors, muted now. A spinning wheel sat in the corner; a wooly thread dangled from a hole, waiting for nimble fingers. "A winter pastime," Senga had explained. To the left of the mirror hung a poster of *The Mermaid* by Waterhouse.

In the mirror, Sebastian watched the pale dawn creep brighter by degrees. The cabin, he'd observed, sat at the base of a hillside, similarly to his aunt's—*mine*, he corrected with melancholy. The sun would eventually rise above the ridge; his grief would likewise abate.

Senga made a swallowing sound. He turned his head to her, then gently lifted the comforter and sheet away so he could view the curve of her back. He quickened simply in noticing the rounding of her backbone, each knob of vertebra articulated in a beautiful sweeping line, like a necklace, or a series of waves. *No. A mountain range from the air. The riven country of Senga.* Her long braid fell to the sheet. He lifted the mussed, feather-like tail of hair to his nose, breathed, and laid it back down. *Peppermint.*

He needed her now.

Rolling over, he pressed his body against hers, skin to skin, his right hand seeking one, and then the other warm breast. And sliding his left arm beneath, he pulled her to him, onto his own body, facing away, the back of her head resting upon his shoulder. Having awakened, Senga murmured words inarticulate but acquiescent. He massaged her left nipple and breast with one hand, and with the other he drew increasingly firmer circles below until she squirmed and bucked with pleasure and feeling. His own senses burst in a paroxysm of longing and hunger. He was overcome, but it was Senga crying out. . .

"Sebastian, now—*please*—"

"*Ingen*, not yet, *mmm*; wait . . . a little," and he continued to rub, stroke, nibble, bite, kiss, *love* her, until she rolled over, panting and laughing.

"Oh God. Enough! No, never enough . . . Oh! *Ooohh*. . ." He pulled her around so she lay on her back and he spread her legs. Sebastian felt he might expire by sheer force of stimulation, but Senga reached below and, drawing his cock, she guided him to her, pressing him against her, and he entered her and, after, they lay spent, like creatures who had wrestled underwater, both inundated by emotion.

Gabe jerked, then sighed deeply. The lighting pulled focus on all, as in a dream. Francesca's grasp softened as she cupped him between her hands. She sat beside him, crossed-legged, *tailor-style*. He wondered where the expression originated, then banished his distracted thoughts. Turning over, he let his eyes fall where they might, anywhere, on her person.

Where to begin? With those breasts and soft belly? With hips made for childbearing? Her dolorous, dark eyes seeing none but him? The thin band of silky dark hair, just visible, when she leaned back now on her arms? And curling his toes to see?

"*Gehb?*" she said, in a tone he recognized as supplicating. She bent over her task.

"Yes, sweet Francesca. . ." he replied, sucking in his breath to her ministrations.

"How soon, I mean, *mmmm* . . . when can you come to Italy? You and Senga? I don't know if . . . *mmmm* . . . I tell Mama about Senga yet. (*Pop!*) I don't want her—Mama—to tell Maria Teresa, do you see? *Mmmm* . . . unless I know Senga comes. . ."

Oh, dear Lord; women and multitasking, he noted. "Ohhh—*mmph!*" He tightened his jaw, then lifted Francesca's hand away.

"Wait! . . . please . . . Uh, I'm not . . . ahh, certain she's going—yet, *chère,*" he managed, as he blew out his cheeks, ". . . and there's still time . . . to apply for passports. Just don't mention it 'til then, okay? Can you do that?"

"*Sì,* I can. Do you think it is money?"

"Could be. I really don't know Senga's means—you know—her finances. For all I know, she could have thousands squirreled away somewhere."

"*Skirled away?* What is this? The animal?" she asked, as she moved her glorious breasts over his chest, clearly enjoying it.

"Oh my . . . and I'm supposed to be able to think, woman?" So he did not; instead, he cupped both hands around the breast he'd nicknamed *La Cupola Una,* after the iconic dome in Florence. "Only fair, after all," he'd told her. And as he suckled her hard nipples, large and brown as acorns (the simile, apt), Gabe forgot all and returned to the primordial noise of a lover's sounds, in abandon so complete that his employers wouldn't know if cats were caterwauling or being skinned alive down at the barn. But he'd probably hear about it.

Senga lay smiling with eyes closed, wishing never to move again. Rarely had she known such peace. A feeling of utter well-being. Spiritual *café au lait,* crusty French bread and chokecherry jam.

Sebastian had risen from the bed, her hands reaching along his arms and backside as he did so. She'd told him to shower first. Leaning over, she stretched her back, stood, then leaned side to side. Needing to use the toilet, Senga plucked her robe off a hook and wondered if—no, she'd go outdoors. *Too soon for some realities.* After filling the kettle with water and turning it on, she stepped outside.

She brought in an armful of split wood from the stack under the porch, noting she'd have to gather more soon. After arranging pinecones, paper and kindling, she struck a match and left the stove door cracked to draw until the wood caught. She made the coffee and set the press in the pan of water on the woodstove to stay warm. Sebastian emerged from the bedroom dressed, shaved and smelling of something green. She couldn't put her finger on it. He was holding one of her bathroom quotes.

"I like this," he said, "'Nothing before, nothing behind. The steps of faith fall on the seeming void and find the rock beneath. . .' Whittier. Ah."

"My Franciscan friend in Montana sent it . . . and the other quote. What's that smell? It's *green.*"

"Hmmm, I do not know what you mean, my dear. . . You are confusing your senses, I fear," he smiled at his rhyme and, moving to her, placed both hands on her cool cheeks and kissed her forehead. ". . . It is a gift from my daughter," she heard him say. "The liquid is clear, I believe. Not green. Would you like to see it?" he asked. "More important, do you like it?"

"Yes, very much." Senga detected sage and lime. Maybe musk.

Sebastian disappeared into the bathroom and returned with a small bottle.

"Ha, it does have a slight color, Senga; I was mistaken— more blue-green. It's *Royal Copenhagen*, but this is all I know. I am glad you like it. *I* do, else I couldn't wear it. Picky about such, you see, and it's not too dear, the price. A good value, we call that."

She noticed he didn't say "cheap." *He grabs things by their smooth handle*, quoting Thomas Jefferson. She would pair the scent with love—no matter what happened. . . *Where did that come from?* she wondered, and shook her head.

"Why do you do that?" he asked as she poured their coffee.

"Do what?"

"You move your head, like so—" and he demonstrated.

"Oh—well, it's just a habit, but ah, one I consider actually helpful. I suppose I do it unconsciously anymore. Let's sit down, shall we?" and she brought the cream and sugar to the table. "I drink a cup before eating . . . is this all right with you?"

"Yes, of course . . . you were saying—"

"I can't remember when I started doing it. All it is . . . I am dismissing a thought, banishing it, I guess. At least it seems to. But here's an interesting thing—there's a technique used to help victims of trauma, particularly post traumatic stress disorder. It's called EMDR."

"Ah, yes, I have heard of this—I am sorry, go on—"

"Then you understand the principle? *Eye Movement Desensitization and Reprocessing* is what it stands for. I do a one-person version and with a slight change in focus as to the object. I'm just trying to stop, or antidote, a pesky thought. Therapists use it to diminish the effects of severe trauma. . . I've experienced . . . too. . ." she added, looking away from him, through the window.

"Senga—" he said now, just her name, calling her back.

"Mmmm. And there's also something called *Recapitulation*," she continued, turning back to him. "It's shamanic in origin.

I'll tell you about it sometime if you like—too heavy for now," and she stood up, moved her head to the side and back, noticing him notice, and stoked the fire.

"Will you tell me about the red cloth?" He was gazing toward the tree.

"Yes. I will. But not today," she said, smiling to soften her refusal. "You don't miss much, do you?" she said, as she twisted to face him.

"I am a photographer, my dear; I notice things."

Rising, she crossed to the kitchen window and opened it to allow fresh air. She counted four crows flying overhead to the west. *Good*, she thought.

CHAPTER 45~LETTERS

Senga's hands (and heart) trembled as she examined the two medals. One in each hand, she closed her fists around them. Beside the yet-unopened letter from her cousin, a one-page letter lay open on the table in invitation, like Grannie's dying, outreached hand. Senga had unlocked her Grannie's box, setting aside a thin packet of envelopes, tied with pink ribbon—the postmarks of which were dated late 1960. *From Mama to Grannie.* She'd save them for later.

May 3, 1975
Fort Bragg, North Carolina

Dear Mrs. Munro,
It is with deepest regret that I must inform you of the death of your husband, Cpl. Andrew Munro, U.S. Army, on April 30, 1975, in the city of Saigon, Viet Nam. His remains are en route to the post for internment, or for burial elsewhere, as per your wishes.
Posthumously, Cpl. Munro will receive the Purple Heart for giving his life in the service of his country, and the Silver Star for valor. These medals are presented to you. The report of the circumstances was forwarded to me and I will try to relay these as best I can.
Cpl. Munro had just helped load a Huey helicopter with evacuees from the city. As

you may know, the United States servicemen and women made many valiant attempts to bring away as many South Vietnamese and American personnel as possible before our departure. The helicopter pilot had just lifted off, when he was jostled by the passengers and he accidentally hit the collective lever (a flight control), changing the pitch of the blade, which then swung the helicopter around. Cpl. Munro was standing below on the ground when the boom struck him.

It appears he perished instantly.

The helicopter pilot recovered the craft and was able to continue his mission of taking the evacuees to safety.

Your husband died while saving others, Mrs. Munro. Please accept our deepest condolences and know we honor his and your family's sacrifice.

Capt. Mary Ann Berg will be in touch regarding the arrival of your husband's remains.

Most respectfully yours,
Col. James C. Pritchard, U.S. Army

Her mother's circumstances in 1975 had overtaken her father's death and his memory, though Senga believed one had led to the other. She'd known nothing regarding the contents of this official letter. A "freakish mishap" was all she'd ever heard. From whom? *Who'd used the phrase?* She thought hard. And it came, like the sound of one popped-corn kernel after it sizzles in a hot pan. An overheard remark at school. One teacher whispering to another, to Senga's turned back. *Freakish mishap? Don't teachers, of all people, realize the impression their language makes on their students?*

Sebastian had gone for a hike after breakfast. Senga had wanted to, but she needed to take care of a couple of matters before going to work, and Caroline had invited them to lunch

330

at the ranch. Mainly to meet Sebastian, Senga knew. Which was as it should be, she'd reasoned.

She replaced her father's medals in the box, along with the official communication, and closed the box. Then, using her pocket knife, she opened Colin's letter. After reading through it once, she had to again to digest *this* content now. She sighed.

> October 10, 2013
>
> Dear Cousin,
>
> I hope you are well. I expect you are surprised to receive all this, but it was time. As you see, your grandparents' house is worse for wear and it is scheduled to be torn down. I am not sure if the new owners will rebuild on the spot or choose another. I loved the view from the porch and we enjoyed living there. I am sorry I haven't kept in better touch, but life sort of steps in.
>
> This is why I am writing, as you may be wondering: Rob McGhee happened by when we were cleaning. He introduced himself and my wife was all nerves—she knew who he was. Seems he has a few CDs out. Old Mountain music mostly. Anyway, he asked about you and I was sad I really didn't know much. He knew you had moved to the country after his and your daughter died, but he didn't have the new address. I reminded him it was a small town so a letter would probably reach you. He didn't seem too concerned. But, he was determined to gather up some things you might have wanted.
>
> What I've sent are thanks to him in large part. He spent most of the day helping us. So, here are the treasures he placed in your pile. I was surprised he didn't want to add a note or something. But no, he said the spirit of the doing was the main thing, saying you'd understand. He added something strange

about your having "taken your spirit basket" when y'all split up. I let that one go too.

I don't know if you are interested in knowing his circumstances, but he seems both at peace and as if he's suffered. I suppose in the end that's what we'll all look like— peaceably haunted. . .

Grannie? When it rains does it need to be a hurricane? Rob had thought of her. He'd done this thing, made this gesture. And it was on account of his actions she might be reunited with her *Nonna* after thirty-eight years.

. . . Also, you will be receiving by registered mail a check made out to you for the sale of the house and property, minus our yearly tax payments through the years. We count our rent paid in the upkeep of the house and buildings, until we had to move away, and, as you can see, it deteriorated quickly, as empty houses can. I hope this is acceptable. Our family enjoyed living there.

This is a large sum, Senga. Property in the western counties has become popular for retirees, for one. Not much tobacco being grown nearby anymore, but folks like their country living. $505,150 should be a nice surprise for you, but beware those capital gain taxes. . . I do this for a living, so if you need help with any aspect of banking, reinvesting, etc., get in touch. And please do anyway. We'd love to hear from you. It's been too long.

I like feeling like Santa Claus. Ho Ho Ho.
Your cousin Colin.
The other one says 'Hey.'

Her chest constricted. Angina or anxiety she couldn't tell. She rose and poured herself a glass of water and drank it, feeling better immediately. *Sometimes that's all it takes.* Hydration.

"Holy shit. . . Oh, fuck—I was going to delete that from my vocabulary, wasn't I?" she spoke to the air.

She picked the bottle of bear root tincture, *Osha*, against shock, and placed five drops under her tongue, relaxing her rule. She went to her bedroom and lay down, placing two pillows under her feet, to rise again for an ever-present bag of frozen peas; then, back in bed, she placed this on her forehead. It was too cold, so a corner of the sheet to her head first, then the bag. Better. She counted breaths to calm herself. *After this, I'll fix a cup of chamomile.*

"Holy *sh*—" No; just—*breathe.*

Caroline had suggested they arrive around 11:30 when she called earlier. Gabe and Francesca were coming too, and, "How did they both sleep on that skinny bed anyway?" And, "You should've heard the cat screeching coming from the barn this morning—between that and the damn crows—woke us up. Our window was open. . . Is it a weird phase of the moon or something? Don't you want a cat, Senga? Take two."

She glanced at her alarm clock. Ten after ten. Calm descended. The moon was waning gibbous and, no, she did not want a cat. Caroline added that Francesca was busy helping Gabe with his morning chores: "He loaned her some gear, and the gal sure filled it out good."

The Stricklands had met Francesca in June. Senga had stayed mum about the engagement and asked Caroline if she could contribute to the meal. Her neighbor told her it'd be more of a brunch—*thank you*—and she had plenty. What Caroline wanted to do, she'd said, was plan the cider pressing; make it sort of a party, since Gabe had persuaded Senga to bring her apples to them, instead of hauling the press to her place. And would she bring that bushel today so she could get started on those pies?

Senga needed to haul several boxes of apples to town for the folks who were picking them up at the library. She'd wait until Thursday to do laundry.

A jiggling on the door latch prompted her to rise from her bed, but Sebastian worked it out, so she lay back down. Just breathing.

She heard him set something on the table, then ask, like a riddle, "Where does the mermaid hide when marooned on dry land?" And Senga smiled, feeling a tide of warmth and peace return to her heart.

EPILOGUE

Journal

A mermaid sky this morning—what Em and I renamed the mackerel variety—tufts of scaly clouds spread heavenward. I remember her coming home from school one day, disgruntled at her teacher for having corrected her vocabulary. "But my Mama says . . ." said she.

No more capitalized faith, hope and love. Give me the generic brand, the ordinary wine, the everyday stuff of life; these virtues are easier to coax into my personal traveling bag.

Random thought #3, from an earlier entry, dated December 19, 1981. I recall writing this; I claim it. I revel in its buoyant, wordful joy:

"It will come—like a star bursting over my head one day—all these twinkling bright lights of recognition, belonging and triumph will sparkle down all around me. And—this—shall be my very own Glory Robe." Papa . . . Grannie . . . Mama . . . Daddy . . . Emily. My Stars of Infinite Magnitude. I greet you in ecstatic stance with Hermione's out-flung arms. . .

Gabe's short story haunts me. The poignancy of the children's painful love for their father. . . Facts and particulars may be altered for a story, but feeling remains, like a *pentimento* on a wall after a long-exhibited painting has been removed. And yet, feelings themselves are still not the truth. Not the whole of it. Both fathers' love is returned—even through the pain of their frailties—perhaps stronger for them, who knows? And who could hold the whole truth, anyway? But we try. Maybe that's the object of a human journey. The tide comes in; the tide goes out. "Mind the gap," they say in England. I've been lonely, but today, what compensation (no exclamation mark).

Rufus and Caroline sported grins on their faces the whole of our visit on Tuesday. They presided as True Elders. Their grandson, Jake, will be spending the summer with them. They haven't seen him in six years.

"The kid wants to learn some rope tricks," Caroline said, meaning, to learn the ropes of running a ranch; "A few, anyway," she added.

They're happy for Gabe and Francesca, and for me. Caroline pulled me over as she scrambled eggs, her eyes shining like black diamonds.

"Sebastian's good to you, and *for* you—I can see that."

"Yes, Caroline, he is."

"And he's so big!"

"Yes, he is that."

"And a *hunka-hunka burnin' love*, I bet?"

"Caroline—" I laughed, and when she lit into Gabe and Francesca about torturing cats earlier, I sneaked away. At table, Gabe told us about their run-in at Earl's and Francesca's bold response. Classier than a Hori Hori. Rufus whooped and hollered. I don't think he's been so entertained in a long time. After we ate, he moved to the porch for his smoke, Gabe and Sebastian in tow, while we women stayed in the kitchen, the usual arrangement. Must segregate gender in the country, else what'll happen? *Aho*, as Joe says, speaking of whom. . .

A letter arrived yesterday from him—a faster than our usual turn-around. Milo, Moona'e and he are coming next month to pray at the Tower, but also to examine the place where I saw the Indian. (I'm waiting to tell Sebastian about it—and the incident in the store.) Milo wants to smudge the spot with sage.

Joe says my drawing resembles a Cheyenne chief who lived in the early 1800s. His name was Wolf on the Hill. (On the side of the hill, in this case.) George Catlin painted him, so there is a record. Joe asked if I'd ever seen this portrait. I haven't. He also said Indians marked their own arrows by design—by color, for instance. Some made their points in a particular way.

Milo wants to search where I saw the buck—where the arrow flew.

Charlie Mays called Gabe to say the Berry place folks "aren't apprehended yet,"—that the South Dakota authorities arrived after the Wild Bunch had left the motel. "Slippery characters," Charlie told Gabe.

"Like snot," I contributed.

The Russian woman and her child will stay on at the shelter for a while. Jim will be pleased, said Francesca. Rufus mentioned another of Gabe's stories that he and Caroline just read. He glowed in relating this, but didn't mention the premise. Gabe told us he's got enough stories for a collection and we all cheered.

We discussed the apple pressing and think Halloween might be a good day for it. If it isn't snowing.

I told Sebastian about the sale of my grandparents' home and that I'd come into some money. He didn't press for details. Now I can make plans to visit my *Nonna*. I vibrate with anticipation—among other things.

In the back of the photo album, I discovered a CD, Rob's latest, judging by the date on the back. I haven't played it yet, but I'm glad he made it. There's a song, "Nothing's Lost, Nothing's Wasted—For Emily and Senga." *Hmmm.*

Sebastian confided what the runic inscription says on his uncle's magnificent door hinges. I think he was disappointed by my response, or lack thereof. It was one of those obvious truths for me, like hearing the song of a robin and knowing what bird made it, but at last I was given to smile—grin actually—and he readjusted his own features. He drew it for me:

ᚤᚿᛀ:ᚦᚿᚤᛁᚠ:ᚤᛀᛀ:ᚦᛁᚠ:ᚿᛀ:ᚦᚿ:ᚤᛁᚱ:ᛀᛀ:ᛀᚤᚦ

Remember me, I remember you.
Love me, I love you.

It's proverbial in Denmark, I was told. I sense the magic in it now, in the writing of it. A Runic spell; a wish. Indeed, a hinge. Sebastian said we are hinged by intent now.

I'll save Mama's letters for winter, the time for stories. It's too soon yet; moon's not right. . . I may be a beached mermaid, but I reside near still waters, and when the tide next turns, I'll be accompanied by creatures fair, belovéd and—rare.

ACKNOWLEDGMENTS

The heartrending loss of a child and what comes after are difficult subject matter to relay in a story. Grannie and Papa Cowry lose their daughter Lucy, Senga's Emily dies in a fall. I have not suffered that heartbreak, but my parents did, as has my sister; as have friends Laura and Dixie. As have so many. Tragedy and joy are dialectics made the more so by intensity, but tempered, it is to be hoped, by a loading dose of love.

Senga's heart was molded by a grandmother who insisted on usefulness, and her lessons in love and healing were squeezed into the young woman's traveling bag when she left Appalachia for Wyoming.

I hope you found something of use—and beauty—in Senga's story. Please leave a review on Amazon and Goodreads if you feel inclined. Tell me what moved you. There's more to follow in the sequel, *STARWALLOW*. Thanks for reading Senga's story and being a part of her journey.

Thank you to my husband Jeff, without whom I wouldn't have discovered the joys of finally working out of a tiny cabin made useful by a small propane heater one Christmas; your love sustains me.

To our daughter, AdriAnne, a first reader—thank you for endless encouragement, legal expertise, and especially, for your Artemis courage. To Joe, thank you for technical assistance, and also for your courage.

To our son John, to Sami, and their beautiful family—thank you for being kind always, for the look at the hunting chapters, for Hammond, and, yes, for your high-flying courage.

Gratitude to my editor, Sarah Pridgeon, who showed me more in two years than all the conferences, articles and web searches could in twenty. You are a brilliant woman. All errors herein are mine.

Deep bows to Dr. Chaim Vanek. As endocrinologist, Dr. Chaim may have wondered, Why depend on a possible remedy when a cure is easily available? I took his forthright suggestion to publish with Amazon. I thank Phil Zuckerman of Applewood Books for suggesting IngramSpark.

To my thoughtful brother and sweet sisters: André, Gabi, Felicia, Alex, and Nancy, and my nieces and nephews, "Love 14." To the memory of our remarkable parents, Paul and Millie Latiolais, I sigh with deep gratitude.

To Gretel Ehrlich, Diana Gabaldon, Morgan Callan Rogers, Louise Penny, Elizabeth Gilbert, Craig Johnson, and Loreena McKennitt, my gratitude. To Charles Mac Kay in Scotland and Micheline Labrousse in France, for 'cross-the-pond friendship. To the memory of Tom Waugh and to his wife, Twylia. To Andi Hummel for southern-accented talks, ice cream runs, a first read and suggestions. To Rob Shively, for legal help, and for cutting through BS in general. To Kevin Sweeney, for reading, encouraging, and offering a good word. To Laura Jones, for reading an early draft and being especially supportive. To Candace Christofferson, first reader, wise and beautiful artist, many thanks for the book cover, and, to all the Gemini Picnickers—*bravas* for the raw material of grace and grit. To Susun Weed, Wise Woman and fierce teacher, gratitude for showing me green allies. To philosopher Patricia Sun, for your work in wholing.

To Tom and Janice Cowell, Jon and Kim McDowell, Kirk and Linda Hughes, Paul and Mel Kuecks, John and Becky Curless, Penny Thompson, Janet Penland, Chris Carrier, Dick and Katinka Nanna, Randy and Lupita Brooks, the Bearlodge Writers, Joan Fullerton, Linda Knudson, long-time friends Linda Spears and Dixie Minor—loving gratitude. Linda is responsible for the "hunka-hunka burnin' love," and, "Ghosts are Petty," in the third volume.

My appreciation to the Wyoming Arts Council, and Neltje, for the professional development grant and the Frank Nelson Doubleday Writing Award.

Finally, to animal friends who have passed on, and the present hug giver, Gabe, our yellow Lab (yes, named after *that* Gabe), and present plant and animal families inhabiting the little piece of the planet we live on—I thank you all for the joy.

~Renée Carrier

READ ON FOR AN EXCERPT FROM

STARWALLOW
by Renée Carrier

Book Two of the Riven Country Series
Available in 2020

PETRIFIED

Sebastian drove to Senga's cabin after the party in silence and waning, sickle-moon darkness, save the light beam ahead. His appetite fully sated with food and drink, he groaned at the wheel.

"Eat too well?" Senga asked.

"How did you know? That was quite possibly the best meal I've eaten in America."

"Helped along by Caroline's aperitif, I expect. . . What a hoot—*watch out!*"

In reaction, he slammed on the brakes as a great horned owl winged low before the windshield from the west, to veer off to their right into the wash of light. It rotated its large round head in their direction, small beak and wide eyes meeting their startled gaze.

"Senga—hoot? Please stop *calling* them," he said under his breath. Owls were portents of doom in his culture.

"*I heard the owl call my name . . .*" she said quietly.

"Pardon?" He'd heard and didn't know if he wanted to pursue the subject. Slowly accelerating, he continued through the darkened landscape. Watchful.

"It's a Northwest Indian tradition . . . not sure if Plains as well. Owls are about something dying, but they don't always represent physical death. Like the hanged man in the Tarot, it can just mean the end of something. That's all." She was watching him, then—

"Here's the turn-off; it can be hard to see at night. See the glow?"

He could, in the near distance. The shrine to her daughter. A year-round Christmas tree near her cabin, illuminated every evening. If away after dark (she'd explained), it served as a "candle in the window," for her homecoming.

Sebastian dismissed the owl and negotiated the drive onto her property.

Indoors, Senga leaned down to light a ready-laid fire. *The night is young*, he recalled the idiom. His English had improved in the three months he had lived in this country. He put away his and Senga's outer garments, then turned to wash out the salad bowl she'd set on the counter. Her hand gently pulled his away from the task. A whisper—"Mine to do." Then, she indicated the woodstove, ". . . but that could be watched and fed. Please."

"As you wish," he replied in courtly manner. He chose a length of split pine from the tub to add to licking flames. After closing the windowed woodstove door, he moved to his chair.

"Who splits your wood for you, my dear?"

"I do it . . . though I dreaded it this year. I have enough for this winter, but next winter I may hire it done. My neighbor fells a dead for me about every other year and saws it into logs." She wiped the wooden bowl dry as he watched her.

Observing Senga had become ritual for him. Her actions proved economical; her intentions, astute. He watched her as if she were a poem; *louder than words* went the saying, yes? But she was quiet. Did everything quietly. *Except in bed*. . . He felt his face flush. The three joys of travel occurred to him: anticipating the travel, the trip itself and, soon after, reviewing it with pleasure. *If all went well*, he amended.

He pushed the thought away and resumed his exercise. She did not seem to mind his scrutiny. Some women might. Some women were self-conscious, he knew. He loved to watch Senga at her toilette, often made in the nude. He did not know if it was her usual practice, or if she did so for his sake.

The crackling fire lulled him. He turned his head sleepily as she spoke from the bedroom.

"There are a couple guys in town who have a wood splitter. That would be great. Mm. Thank you, Papa and Grannie," she said as she returned to the room and began filling the electric kettle with water for tea. She had changed into her robe; she needed a new one, he noticed. Hers was clean but worn. *Aunt's bright silk one suits her better.*

"Indeed," Sebastian said as he stood, then stepped, to one of the candles on the sill to light it. Then another, and another, until the cabin glowed like the votive stands in cathedrals he'd visited. He enjoyed candlelight at dawn and dusk, a practice in his country. The glow from the juniper shone beyond the periphery of the large window; no other light was necessary for their purposes.

While the water heated, Senga sat in her chair and closed her eyes for a moment. She opened them and smiled, eyes resting on an object on the table. "I've left it where you put it," she told him, "as you can see, but what *is* it, please? It looks petrified."

"Ah. Well. This is one of those moments when I wish Uncle Harold were still alive. It is old. Prehistoric, I believe. I found it when I was walking along the creek bed that day," and he inclined his head toward the west. "Do you know the place where dark gray soil slopes to the creek? A very steep bank?"

She nodded.

"I stood, wondering whether to descend, when sunlight fell on this. It was partially hidden in soil." Sebastian picked up the object, still covered with powdery silt. He moved to the sink and turned on the tap.

"Do you have a cleaning brush, my dear?"

"Under the sink to the left. . . So what do you think it is?"

"I'll photograph it and make some inquiries, Senga. See how the bone has, *hmm*—"

Senga rose and stepped to the sink. She reached for the light switch and turned it on. "Better?" Then, "May I?" as she reached for the piece.

Cleaned of its debris, it measured four or five inches across, the same in length. A rounded cavity marked the middle, with sides like small wings. Sebastian recognized *lacunae* or, pock-marks of time on bone. Senga hefted the piece for its weight then brought it closer to better examine it.

"It's a vertebra," she declared.

Sebastian looked at it, then to Senga and back to the bone. His face broke into a wide grin. "Yes! I think so, too. Of course it is—I can see it now. But you astound me." He reached over and kissed her temple.

"One of my studies was paleontology . . ." she explained, "But a vertebra to what? You didn't see others? Seems the whole beast should be there."

"Parts could have washed down the creek—or river—if it ever was, eons ago. But yes, it could still be intact. Or, it could have been left as a kill by another animal and simply dropped there."

"Hadn't thought of that. Good point. Nice find, Sebastian. You'll have to show me the spot."

The kettle whistled and she took down two mugs for their usual tisane.

"Chamomile or linden tonight?"

"Linden, please," he said as he scanned the room for a place to put the bone. "Where do you want this?"

"Oh, take it with you—to photograph, right?" She set the timer to brew the tea.

"I have my camera; I'll do it tomorrow. Here—is this a good place?" he asked as he lifted the bone to a spot on the shelf above the window.

"Perfect." When the timer beeped, she turned it off and stirred milk and honey into hers, while he preferred his plain. After sweeping the dirt off the table with a hand, she brought the mugs and set them down, then arranged her only upholstered chair, an old blue wingback, to face the fire. They were settled.

The Black Hills, circa 1820.

High Wolf returned to the camp disgruntled, having missed his quarry. The large deer, a drop tine on his right antler, had acknowledged him and blithely bounded off to live another day. *Inconceivable* that he had missed, he thought, and he should have searched for the arrow. *No time;* the sun was setting, and so he marked the area in his mind: beneath the horned escarpment, about ten paces from an old juniper.

His wife would have liked to have watched him stroll into camp carrying the beast across his broad shoulders. Alas, not this evening. He was glad She Who Bathes Her Knees was even-tempered and not prone to sarcasm, as were some wives of his friends. No, this wife was affectionate. They had as yet no children, but hoped to soon.

She would offer to return with him to search for his arrow. He knew this about her.

Her sister, called Lona (meaning "beautiful" in the *Tsitsistas* language), was causing a stir among the elders and talk among the rest. She had met a Little Eagle man and they had professed their love. This would have been accepted by her band, were she not promised to another *Tsitsistas*. Her betrothed had challenged the Little Eagle man, who would surely lose—given his size and lack of experience. Lona had wept as she related the circumstances to her sister and brother-in-law. Their mother took a hard stance and refused to back down, clearly preferring the *Tsitsistas*.

If only Father were here, She Who Bathes Her Knees lamented. A sickness took him in the cold time. Their mother was only being pragmatic; the tribesman would provide better for her daughter, hence, for her.

To distract Lona from the situation, Bathes Her Knees asked her along to help them find the arrow. They set off in the morning—a chill forecasting the coming season. High Wolf explained the distance. Bathes Her Knees carried a small bag of leftover meat from last night's meal.

"Will you keep your eyes open for that drop tine buck, or *any* game? And no chatter. The leaves are crisp as it is," he said. He wanted to take an animal before the moon was full, another eight days. It was his responsibility now to provide for his wife's family, as well as his own mother and a child she had adopted. He would surely welcome another hunter. *Pray it be soon.* But he kept his thoughts to himself regarding his wife's sister's affairs. The tribesman was a hard man, he knew. Not kind. Not gentle. Not a friend.

After trekking over hills and valleys for nearly two hand widths of time, High Wolf spotted the sheer rock face of the cliff to the east. It formed the curved end of a wide crescent of rim rock. Across the valley to the west, a similar abutment stood, but not as remarkable in appearance. Below, a dry creek bed meandered through the narrow valley. Here High Wolf turned to look at his wife and her sister.

"Do you see that dark soil rising from the creek bed?" High Wolf asked quietly, almost whispering. "The charcoal shade that reaches the shrubs?" He pointed with his lips. "When I was young, my father and I discovered a large bone there, like a gift sticking out of the earth. From the backbone of some ancient beast, he told me. I wanted to continue digging, but he said we would never be finished. That it was a task for those who came after us, and to leave it to them. But he allowed me to carry home the one bone. I still have it, do you know?"

"Yes, I do know. It is heavy," his wife smiled at him as she too whispered. She understood the bone as touchstone, in memory of his father, so she did not complain more than this simple assertion. He admired her patience. And now, he'd revealed where he had found it with his father. This was important.

Lona raised her eyes to the rim above the smooth wall and shuddered.

"What is it? Did you see something?" Bathes Her Knees asked the girl in a low tone.

"No, Sister. But I felt . . . I *feel* a coming fear."

High Wolf looked at his wife, but said nothing. He frowned as he turned east, toward the hillside from where he had aimed at the unusual buck. The women followed deftly to avoid the dry leaves.

In late fall, the pungent smell of sagebrush mixed with tang of deer or elk. They had passed several beds where dry grasses lay matted down near scattered, brown pellets. High Wolf tried to concentrate on their purpose, but presentiments unnerved him. When he turned to look at Lona, her eyes were lifted once more to the top of the rock face.

"Look where you step," he warned her.

As a child, Renée Carrier lived in France and five Southern states, "migrating" to Wyoming at eighteen to attend the university, where she earned a B.A in French. "Having lived in rural Wyoming for over four decades, I remain its student of *place.*"

A collection of creative non-fiction essays, *A Singular Notion*, was published in 2006 by the Higher Shelf imprint of Pronghorn Press. In 2010 she compiled, edited, and published her fighter-pilot father's early aviation memoir as a short run, currently out of print. She and her husband, a retired school superintendent, tend an apple farm, a too-large garden, raise garlic and herbs—medicinal and culinary. Their children are grown and live out-of-state.

In 2018, she was awarded the Frank Nelson Doubleday Writing Award by the Wyoming Arts Council. "I continue to sing and play the odd musical performance and I practice family herbalism, which wends its way into my writing, like a possessed vine. At present, I'm working on a homestead manual/memoir, and formatting the third book in my Riven Country Series.

To inquire about booking Renée for a speaking engagement, please visit the following links: reneecarrier.wordpress.com; Twitter@reneecarrier12

The Riven Country of Senga Munro

CPSIA information can be obtained
at www.ICGtesting.com
Printed in the USA
LVHW111502191219
641063LV00001B/233/P